NATURAL RESOURCES MANAGEMENT AND AGRARIAN DEVELOPMENT

By the Same Author

—Emerging Africa : Potential and Challenges
—Farm Management : Theory and Practice

About the Author

Dr. Reji D. Nair is Assistant Professor in the Department of Economics, Arba Minch University, Ethiopia. He was officer in the Kerala State Planning Board, India. Dr. Nair has published many books including *Africa in the New Millennium: Challenged and Interventions, Land Economics : Issues in Land Use, Natural Resources Management and Agrarian Development and Environment Conservation in the Twenty First Century* (Malayalam). He is a recipient of Dr. B.R. Ambedkar Fellowship Award (2006) of the Bharathiya Dalit Sahitya Academy. He is a notable writer in Malayalam and has published many literary works including children's literature, science fiction and short stories. Dr. Reji has shown his calibre in the fields of teaching, research, planning and social activities.

Natural Resources Management
and
Agrarian Development

REJI D. NAIR

CONCEPT PUBLISHING COMPANY PVT. LTD.
NEW DELHI-110 059

ISBN-13: 978-81-8069-712-8 (HB)
ISBN-13: 978-81-8069-713-5

First Published 2010

Published and Printed by

Concept
Since 1974

Concept Publishing Company Pvt. Ltd.
Regd. Office:
A/15-16, Commercial Block, Mohan Garden
New Delhi-110059 (India)
Phones : 25351460, 25351794, *Fax* : 091-11-25357109
Email : publishing@conceptpub.com
Website : www.conceptpub.com

Editorial Office:
H-13, Bali Nagar, New Delhi-110 015, India.

Cataloging in Publication Data--*Courtesy:* D.K. Agencies (P) Ltd. <docinfo@dkagencies.com>

Nair, Reji D.
Natural resources management and agrarian development / Reji D. Nair.
p. cm.
Includes bibliographical references (p.) and index.
ISBN 9788180697128

1. Natural resources--Developing countries--Management. 2. Environmental economics--Developing countries. 3. Agriculture--Economic aspects--Developing countries. 4. Rural development--Developing countries. 5. Sustainable development--Developing countries--Mathematical models. I. Title.

DDC 333.7091724 22

Preface

Issues about environment, economics and politicr are interrelated through the way humans interact with their surroundings and with each other. Biological diversity allows a variety of species to live together to help maintain the environment without costly human intervention. We benefit because the environment sustains us with the variety of resources produced. However, there is often a mainstream belief that for poor countries to develop, environmental concerns have to be sacrificed, or is a luxury to address once poverty is alleviated. Therefore, the approaches to such issues require rethinking. The overloaded phrase "sustainable development" must recognize the interrelations between human beings and the environment if true environmental and social justice is to be obtained.

The number of species of plants, animals, and microorganisms, the enormous diversity of genes in these species, the different ecosystems on the planet, such as deserts, rainforests and coral reefs are all part of a biologically diverse Earth. Appropriate conservation and sustainable development strategies attempt to recognize this as being integral to any approach. Almost all cultures have in some way or form recognized the importance that nature, and its biological diversity has had upon them and the need to maintain it. Yet, power, greed and politics have affected the precarious balance. Biodiversity actually boosts ecosystem productivity where each species, no matter how small, have an important role to play and that it is this combination that enables the ecosystem to possess the ability to prevent and recover from a variety of disasters. This is obviously useful for mankind as a larger number of species of plants means more variety of crops and a larger number of species of animals ensure that the ecosystem is naturally sustained.

It is feared that human activity is causing massive extinctions. From various animal species, forests and the ecosystems that forests support to marine life. The costs associated with deteriorating or vanishing ecosystems will be high. However, sustainable development and consumption would help avert ecological problems. The World Resources Institute reports that there is a link between biodiversity and climate change. Rapid global warming can affect ecosystems chances to adapt naturally.

With global warming on the increase and species and their habitats on the decrease, chances for ecosystems to adapt naturally are diminishing. Many are agreed that climate change may be one of the greatest threats facing the planet. Recent years show increasing temperatures in various regions, and/or increasing extremities in weather patterns.

Research has shown that air pollutants from fossil fuel use make clouds, which reflect more of the sun's rays back into space. This leads to an effect known as global dimming whereby less heat and energy reaches the earth. At first, it sounds like an ironic saviour to climate change problems. However, it is believed that global dimming caused the droughts in Ethiopia in the 1970s and 1980s where millions died, because the northern hemisphere oceans were not warm enough to allow rain formation. Global dimming is also hiding the true power of global warming. By cleaning up global dimming-causing pollutants without tackling greenhouse gas emissions, rapid warming has been observed, and various human health and ecological disasters have resulted, as witnessed during the European heat wave in 2003, which saw thousands of people die.

Both environmental degradation and poverty alleviation are urgent global issues that have a lot in common, but are often treated separately. As Delhi-based environment organization, the Centre for Science and Environment, points out, if the poor world were to develop and consume in the same manner as the West to achieve the same living standards, "we would need two additional planet Earths to produce resources and absorb wastes ... and good planets are hard to find!"

Poverty and third world has been shown to result in resource stripping just to survive or pay off debts. See the Box 1 for a close look at the severity of poverty in the World.

Box 1: Poverty Extent in the World

- Half the world—nearly three billion people—live on less than two dollars a day.
- The GDP (Gross Domestic Product) of the poorest 48 nations (*i.e.* a quarter of the world's countries) is less than the wealth of the world's three richest countries combined.
- Nearly a billion people entered the 21st century unable to read a book or sign their names.
- Less than one per cent of what the world spent every year on weapons was needed to put every child into school by the year 2000 and yet it didn't happen.
- One billion children live in poverty (1 in 2 children in the world), 640 million live without adequate shelter, 400 million have no access to safe water, 270 million have no access to health services; 10.6 million died in 2003 before they reached the age of 5 (or roughly 29,000 children per day).
- The United Nations' 1998 Human Development Report reveals that, "Globally, the 20 per cent of the world's people in the highest-income countries account for 86 per cent of total private consumption expenditures—the poorest 20 per cent a minuscule 1.3 per cent."
- To highlight this inequality further, consider that approximately 1 billion people suffer from hunger and some 2 to 3.5 billion people have a deficiency of vitamins and minerals.

For example, Nepal and Bangladesh have suffered from various environmental problems such as increasingly devastating floods, resulting from large-scale deforestation. Forests around the world face increased pressures from timber companies and agricultural businesses.

Some environmentalists, from rich nations especially, also raise concerns about increasing populations placing excessive burdens on the world's resources as the current major source of environmental problems. This makes for a worrying situation for third world development and poverty alleviation. However, an environment-only approach risks "blaming the victims." While humans are largely responsible for many problems of the planet today, not all humans have the same impact on the environment. It is important to consider, for example, that the consumption of just the worlds wealthiest fifth of humanity is so much more than the rest of the world, as highlighted at the beginning.

Thus, putting emphasis on population growth in this way is perhaps over-simplistic. However, this does not mean we can be complacent about future population burdens. Sustainability is critical for the world's majority to develop without following the environmentally damaging processes of the world's currently industrialized nations.

Mainstream economists and politicians have long been criticized for concentrating on economic growth in ways that ignores humanity and the environmental costs. Perhaps one of the harshest ironies is how food and farm products flow from areas of hunger and need, to areas where money and demand is concentrated. Farm workers, and women especially, are amongst the worlds most hungry.

It is perhaps natural to assume that we are growing food to feed people, but are struggling to keep up. Reasons are frequently attributed to the effects that rapid population growth places of poor countries as the ultimate cause. However, we make more than enough food to keep up with population growth, although environmentally damaging industrial agriculture threatens future sustainability. Yet, how is it that there is so much hunger, and that farm workers are usually the hungriest people in the world?

An indication of the answer lies in what is less discussed in the mainstream: the purpose of agriculture in today's world. Like many other markets, food is available to those who can afford it, not necessarily those who need it. Most food is, therefore, produced to meet consumer demands, not the needs of the poor or hungry. This leads to a major diversion, and even wastage, of environmental resources from productive uses to non-productive uses. For poor countries that need to earn foreign exchange to pay off huge debts, cash crops offer the chance of money. For elite landowners, this is the only way they can make money, as the poor have little. As professor of anthropology, Richard Robbins, summarizes:

'To understand why people go hungry you must stop thinking about food as something farmers grow for others to eat, and begin thinking about it as something companies produce for other people to buy.'

Box 2: Agriculture and the Humanity

- Much of the best agricultural land in the world is used to grow commodities such as cotton, sisal, tea, tobacco, sugar cane, and cocoa, items which are non-food products or are marginally nutritious, but for which there is a large market.
- Millions of acres of potentially productive farmland is used to pasture cattle, an extremely inefficient use of land, water and energy, but one for which there is a market in wealthy countries.
- More than half the grain grown in the United States (requiring half the water used in the U.S.) is fed to livestock, grain that would feed far more people than would the livestock to which it is fed.

Box 2 just scratches the surface, but highlights the interconnectedness of humanity, the environment and all other forms of life. We cannot take the environment for granted. Humanity has a responsibility not only to each other, but to the environment as well, as the environment has long sustained us and can only continue to do so if we do not destroy it.

Providing enough food for the world's poor is a continuing challenge. According to a study conducted by the International Food Policy Research Institute, by 2020 world population will increase to at least 8 billion. Most of this growth will take place in the developing world and will account for about 85 per cent of the increase in demand for cereals and meat. Already, almost 1 billion people live in poverty and suffer chronic hunger—about two-thirds of whom are farmers.

The amount of arable land available to meet increased demand from a burgeoning population is limited. Only about 10 per cent of the world's land surface is suitable for farming, and soil erosion and over-farming are becoming problems in some areas. With no significant room to expand areas of cultivation, increased demand for food in developing countries will have to be met through improved yields of the most widely grown staple crops at a time when the rapid yield growth that characterized the Green Revolution is beginning to peak.

The lack of arable land also can lead to environmental problems. In many developing countries, for example, biodiversity is threatened because wilderness areas such as tropical rainforests are being converting to farmland to meet the demand of food production. Therefore, farmers need to find new ways to boost production using fewer natural resources.

Today, the Millennium Development Goals are a guiding light for international cooperation for development, in particular the target to halve the proportion of hungry and extremely poor people by 2015. But the starting point to achieve this target must be the recognition that poverty is predominantly rural. Three quarters of the world's poor, about 900 million people, live in rural areas where they depend on agriculture and related activities for their livelihood. The reality is that the Millennium poverty target cannot be met unless the world addresses rural poverty.

In most poor countries, agriculture is the largest employer, job creator and export earner. Historically, reforms in this critical sector have been the foundation for overall economic development and poverty reduction. Whether we consider Europe and the United States in the nineteenth century, or Japan and the miracle economies in South East Asia in the twentieth century, agriculture has been the engine that has driven economic growth in many countries. For every dollar invested in agriculture, another two dollars is generated for a developing country's national economy. It has been the often dramatic progress in agricultural development, translated into increases in productivity, that has generated increased income, which leads to savings and investments, and finally to greater demand for goods and services.

Yet, despite these obvious connections, the share of official development assistance for agriculture and the rural sector has fallen steadily since 1988. Today, only about eight per cent of bilateral official development assistance (ODA) goes to rural development. This situation must be reversed. Fortunately, there are clear indications that both developing countries and donor countries are recognizing the importance of rural and agricultural development in the fight to end hunger and poverty.

The new emphasis on rural development was also seen at the 2003 sessions of the High-Level Segment of the United Nations Economic and Social Council, which focused on promoting an integrated approach to rural development in developing countries for poverty eradication and sustainable development.

Developing countries, for their part, also need to assign a higher priority to rural and agricultural development, and this must be reflected in both policy and investment. The declaration on agriculture and food security in Africa, made by the African Union at its July 2003 summit in Maputo, is an encouraging sign of greater commitment to poverty eradication in rural areas. African leaders resolved to allocate at least 10 per cent of their national budgets to implement sound policies for agricultural and rural development within five years.

The challenge now is to ensure that it translates into more resources for rural development and poverty eradication and more effective use of these investments.

While higher productivity and output are prerequisites for sustained poverty reduction, without access to efficient markets, small-scale farmers and entrepreneurs in developing countries are at an enormous disadvantage. Today, many markets are hostile or inaccessible to the rural poor. And the efforts of poor farmers in some of the most remote areas of the world can be undone by international processes far beyond their control. It is now widely recognized that subsidies and protectionist trade policies of the industrialized countries are damaging for developing countries. For example, cotton farmers in Western and Central Africa lost US$ 301 million in 2001 because they could not compete in world markets against cotton producers in the US, who received US$ 3.4 billion in subsidies. Small farmers are hardest hit when these subsidies encourage over-production and drive down world prices, even though they can produce cotton at one-fourth of the cost to their US counterparts.

Broad-based agricultural and rural development in developing countries must be founded on higher productivity by small-scale farmers. More secure access to land, water, technology, financial and other institutions that support and reward efforts of poor farmers are essential. At the same time, better transport and communication infrastructure and facilities for storage, crop processing and marketing are needed so that higher yields and good harvests are not followed by a collapse in prices. Perhaps most important, small-scale farmers need to be able to organize themselves so that they can access markets and gain a stronger voice in decision-making processes.

Vibrant rural economies are vital not only to eradicating poverty in rural communities, but to economic growth in poor countries as a whole. Furthermore, poverty eradication is the foundation for global peace and security and quality of life for all. The public, private and civil sectors must work together, coherently and efficiently, to translate their commitment to rural development into policies, action and investments that improve the daily lives of the rural poor and enhance their power to chart and lead their own development into the future.

The idea of sustainable development grew from numerous environmental movements in earlier decades. Summits such as the Earth Summit in Rio, Brazil, 1992, were major international meetings to bring sustainable development to the mainstream. It has economic, environmental and social perspectives in its efforts towards the unending target. However, the record on moving towards sustainability so far appears to have been quite poor. The concept of sustainability means many different things to different people, and a large part of humanity around the world still live without access to basic necessities.

The present book is a theoretical account of the three inter-related areas of environment, agriculture and rural development. It underlies different basic theories covering natural resources management, agriculture development and rural development. The book consists of three parts. Part I is exclusively related to the theories of natural resources and environmental management; Part II captures that of agriculture development and Part III of rural development. Even though agriculture development and rural development are inter-related, the present work gives special emphasis and focus to both the areas.

Part I consists of seven chapters, which discusses the classification and allocation of natural resources; how efficiency, property rights and market failures affect the environment; efficient allocation of pollution and market allocation of pollution; impact of population growth and economic growth on environment and the concept of sustainable development; various policy instruments to combat environmental degradation; and also the important environmental valuation techniques.

Part II examines the role of agriculture in economic development; farm production decisions including production function, cost functions and farm organizations; principles and determinants of land utilization; agriculture policy and government intervention; food security and challenges; and the relevance of world trade and agriculture. All these areas in this part are covered in seven chapters.

Part III consists of seven chapters, which details the concept of rural development, including basic concepts. Other areas of discussion in this section include different measures of rural development; population and rural-urban migration; agriculture transformation and the resultant effect on rural societies; land, labour and credit as factors of rural growth; and various policies, strategies and instruments underlying rural development.

This book will be of immense help to both graduate and post-graduate students, who are studying courses such as Environmental Economics, Agriculture Economics and Rural Development. It is also a reference book to the practitioners and policy makers in the areas of planning, environment, agriculture and rural development.

REFERENCES

ADB (2001), *Agricultural Biotechnology, Poverty Reduction, and Food Security*, Working Paper, May.

Ismail Serageldin and G.J. Persley (2000), *Promethean Science: Agricultural Biotechnology, the Environment, and the Poor*, CGIAR.

Lawrence Summers (1992), 'Let them eat pollution', *The Economist*, February.

Per Pinstrup-Andersen, Rajul Pandya-Lorch, and Mark W. Rosegrant (1999), *World Food Prospects: Critical Issues for the Early Twenty-First Century*, IFPRI (October).

Richard Robbins (1999), *Global Problems and the Culture of Capitalism*, Allyn and Bacon.

Richard H. Robbins, *Readings on Poverty, Hunger, and Economic Development*.

UNDP (1998), *Poverty facts and Statistics: Loss of Biodiversity, Climate Change and Global Warming*.

U.N. Population Division (2001), *World Population Prospects: The 2000 Revision*.

Vandana Shiva (2000), *Stolen Harvest*, South End Press.

Contents

PART II: AGRICULTURAL ECONOMICS

PART III: RURAL DEVELOPMENT

List of Tables

PART I

PART II

PART III

List of Figures

PART I

PART II

PART III

List of Boxes

PART II

PART III

PART I
NATURAL RESOURCES AND ENVIRONMENTAL ECONOMICS

1

Introduction to Natural Resources and Environmental Economics

Introduction

Environment is defined as the complex of physical, chemical and biotic factors (as climate, soil and living things) that act upon an organism or an ecological community and ultimately determine its form and survival. It is the aggregate of an individual or community.

In economics the environment is viewed as a composite asset that provides a variety of services. It includes raw materials, which are transformed into consumer products by the production process, and energy, which fuels this transformation. These raw materials and energy return to the environment as waste products. Environment also provides services directly to consumers; the air we breathe, the nourishment we receive from food and drink, and the protection we derive from shelter and clothing and all benefits we receive either directly or indirectly from the environment.

If the environment is defined broadly, the relationship between the environment and the economic system can be considered a 'closed system'. Here it means no inputs (energy, matter, and so on) are received from outside the system and no outputs are transferred outside the system. In contrast, an 'open system' is one in which the system imports or exports matter or energy (Fig. 1.1).

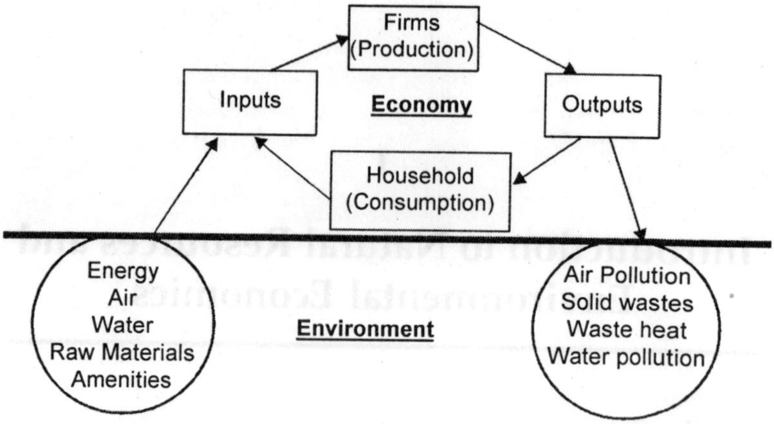

Fig. 1.1: Economic System and the Environment

Emergence of Natural Resources and Environmental Economics

Here we examine the development of resource and environmental economics from the time of the industrial revolution to its modern form.

Classical Economics

A central interest of the classical economists was the question of what determined standards of living and economic growth. Natural resources were seen as important determinants of national wealth and growth. A strand running through classical political economy concerns the prospects for living standards in the long-term for an economy subject to constraints on the supply of land. Land (natural resources in general) was viewed as limited in its availability. When to this were added the assumption that land was a necessary input to production and that it exhibited diminishing returns; the early classical economists came to the conclusion that economic progress would be a transient feature of history, and the inevitability of an eventual stationary state, in which the prospects for the living standard of the majority of people were bleak.

To Malthus, a fixed land quantity, and assumed tendency for continual positive population growth, and diminishing returns in agriculture implied a tendency for output per capita to fall over time. So that, there is a long run tendency for the living standards of the mass to be driven down to a subsistence level. At the subsistence wage level, conditions would permit reproducibility of the population at an unchanging level, and the economy would attain a steady state. This notion of a steady state was formalized and extended by David Ricardo.

Mill's work utilizes the idea of diminishing returns, but recognizes the countervailing influence of the growth of knowledge and technical progress in agriculture and production.

Neo-classical Economics

The neo-classicals have little of intrinsic interest to environmental economics. What is noticeable in early neo-classical growth models is the absence of land, or any natural resources, from the production function used in such models. Classical limits to growth arguments, based on a fixed land input, did not have any place in early neo-classical growth modelling.

The introduction of natural resources into neo-classical models of economic growth occurred in the 1970s, when neo-classical economists first systematically investigated the efficient and optimal depletion of resources. This body of work, and the developments that have followed from it, is natural resources economics.

Welfare Economics

The final development in mainstream economic theory that needs to be briefly addressed here is the development of a rigorous theory of welfare economics. Economists have attempted to find a method of ranking different states of the world, which does not require the use of a social welfare function, makes little use of ethical principles, but is nevertheless useful in making prescriptions about resource allocation.

Where the conditions do not have markets do not attain efficiency in allocation, and a state of 'market failure' is said to exist. One manifestation of market failure is the phenomenon of externalities. The problem of environmental pollution entered economics as a particular example of the general class of externalities.

Ecological Economics

Ecological economics is a new inter-disciplinary field. In the 1980s a number of economists and natural scientists came to the conclusion that if progress was to be made in understanding and addressing environmental problems it was necessary to study those in an inter-disciplinary way, which they decided to call ecological economics. The first issue of a journal with that title appeared in 1989.

Ecological economics treat the economic system as part of the larger system that is planet earth. It starts from the recognition that the economic and environmental systems are interdependent, and studies the joint economy—environment system in the light of developments in the natural sciences, particularly thermodynamics and ecology, over the last two centuries.

Fundamental Themes

There are three fundamental themes in the natural resources and environmental economics.

Efficiency

One way of thinking about efficiency is in terms of missed opportunities. If resource use is wasteful in some way then opportunities are being squandered; eliminating that waste (or inefficiency) can bring net benefits to some groups of people. An example is energy inefficiency. A substantial part of environmental economics is concerned with how economies might avoid inefficiencies in the allocation and use of natural and environmental resources.

Optimality

Optimality is related to efficiency, but is nevertheless conceptually distinct from it. To understand the idea of optimality we need to have in mind:

(a) A group of people taken to be the relevant society.
(b) Some overall objective that this society has and in terms of which we can measure the extent to which some resource use decision is desirable from that society's point of view.

Resource use choice is socially optimal if it maximizes the objective given any relevant constraints that may be operating.

Sustainability

The third theme is sustainability. It involves taking care of posterity. An allocation of resources is socially optimal and then surely it must also be sustainable. If sustainability matters, then presumably it would enter into the list of society's objectives and be taken care of in achieving optimality. The pursuit of optimality as usually considered in economics will not necessarily take care of posterity. If taking care of posterity is seen as a moral obligation, then the pursuit of optimality will need to be constrained by a sustainability requirement.

Fundamental Features in the Economic Approach to Natural Resources and Environmental Economics

There are three important features of economic approach to resource and environmental issues.

Property Rights, Efficiency and Government Intervention

Regarding allocative efficiency the central issue is the role of markets and prices. It is expected that the markets will bring about efficiency in allocation. However, well-defined and enforceable private property rights are one of the necessary conditions for efficiency. Many environmental resources fail to allocate efficiently, because there are no clearly defined property rights. In such circumstances, price signals fail to reflect true social costs and benefits, and a *prima facie* case exists for government policy intervention to seek efficiency gains.

Time Dimension of Economic Decisions

Many environmental resources exist as stocks, which from an economic perspective are assets yielding flows of environmental services overtime. In considering the efficiency and optimality of their use, we must take account not only of use at a point in time but also of the pattern of use over time. That is, efficiency and optimality have an inter-temporal or dynamic dimension as well as an intra-temporal or static dimension. The relations between rates of return to capital as generally discussed in economics and the rates of return on environmental assets must be taken into account in trying to identify efficient and optimal paths of environmental resource use over time.

Exhaustibility, Sustainability and Irreversibility

Natural resource stocks can be classified in various ways. A useful first cut is to distinguish between renewable and non-renewable resources. Renewable resources are biotic, plant and animal populations, and have the capacity to grow in size overtime, through biological reproduction. Non-renewable resources are abiotic, stocks of minerals, and do not have that capacity to grow over time. The distinction is sometimes made between exhaustible or depletable, and inexhaustible or non-depletable resources. Renewable resources are exhaustible if harvested for too long at a rate exceeding their regeneration capacities.

Another property of natural resources is the extent to which they are substitutable for one another. Matter of central importance is the degree to which environmental resources can be substituted for by other inputs, especially the man-made capital resulting from saving and investment.

REFERENCES

Blaug (1985), *Economic Theory in Retrospect*, Cambridge University Press, Cambridge.

Dorfman, Robert and Nancy S. Dorfman (1993), *Economics of the Environment: Selected Readings*, W.W. Norton, New York.

Kneese, Allen V. *et al.* (1970), *Economics and the Environment: A Material Approach, Resources for the Future*, Washington DC.

Tietenberg, Tom (1996), *Environmental and Natural Resources Economics*, Harper Collins College Publishers, New York.

2

Natural Resources
Classification and Allocation

Introduction

The efficient allocation of substitutable, depletable and renewable resources depends on the circumstances. When the resources can be extracted at a constant marginal cost, the efficient quantity of the depletable resources extracted declines overtime. In an efficient market allocation, the transition from depletable to renewable resources is smooth and exhibits none of the overshoot and collapse characteristics of the 'Limits to Growth' view of the world. In the present chapter we will discuss the broad classification of natural resources and the possibility of substitution towards renewable resources.

Depletable and Renewable Resources

In the "Limits to Growth' vision of the future, society's demand for resources suddenly exceeds their availability. Rather than anticipating a smooth transition to a steady state, the vision estimates that the system will overshoot the resource base, precipitating a collapse. Is this realistic? We approach this question in the following sections.

Resource Taxonomy

Following three important concepts are used to classify the stock of depletable resources.

(a) *Current reserves*: Defined as the known resources that can profitably be extracted at current prices.
(b) *Potential reserves*: The amount of reserves potentially available depends upon the price people are willing to pay for those resources—the higher the price, the larger the potential reserves.
(c) *Resource endowment*: It represents the natural occurrence of resources in the earth's crust. Since prices have nothing to do with the size of the resource endowment, it is a geological rather than an economic concept.

A model categorization of resources is given in Fig. 2.1.

Depletable resources are those for which natural replenishment feedback loop can safely be ignored. The rate of replenishment for these resources is so low that it does not offer a potential for augmenting the stock in any reasonable time frame. Recyclable resources are those which, although currently being used for some particular purpose, exists in a form allowing its mass to be recovered once that purpose is no longer necessary or desirable. The current reserves of depletable, recyclable resources can be augmented by economic replenishment, as well as by recycling.

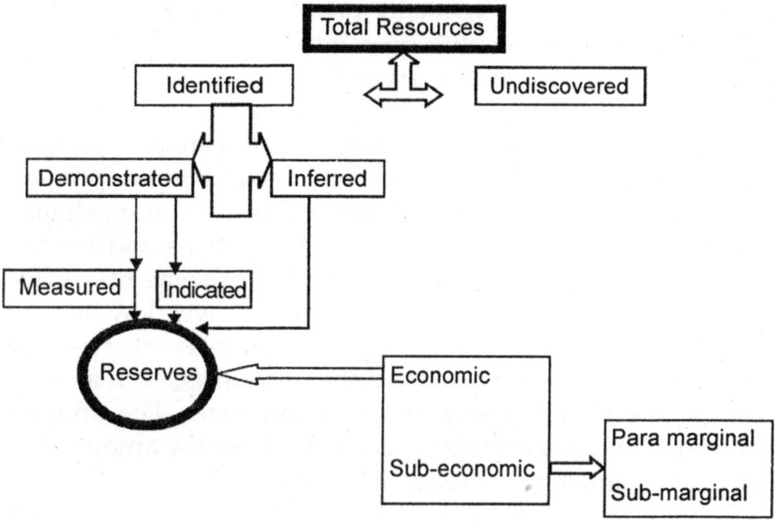

Fig. 2.1: Categorization of Resources

Notes to Fig. 2.1

(a) *Identified Resources*: Specific bodies of mineral-bearing material whose location, quantity and quality are known from geologic evidence, supported by engineering measurements.
(b) *Measured Resources*: Material for which quantity and quality estimates are within a margin of error of less than 20 per cent, from geologically well known sample sites.
(c) *Indicated Resources*: Material, which quantity and quality have been estimated partly from sample analysis and partly from reasonable geological projections.
(d) *Inferred Resources*: Material in unexplored extensions of demonstrated resources based on geological projections.
(e) *Undiscovered Resources*: Unspecified bodies of mineral-bearing material surmised to exist on the basis of broad geological knowledge and theory.
(f) *Hypothetical Resources*: Undiscovered materials reasonably expected to exist in a known mining district under known geological conditions.
(g) *Speculative Resources*: Undiscovered materials that may occur either known types of deposits in favourable geological settings where no discoveries have been made, or in yet unknown types of deposits that remain to be recognized.

The other side of the recyclable resources is that their potential reserves can be exhausted. The depletion rate is affected by the demand for and the durability of the products built with the resource, and the ability to reuse the products. Except where demand is totally price inelastic higher prices tend to reduce the quantity demanded. For some resources, the size of the potential reserves depends explicitly on our ability to store the resource.

Renewable resources are differentiated from depletable resources primarily by the fact that natural replenishment augments the flow of renewable resources at a non-negligible rate. Solar energy, water, cereal grains, fish, forests, and animals are all examples of renewable resources. For some renewable resources, the continuation and volume of their flow depend crucially on humans. Soil erosion and nutrient depletion reduce the flow of food. For other renewable resources, such as solar energy, the flow is independent of humans. The amount consumed by one generation does not reduce the amount that can be consumed by subsequent generations.

Some renewable resources can be stored, others cannot. For those that can, storage provide a valuable way to manage the allocation of the resources over time. We are not left simply at the mercy of nature and flows of the resources. Food without proper care perishes rapidly, but with storage can be used to feed the hungry in times of famines.

Managing renewable resources presents a different challenge than managing depletable resources, though an equally significant one. The challenge for depletable resources involve allocating dwindling stocks among generations while meeting the ultimate transition to renewable resources. In contrast, the challenge for managing renewable resources involve the maintenance of an efficient sustainable flow.

Efficient Inter-temporal Allocation

If we are to judge the adequacy of market allocations, we must define what is meant by efficiency in relation to the management of depletable and renewable resource allocations. Because allocation over time is the crucial issue, dynamic efficiency becomes the core concept. The dynamic efficiency criterion assumes that society's objective is to maximize present values of net benefits coming from the resources. For depletable, non-recyclable resources this requires a balancing of the current and subsequent uses of the resource.

The N-period Constant Cost Case

Here we analyze the efficient allocation of the depletable resource over time when the number of time periods for extraction is unlimited. This is a more difficult calculation because how long the resource will last is no longer predetermined, the time of exhaustion must be derived as well the extraction path prior to exhaustion of the resource.

The equation describing the allocation which maximizes the present value of benefits is:

$$\frac{a - bq_t - c}{(1+r)^{t-1}} - \lambda = 0, t = 1, 2, ..., T$$

$$\sum_{t=1}^{T} q_t = Q' = 0$$

Where, $a-bq_t$ is the inverse demand curve in year '*t*', and marginal cost of extracting that resources is a constant '*c*'. Total available amount of the resource is '*Q*', and '*r*' the appropriate interest rate; λ marginal user cost.

Figure 2.2a demonstrates how the efficient quantity extracted varies over time, while Fig. 2.2b shows the behaviour of the marginal user cost and the marginal cost of extraction. Total marginal cost refers to the sum of the two. The marginal cost of extraction is represented by the lower line, and the marginal user cost is depicted as the vertical distance between the marginal cost of extraction and the total marginal cost.

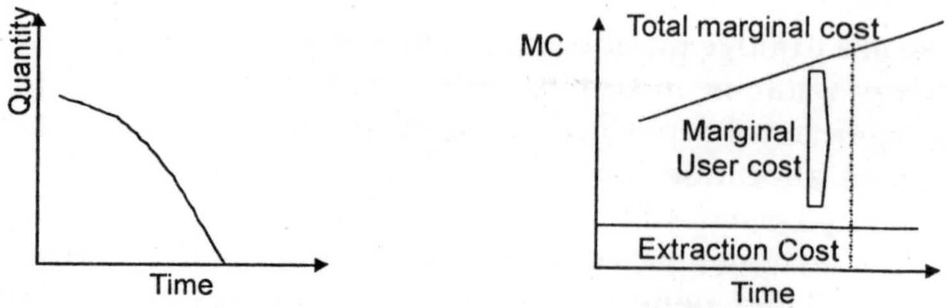

Fig. 2.2a **Fig. 2.2b**

Fig. 2.2: Efficient Inter-temporal Allocation

Transition to a Renewable Substitute

Here we consider the nature of an efficient allocation when a substitute renewable resource is available at constant marginal cost. For example, efficient allocation of oil or natural gas with solar substitute or the efficient allocation of exhaustible ground water with surface water substitutes.

If we assume the existence of a perfect substitute for the depletable resource which is infinitely available at a cost, say \$6 per unit. The transition from the depletable resource to this renewable resource would ultimately transpire because its marginal cost (\$6) should be less than the maximum willingness to pay (say \$8).

The total marginal cost for the depletable resource in the presence of a $8 perfect substitute would never exceed $6, because society could always use the renewable resource instead, whenever it was cheaper. Thus, while the maximum willingness to pay (choke price) sets the upper limit on total marginal cost when no substitute is available, the marginal cost of extraction of the substitute sets the upper limit when one is available at a marginal cost lower than the choke price.

In the efficient allocation the transition is smooth. Quantity extracted is gradually reduced as the marginal user cost rises until the switch is made to the substitutes. No abrupt change is evident in either marginal cost or quantity profiles.

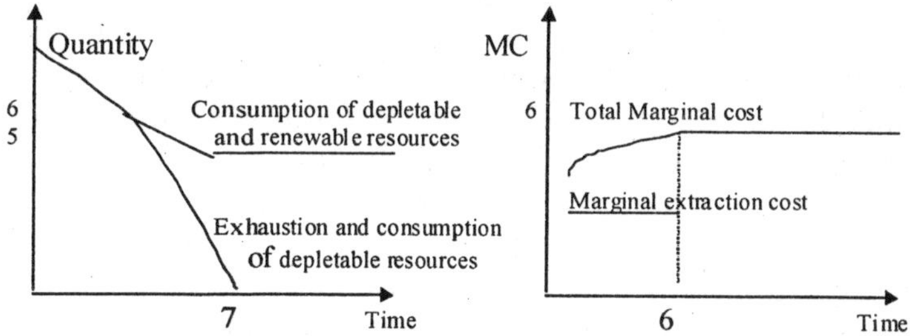

(a) *Quantity Profile* (b) *MC Profile*

Fig. 2.3: Combined Marginal Extraction Cost with Substitution of Resources

At the transition point, called the 'switch point', consumption of renewable resources begins. Prior to the 'switch point', only the depletable resource is consumed, while after the switch point, only the renewable resource is consumed. This sequencing of consumption pattern results from the cost patterns. Prior to the switch-point, the depletable resource is cheaper. At the switch point, the MC of depletable resource (including marginal user cost) rises to meet the MC of the substitute, and the transition occurs. Due to the availability of the substitute resources, consumption never drops below 5 units in any time period. This level is maintained because 5 is the amount which maximizes the net benefit when the MC equal $6 (the price of the substitute).

Environmental Costs

One of the most important situation in which property right structures may not be well defined is that in which the extraction of a natural resource imposes an environmental cost on society not internalized by the producers. The health risks associated with uranium tailings, and the acids leached into streams from mine operations are all examples of associated environmental costs.

The extraction of a depletable resource causes damage to the environment not adequately reflected in the costs faced by the extracting firms; which would be an external cost. The cost of getting the resource out of the ground, as well as processing and shipping it, is borne by the resource owner and considered in the calculation of how much of the resource to extract. However, the environmental damage is not borne by the owner and, in the absence of any outside attempt to internalize that cost, will not be part of the extraction decision.

The result of including environmental cost on the timing of the switch point is interesting because it involves two different effects that work in opposite directions. On the demand side, the inclusion of environmental costs results in higher prices, which tend to dampen demand. This lowers the rate of consumption of the resource, which would make it last longer.

The higher marginal cost also means that a smaller cumulative amount of the depletable resource would be extracted in an efficient allocation.

Renewable Resources

Forest and Management

Forests represent an example of storable, renewable resource; it provides a variety of products and services. The raw materials for housing and wood products are extracted from the forest. In many parts of the world wood is an important fuel. Paper products are derived from wood fibre. Trees cleanse the air by absorbing carbon dioxide and adding oxygen. Forests provide shelter and sanctuary for wild life and they play an important role in maintaining the water sheds that supply much of our drinking water.

Typically tree stands go through three distinct growth phases—slow growth in volume in the early stages, followed by rapid growth in the middle years and slower growth as the stand reaches full maturity. From an economic point of view, the efficient time to harvest a stand of timber is when the present value of net benefits is maximized. The present value of net benefits is maximized when the marginal gain from delaying the harvest one more year is equal to the marginal cost of the delay. For longer than efficient delays the additional costs outweigh the increased benefits, while for earlier than efficient harvest more benefits (increased value of timber) are given up than costs saved.

The efficient harvest age depends on the circumstances the owner faces. When the plot is to be left fallow after the harvest, the efficient harvest occurs later than when the land is immediately replanted to initiate another cycle. With immediate replanting, delaying the harvest imposes an additional cost—the cost of delaying the next harvest—which, when factored into the analysis, makes it more desirable to harvest earlier.

Inefficient deforestation has been encouraged by a failure to incorporate global benefits from outstanding forests, by concession agreements which provide incentives to harvest too much, too soon, and which fail to provide adequate incentives to protect the interests of future generations, by land property right systems that make the amount of land acquired by squatters a multiple of cleared forest land, and by tax systems which discriminate against standing forests.

Substantial strides towards restoring efficiency as well as sustainability can be achieved simply by recognizing and correcting the perverse incentives, actions which can be and should be taken by the tropical forest nations. But these actions will not, by themselves, provide adequate protection for the global interests in the tropical forests. Following three schemes are designed to internalize some of these benefits.

(a) Debt Nature Swaps

To reduce the pressure on the forests caused by the international debt, especially by many developing countries, one of the more innovative polices has been the Debt Nature Swaps programme. It involves the purchasing of a developing country debt at a discount rate, usually by a NGO, which offers to cancel the debt in return for an environmentally related action on the part of the debtor nation. It swap the face value of the debt with the Central Government (debtor) in return for an agreement to put together a public-private partnership. This partnership would develop a programme that combines ecosystem conservation and regional development planning. The main advantage of this to the debtor nation is that a significant foreign exchange obligation can be paid off with domestic currency.

(b) Extractive Reserves

This is designed to protect the indigenous people of the forest as well as to prevent deforestation involves the establishment extractive reserves. These areas would be reserved for the indigenous people to engage in the traditional hunting, gathering activities.

(c) Establishing Conservation Easements

In this system a common global fund is raised mainly from industrial nations, which is used for protecting biodiversity. For example, the World Heritage Fund is used to protect environments of outstanding universal value.

All these measures involve recognition of the fact that resolving the global externalities component of deforestation requires a rather different approach than resolving the other aspects of deforestation problem.

Fisheries and its Efficient Allocation

Renewable resources are those for which the stock can be continuously replenished. Biological populations such as fish belong to a class of renewable resource, known as 'interactive resources,' wherein the size of the resource stock is determined jointly by biological consideration and by actions taken by society. Unrestricted access to commercially valuable species will generally result in over exploitation. This over exploitation, in turn results in over capitalization, depressed incomes for fishermen, and depleted fish stocks. Even extinction of the species is possible, particularly for fisheries characterized by particularly low extraction costs.

Efficient Allocation

(a) Schaefer Model

This biological model was proposed by Schaefer (1957). The Schaefer model posits a particular average relationship between the growth of the fish population and the size of the fish population. In Fig. 2.4, the size of population is represented

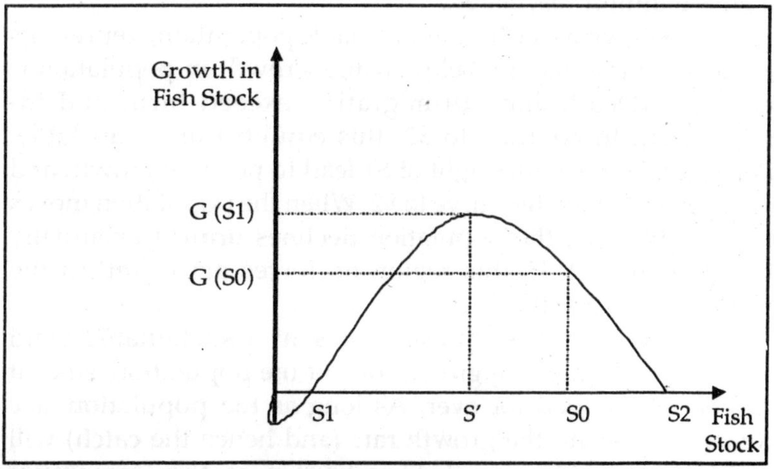

Fig. 2.4: Schaefer Model

on the horizontal axis and the growth of population on the vertical axis. The *S*1*S′* part of the function shows a range of population size, where population growth increases as the population increases and a range (*S′S*2) where initial increases in population lead to eventual decline in growth.

*S*2 is known as the 'natural equilibrium', since this population size which would persist in the absence of outside influences. Reductions in the stock due to mortality or out-migration would be exactly offset by increases in the stock due to births, growth of the fish in the remaining stock, and in-migration.

This natural equilibrium would persist because it is stable. A 'stable equilibrium' is one in which movements away from this population level set forces in motion to restore it. For example, if the stock temporarily exceeded *S*2, it would be exceeding the capacity of its habitat (called carrying capacity). As a result, mortality rates or out-migration would increase until the stock was once again within the confines of the carrying capacity of its habitat at *S*2. On the same manner if the population is temporarily reduced below *S*2. Now the stock is smaller and the growth positive; so that the stock would increase until it reaches *S*2.

*S*1, known as the 'minimum viable population,' represents the level of population, below which growth in population is negative (Death and out-migration exceed birth and in-migration). In contrast to *S*2, this equilibrium is unstable. Population sizes to the right of *S*1 lead to positive growth and a movement along the curve to *S*2. When the population moves to the left of *S*1, the population declines until it eventually becomes extinct. In this region no forces act to return the population to a viable level.

A catch level is said to represent a sustainable yield whenever it equals the growth rate of the population, since it can be maintained for ever. As long as the population size remains constant, the growth rate (and hence the catch) will remain constant as well. *S′* is known as the 'maximum sustainable yield' population, defined as that population size which yields the maximum growth; hence, the maximum sustainable yield is equal to this maximum growth and it represents the largest catch that can be perpetually sustained. *G* (*S*0) is the sustainable yield for population size. Since the catch is equal to the growth, population size (and next year's growth) remains the same. *G*(*S′*) is the maximum sustainable yield. Larger catches would be possible in the short run, but these could not be sustained; they would lead to reduced population sizes and eventually to the extinction of the species.

(b) Static Efficient Sustained Yield

The static efficient sustainable yield is the catch level which, if maintained perpetually, would produce the largest annual net benefit. Following three assumptions distinguish it from the dynamic efficient sustainable yield, which incorporates discounting:

(i) The price of fish is constant and does not depend on the amount sold;
(ii) The marginal cost of a unit of fishing effort is constant; and
(iii) The amount of fish caught per unit of effort expended is proportional to the size of fish population (the smaller population, the fewer fish caught per unit of effort).

In any sustainable yield, catches, population, effort levels, and net benefits remain constant over time. The static efficient sustainable yield allocation maximizes the constant net benefits. In Fig. 2.5, the benefits (revenues) and costs are portrayed as a function of fishing effort. The shape of revenue function is dictated by the shape of the function in Fig. 2.4, since the price of fish is assumed constant. Notice that increasing fishing effort in Fig. 2.4 would result in smaller population sizes and would be recorded as a movement from right to left. Because the variable on the horizontal axis in Fig. 2.5 is effort, and not population, an increase in fishing effort is recorded as a movement from left to right.

As sustained levels of effort are increased, eventually a point is reached (Em), where further effort reduces the sustainable catch and revenue for all years.

The net benefit is presented as the difference between benefits (prices times the quantity caught) and costs (the constant marginal cost of effort times the units of effort expended). The efficient level of effort is *Ee,* where vertical distance between benefits and costs are maximized.

At this level *MB* = *MC*

The maximum sustainable yield would be efficient only if the marginal cost of additional effort were zero. If this is not, the efficient level of effort is less than that necessary to harvest the maximum sustainable yield. Thus the static efficient level of effort leads to a larger fish population than the maximum sustainable yield level of effort.

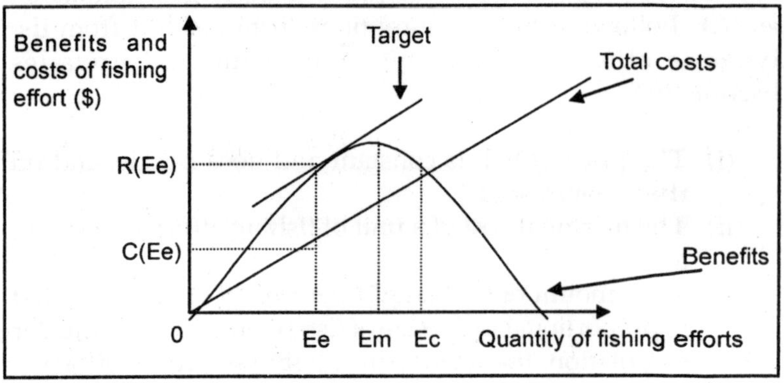

Fig. 2.5: Static Efficient Yield

Conclusion

The efficient allocation of an increasing marginal cost of resources is similar in that the quantity extracted declines over time, but differs with respect to the behaviour of marginal user cost and the cumulative amount extracted. Market allocations of depletable resources can, when property right structures are properly defined, be efficient. Regarding the renewable resources like forests substantial strides towards restoring efficiency as well as sustainability can be achieved simply by recognizing and correcting the perverse incentives, actions which can be and should be taken by the tropical forest nations.

Unrestricted access to commercially valuable species will generally result in over exploitation of fisheries, which in turn results in over capitalization, depressed incomes for fishermen, and depleted fish stocks. Creative strategies for sharing the gains from moving to an efficient level of use could prove to be a significant weapon in the arsenal of techniques designed to protect a broad class of biological resources from over exploitation.

REFERENCES

Anderson, Lee G. (1977), *The Economics of Fisheries Management*, John Hopkins University Press, Baltimore.

Conrad, John M. and Colin W. Clark (1987), *Natural Resources Economics: Notes and Problems*, Cambridge University Press, Cambridge.

Dasgupta, P.S. and G.M. Heal (1979), *Economic Theory and Exhaustible Resources*, Cambridge University Press, Cambridge.

Price, Colin (1989), *The Theory and Application of Forest Economics*, Basil Blackwell, Oxford.

Scott, Anthony (1985), *Progress in Natural Resources Economics*, Clarendon Press, Oxford.

3

Environment and Welfare Economics

Introduction

Environmental economics places considerable importance on economic efficiency in resources allocation, due to limited supply. This is evidently true for non-renewable stock resources, such as mineral deposits and fossil fuels. In the case of renewable resources also there are limits to the quantities that can be harvested in any period of time. If harvesting is persistently above sustainable level, the possibility of the stock irreversibly collapsing to zero arises.

Mainly two sets of choices we have regarding how the resources are allocated among competing uses.

(a) At any point in time there are many uses to which resources could be put and many different ways in which they could be distributed over individuals and between nations.
(b) Choices relate to the patterns of use over time—the inter-temporal allocation of resources.

Any sensible allocation will involve resources being used efficiently.

Economic Efficiency

An allocation of resources describes what goods are produced, which combinations of inputs are used in producing those goods, and how the outputs are distributed between persons. A static allocation of resources refers to the allocation at some single point in time. Resource allocation over time is known as the inter-temporal allocation of resources.

Static Efficiency

For some particular initial distribution, an allocation of resources is said to be efficient if it is possible to make one or more persons better off, without making at least, one other person worse off. If our economy consists of two persons (*A* and *B*), two goods are produced (*X*, *Y*); and production of each good uses two inputs (*K* and *L*) available in fixed quantity.

Consumption efficiency requires that the ratio of the marginal utilities of goods X and Y are the same for each consumer:

$$\frac{U^A{}_X}{U^A{}_Y} = \frac{U^B{}_X}{U^B{}_Y}$$

Efficiency in production requires that the ratio of the marginal product of each input be identical in the production of both goods:

$$\frac{MP^X{}_L}{MP^X{}_K} = \frac{MP^Y{}_L}{MP^Y{}_K}$$

The final condition necessary for economic efficiency is product-mix efficiency. It requires that the rate at which consumers value one good in terms of another is equal to the opportunity cost of one good in terms of the other in production.

$$\frac{U_X}{U_Y} = \frac{MP^Y{}_K}{MP^X{}_K} = \frac{MP^Y{}_L}{MP^X{}_L}$$

Social welfare is maximized when the resources are allocated in a socially optimal way at the point on the utility possibility frontier associated with the highest level of social welfare.

Inter-temporal Economic Efficiency

An allocation of resources over time is inter-temporally efficient, if, for some given level of utility at the present time, utility at all future points in time are as high as is economically feasible. That is, future utility can only be increased at the expense of current utility.

Let δ denote a real rate of return on a single homogenous asset, and suppose that there are *M* different sectors of the economy in which the asset can be used as a productive input, call δ_i the return on this asset in the *i*th sector (where $i = 1, 2, \ldots, M$).

The first inter-temporal efficiency condition states that the real rate of return on assets is equalized across all sectors and between all assets at any point in time.

$$\delta_i = \delta \text{ for all } i, i = 1, 2 \ldots M$$

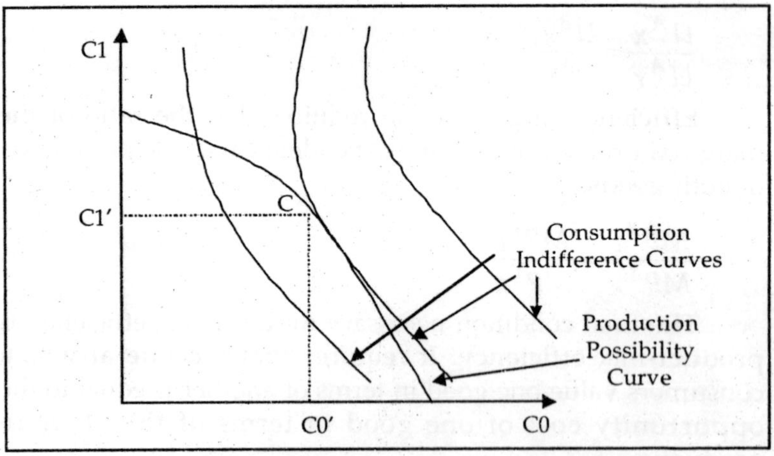

Fig. 3.1: Inter-temporal Economic Efficiency

The second necessary condition for the efficient inter-temporal allocation of resources is that the real rate of return on investment (δ) equal to the consumption discount rate (r). This condition is illustrated in Fig. 3.1. The consumption indifference curve is a locus of all combinations of consumption in the current period (C0) and consumption in the next period (C1) that confer a constant amount of utility. At any point, the slope of this indifference curve is given by $-(1+r)$; as we move along any indifference curve its slope changes and so 'r' also changes. The production possibility frontier shows the combinations of consumption goods that can be produced in each period; its slope at any point is given by $-(1+ \delta)$; as we moves along any production possibility frontier its slope changes and so δ changes.

An efficient inter-temporal consumption allocation is at point 'C' at which the slopes of the inter-temporal production possibility frontier and the consumption indifference curve are equalized; and the highest possible consumption indifference curve is attained.

That is, $r = \delta$

An allocation of resources overtime is efficient if, for any given level of utility today, further utilities are at their maximum feasible levels.

Efficient Allocation in a Market Economy

Welfare economics theory points to a set of circumstances such that, if they prevailed, markets would sustain an efficient allocation of resources. The institutional arrangements required for an efficient allocation of resources include the following:

(a) Markets exists for all goods and services exchanged.
(b) All markets are perfectly competitive.
(c) All transactions have perfect information.
(d) Property rights are fully assigned.
(e) No externalities exist.
(f) All goods and services are private goods. That is no public good exist, nor are any resources common property resources.
(g) Long-run average costs are non-decreasing. If production is characterized by economies of scale, then natural monopolies would exist, and a competitive equilibrium could not be sustained.

An efficient static and inter-temporal allocation would be sustained if the above institutional circumstances generalized to refer to all points in time now and in the future were satisfied.

Static efficiency conditions in a competitive market include:

(i) Efficiency in consumption:

$$\left(\frac{U_X}{U_Y}\right)^A = \left(\frac{U_X}{U_Y}\right)^B = \left(\frac{P_X}{P_Y}\right)$$

(ii) Efficiency in production:

$$\left(\frac{MP_L}{MP_K}\right)^X = \left(\frac{MP_L}{MP_K}\right)^Y = \left(\frac{P_L}{P_K}\right)$$

(iii) Product-mix efficiency:

$$\left(\frac{U_X}{U_Y}\right) = \left(\frac{MP^Y{}_K}{MP^X{}_K}\right) = \left(\frac{MP^Y{}_L}{MP^X{}_L}\right); \qquad P_X = MC_X \quad P_Y = MC_Y$$

$$\left(\frac{P_K}{MP_K}\right)^X = \left(\frac{P_L}{MP_L}\right)^X$$

$$\left(\frac{P_K}{MP_K}\right)^Y = \left(\frac{P_L}{MP_L}\right)^Y$$

The inter-temporal efficiency condition is:

$r_t = r;$ $\quad t = 1....M$

$\delta = r;$ $\quad r$-consumption discount rate

Market Failure and Natural Resources

Markets cannot allocate resources efficiently, where markets do not exist. Many environmental resources are not transacted at all through market processes, or the markets in which they are exchanged are incomplete in some way. That is,

(a) Unregulated private market behaviour can, in principle, lead to efficient outcomes. However, in practice, some of the institutional arrangements required for market economies to allocate resources efficiently are not satisfied.

(b) The special characteristics of environmental resources play an important part in preventing the necessary institutional arrangements from existing or being likely to exist in any economy.

(c) If these two assertions are correct, market economies will not allocate resources efficiently, that is, the economy will be characterized by market failure.

(d) Even through markets by themselves may fail to allocate resources efficiently; public sector intervention offers the prospect of establishing alternative institutional arrangements that will, by altering behaviour, lead to efficient patterns of resources allocation.

The pervasive presence of public goods and externalities implies failure of the static efficiency conditions, and the risks and uncertainties introduced whenever markets are incomplete suggest that it is very unlikely that resource allocation over time will be efficient.

Externalities and Efficiency

An external effect, or externality, is said to occur when the production or consumption decisions of one agent affect the utility or production possibilities of another agent in an unintended way, and when no compensation is made by the producer of the external effect to the affected party. In real practice consumption and production behaviour by some agents does affect, uncompensated way, the utility gained by other consumers and the output produced by other producers. Economic behaviour does involve external effects.

Externalities may be positive or negative; former is beneficial and latter adverse. Another dimension of externality is public and private, depending upon whether the externality effect is a public good or bad, or private good or bad.

In order to analyze the efficiency under externality following notations are required:

PMP_L—Private marginal product of labour
EMP_L—External marginal product of labour
SMP_L_Social marginal product of labour

An equivalent notation applies to capital.

These three measures of marginal product of labour are related as follows:

$$PMP_L + EMP_L = SMP_L$$

When a firm chooses to employ an additional unit of labour, the marginal product of labour to that firm is PMP_L. If this employment of labour has an external effect on others, we denote that external effect as EMP_L. The total, net, or social marginal product is the sum of these two. The productive efficiency condition for an economy in which external effects occur can be written as:

$$\frac{SMP_L{}^X}{SMP_K{}^X} = \frac{SMP_L{}^Y}{SMP_K{}^Y}$$

$$\frac{PMP_L{}^X + EMP_L{}^X}{PMP_K{}^X + EMP_K{}^X} = \frac{PMP_L{}^Y + EMP_L{}^Y}{PMP_K{}^Y + EMP_K{}^Y}$$

We can now see why private profit maximizing behaviour will fail to allocate resources efficiently in the presence of externalities. Left to act in their individual self-interests, firms will only take account of private marginal products. So profit maximization will result in the ratio of private-marginal products being equalized between goods. An efficient allocation in a market economy is achieved at that point these private marginal products ratios will be equal to the price ratios of factor inputs.

$$\frac{PMP_L{}^X}{PMP_K{}^X} = \frac{PMP_L{}^Y}{PMP_K{}^Y} = \frac{P_L}{P_K}$$

Except in the unlikely event that external effects are exactly offsetting in arithmetic terms, the equalization of private marginal product ratios will yield a different allocation of resources from that which derives from the equalization of social marginal product ratios. As the latter is required for efficiency, private market behaviour will be inefficient in the presence of externalities.

Public Goods and Efficiency

The term public goods is used in two ways. Some define a goods to be public if it is both indivisible and non-excludable. Others use the term to refer to any goods which is indivisible in consumption, irrespective of whether it is also excludable or not. It is probably the case that most indivisible (public) goods are also non-excludable. Moreover, it is this latter aspect which is of most relevance to the place of public goods in market economies; if an owner was unable to exclude another person from consuming goods; it is difficult to see how the owner could sell the goods at any positive price. But if prices cannot be charged for goods, it is difficult to imagine how a market could exist for that goods. That is non-excludable public goods are unlikely to be provided in pure market economies.

The efficiency conditions for two private goods (*X* and *Y*) and one public good (*X*) and one private good (*Y*) are given in Table 3.1.

Table 3.1: Consumption Efficiency: Private and Public Goods

Goods	*Conditions*
1. Private goods X and Y	$\frac{U_X^A}{U_Y} = \frac{U_X^B}{U_Y} = \frac{MP^Y{}_K}{MP^X{}_K} = \frac{MP^Y{}_L}{MP^X{}_L} = \frac{P_X}{P_Y}$
2. Private goods Y and Public goods X	$\frac{U_X^A}{U_Y} + \frac{U_X^B}{U_Y} = \frac{MP^Y{}_K}{MP^X{}_K} = \frac{MP^Y{}_L}{MP^X{}_L} = \frac{P_X}{P_Y}$

In the case of private goods (both *X* and *Y*) $\frac{U_X{}^A}{U_Y}$ is the number of units of goods *Y* that *A* is willing to pay for an additional unit of X. As the consumption of X is divisible, and so only one person can consume it, the social willingness to pay (*WTP*) for one unit of X is equal to one consumer's *WTP*. Given fixed market prices (P_X and P_Y) this measure of *WTP* will be identical over all consumers. The expressions involving marginal product refers to the reduction in production of *Y* that would result from transferring resources into the production of an extra unit of X. In other words, it is the opportunity cost of X in terms of *Y*. Efficiency requires that the individual *WTP* for X in units of *Y* is equal to the opportunity cost of X in units of *Y*.

When *Y* is private goods and X is public goods, the relevant efficiency condition is given in the lower part of Table 3.1. As the consumption of X is non-divisible, the social willingness to pay for one unit of X is the sum over all consumers of each person's *WTP*, rather than being equal to one person's *WTP*. This efficiency in the allocation of resources requires that the sum of all individual's *WTP* is equal to the opportunity cost of X in terms of *Y*. In a competitive market economy the opportunity cost of X in terms of *Y* is equal to the ratio of output prices P_X/P_Y. That is for one public and one private good economic efficiency requires that:

$$\sum \frac{U_X}{U_Y} = \frac{P_X}{P_Y}$$

Property Rights, Common Property Resources and Environmental Resources

The extent in which an economy is able to reach an efficient allocation of resources will depend upon the nature of the property rights that prevail. Hartwick and Olewiler (1986) define property right as, 'a bundle of characteristics that convey certain powers to the owner of the right.'

These characteristics concern conditions of appropriability of returns, the ability to divide or transfer the right, the degree of exclusiveness of the right, and the duration and enforceability of the right. Where a right is exclusive to one person or corporation, a private property right is said to exist.

In these circumstances, markets will tend to exist and efficient allocation of resources will be possible without government intervention. For several classes of environmental resources, well defined property rights do not exist. Outcomes cannot be socially optimal in these circumstances.

Where property rights are non-exclusive, these are common property or open access rights. The title 'common property resources' is used whenever some customary procedures or conventions govern use of the resource in question. This is not implied by the 'open access resources'. In the presence of open access, markets cannot by themselves allocate resources efficiently. It is possible, though unlikely, that resources will be allocated efficiently where common property rights prevail.

Many environmental resources are not privately owned being characterized by either common property regimes or open access in which ownership is either ill defined or non-existent. In these circumstances, there are several sources of inefficiency in the use of the resource. Not surprisingly, the major problem arises from the fact that stewardship of the asset is likely to be poor where users can't expect to receive the fruits of investment in the resource.

A rapacious attitude often characterizes behaviour in the absence of regulatory control. However, since common property resource issues are intimately bound up with the use of resources overtime, and because they are characteristic of many renewable resources, these conclusions will not be always justified.

Cost-Benefit Analysis (CBA)

CBA is a widely practiced technique of project appraisal. It is used in circumstances where it is felt that important components of either the real costs or the real benefits of a project would not be adequately represented by market prices, or would not be traded through markets at all (and so do not have market prices). In these circumstances, markets are failing to value all relevant flows correctly, and so a non-market evaluation procedure is required to assess the net worth of the project.

The key principle that underpins CBA is very simple. The impact of the project on each affected person at each point in time is identified. The value to each person of any gain or loss is then estimated. In principle, these valuations should be based on the preferences of the affected individuals, and ideally should reflect each person's willingness to pay for an improvement or compensation willingly accepted for a loss.

Imagine that three individuals (*A*, *B* and *C*) are affected in each of four consecutive intervals of time, labelled 0, 1, 2, 3, where 0 represents the present period. Table 3.2 presents the impacts on each person's utility at each time. Thus ΔU_{B2} denotes the changes in utility (post project utility minus pre-project utility) experienced by individual *B* during time period 2.

Table 3.2: Changes in utility (ΔU) for Individuals A, B and C Over Four Consecutive Time Periods

Individual	*Time Period*				
	0	1	2	3	Over all
A	ΔU_{A0}	ΔU_{A1}	ΔU_{A2}	ΔU_{A3}	ΔU_{A}
B	ΔU_{B0}	ΔU_{B1}	ΔU_{B2}	ΔU_{B3}	ΔU_{B}
C	ΔU_{C0}	ΔU_{C1}	ΔU_{C2}	ΔU_{C3}	ΔU_{C}
Society	ΔU_{0}	ΔU_{1}	ΔU_{2}	ΔU_{3}	

However, utilities are unobservable, and not all economists believe that utilities are comparable across people. As a result, the usual practice in CBA is to assess changes in terms of observable consumption (or output) gains and losses. Then defining the net benefit (NB) as the gross benefit from the project less the costs associated with the project, both being measured in units of consumption, as given in Table 3.3.

The net value (NV) of the project is defined as:

$$NV = NB_0 + NB_1 + NB_2 + NB_3$$

In this measure of net value, the gains or losses of each individual are weighted equally in arriving at the social net benefit for each time period, irrespective of characteristics or circumstances of the individuals concerned.

That is $NB_0 = NB_{A0} + NB_{B0} + NB_{C0}$

Table 3.3: Net Benefit (NB) of Project for Individuals A, B and C Over Four Consecutive Time Periods

Individual	*Time Period*				
	0	1	2	3	Over all
A	NB_{A0}	NB_{A1}	NB_{A2}	NB_{A3}	NB_A
B	NB_{B0}	NB_{B1}	NB_{B2}	NB_{B3}	NB_B
C	NB_{C0}	NB_{C1}	NB_{C2}	NB_{C3}	NB_C
Society	NB_0	NB_1	NB_2	NB_3	NV

Generally, for 'T' time periods (T>0) the net value of a project is given by

$$NV = NB_0 + NB_1 + NB_2 + \ldots\ldots\ldots\ldots + NB_T$$

The net present value (NPV) of a project is then defined as:

$$NPV = NB_0 + \frac{NB_1}{(1+r_1)} + \frac{NB_2}{(1+r_1)(1+r_2)} + \ldots\ldots\ldots\ldots + \frac{NB_T}{(1+r_1)(1+r_2)\ldots\ldots(1+r_T)}$$

Because we are summing the consumption over a sequence of periods, if a discount rate is deemed to be relevant the appropriate rate should be the consumption rate of discount. The above expression of NPV allows for varying consumption discount rates. However, if the rates are constant, so that $r_t = r$, for t = 1,.... T, as it is commonly assumed to be when CBA is undertaken in practice, and then we can express the NPV of a project as:

$$\text{NPV} = t = \sum_{t=0}^{t=T} \frac{NB_t}{(1+r)^t}$$

The CBA decision rule is that:

Do the projects if NPV > 0, otherwise do not do the project.

Conclusion

The economies in practice do not satisfy the conditions of an ideal competitive economy. Markets are often not perfectly competitive, information is not perfect, and consumption and production behaviour does generate uncompensated external effects upon others. These failures will result in inefficient allocation of resources. If there were no market failure, appraisal of investment projects could, at least as far as efficiency goes, be left to private agents using market prices. But when there is market failure, as these generally is in relation to projects with environmental impacts, the selection of projects in a manner consistent with efficiency requires appraisal by a public agency in a way that corrects the failure.

REFERENCES

Berndt, E. and Field, B. (eds.) (1981), *Measuring and Modeling Natural Resources Substitution*, MIT Press, Cambridge.

Bockstael, N.E. and McConnell, K.E. (1993), 'Public-goods as Characteristics of Non-Market Commodities,' *Economic Journal*, 103, 1244.

Common, M.S. (1996), *Environmental Resources Economics: An Introduction*, Longman, Harlow.

Hanley, N. and Spash, C. (1993), *Cost-Benefit Analysis and the Environment*, Edward Elgar, Alder Shot.

Johanson, P.O. (1987), *The Economic Theory and Measurement of Environmental Benefits*, Cambridge University Press, Cambridge.

4

Economics of Pollution Control

Introduction

In the first chapter we described the schematic relationship between the environmental and the economic systems. It depicted the flow of mass and energy to the economic system, and the flow of waste products back to the environment. The major agenda in Environmental economics is with regard to achieving a balance set of mass and energy flows; including the flow of waste products back to the environment. Because the waste flows are inexorably intertwined with the flow of mass and energy into the economy, establishing a balance for waste flows will have feedback effects on the input flows as well.

In this chapter two questions must be addressed:

(i) What is the appropriate level of flow?
(ii) How should the responsibility for achieving this flow level be allocated among the various sources of the pollutant when reductions are needed?

A Pollutant Taxonomy

The amount of waste products emitted determines the load upon the environment. The damage done by this load depends on the capacity of the environment to assimilate the waste products, as given in Fig. 4.1. The ability of the environment to absorb pollutants is called as its 'absorptive capacity'. If the emissions load exceeds the absorptive capacity, then the pollutant accumulates in the environment.

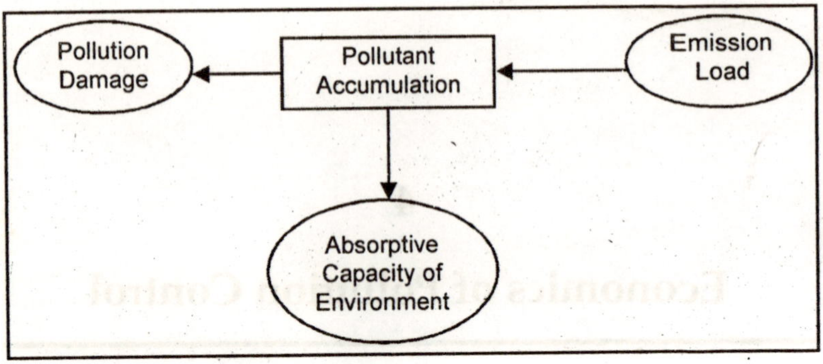

Fig. 4.1: Relationship between Emissions and Pollution Damage

Pollutants for which the environment has little or no absorptive capacity are called 'stock pollutants'. Stock pollutants accumulate over time as emissions enter the environment. Examples of stock pollutants include non-biodegradable bottles tossed by the roadside, heavy metals, such as lead, which accumulate in the soils near the emission source, etc.

Pollutants for which the environment has some absorptive capacity are called 'fund pollutants'. For these pollutants, as long as the emission rate does not exceed the absorptive capacity of the environment, the pollutants do not accumulate. Many organic pollutants injected into an oxygen-rich stream will be transformed by the resident bacteria into less harmful inorganic matter. Carbon dioxide is absorbed by plant life and the oceans. That is, when fund pollutants are injected into the air or water, they may be transformed into substances that are not considered harmful to people or to the ecological system or they may be so diluted or dispersed that the resulting concentrations are not harmful.

Pollutants are also be classified by their zone of influence, defined both horizontally and vertically. The horizontal dimension deals with the domain over which damage from emitted pollutants is experienced. The damage caused by 'local pollutants' is experienced near the sources of emission, while the damage from 'regional pollutants' is experienced at greater distances from the source of emission.

The vertical zone of influence describes whether the damage is caused mainly by ground-level concentrations of an air pollutant or by concentrations in the upper atmosphere. When the damage caused by a pollutant is determined mainly by concentrations of the pollutant near the earth's surface, it is called a 'surface pollutant'. When its damage is related more to its concentration in the upper atmosphere, the substance is called a 'global pollutant'. Water pollutants are obviously surface pollutants, but air pollutants can be surface pollutants, global pollutants, or both. One common global pollutant, carbon dioxide injected into the atmosphere as a product of fossil-fuel combustion, has been implicated in raising global temperature *via* the 'greenhouse effect'. In addition chlorofluorocarbon emissions play a role in the destruction of the ozone layer, which protects the earth's surface from harmful solar radiation.

Efficient Allocation of Pollution

Pollutants are the residuals of production and consumption. These residuals must eventually be returned to the environment in one form or another. Since their presence in the environment may depreciate the service flows received, an efficient allocation of resources must take this cost into account. Efficient allocation of pollution depends on the nature of the pollutant.

Stock Pollutants

The efficient allocation of a stock pollutant must take into account the fact that the pollutant accumulates in the environment over time and that the damage caused by its presence increases and persists as the pollutant accumulates. Stock pollutants can create a burden for future generations by passing on a damage cost which persists well after the benefits received from incurring that damage cost have been forgotten. The analysis of efficient allocation of stock pollutants requires the following assumptions:

(i) The commodity produced is X.
(ii) Production of X involves the generation of proportional amount of a stock pollutant.
(iii) The damage caused by the presence of the pollutant in the environment is proportional to the size of the accumulated stock.

The efficient allocation is the one which maximizes the present value of the net benefit. In this case the net benefit at any point in time *'t'* is equal to the benefit received from the consumption of X *minus* the cost of the damage caused by the presence of the stock pollutant in the environment.

This damage is a cost that society must bear, and in terms of its effect on the efficient allocation, this cost is not unlike that of extracting minerals or fuels. While for minerals the extraction cost rises with the cumulative amount of the depletable resources extracted, the damage cost associated with a stock pollutant rises with the cumulative amount deposited in the environment. The major difference is that the extraction cost is borne only at the time of extraction, while damage is borne as long as the stock pollutant exists in the environment.

When extraction cost rises, the efficient quantity of a depletable resource extracted and consumed declines overtime. Similarly, the efficient quantity of X (and, therefore, the addition to the accumulation of this pollutant in the environment) would decline over time as the marginal cost of the damage rises. The price of X would rise over time, reflecting the rising social cost of production. To cope with the increasing marginal damage, the amount of resources committed to controlling the pollutant would increase overtime. Ultimately, a steady state would be reached where additions to the amount of the pollutant in the environment would cease and the size of the stock would stabilize. At this point all further emission of the pollutant created by the production of X would be controlled (through recycling). The price of X and the quantity consumed would remain constant. The damage caused by the stock pollutant would persist.

However, technological progress could reduce the amount of pollutant generated per unit of X produced; it could create ways to recycle the stock pollutant rather than injecting it into the environment; or it could develop ways of rendering the pollutant less harmful. All of these responses would lower the marginal damage cost associated with a given level of production of *X*.

Fund Pollutants

To the extent that the emission of fund pollutants exceeds the assimilative capacity of the environment, they accumulate and share some of the characteristics of stock pollutants. When the emission rate is low enough, however, the discharges can be assimilated by the environment with the result that the link between present emissions and future damage may be broken.

Generally the marginal damage caused by a unit of pollution increases with the amount emitted. When small amounts of the pollutant are emitted, the marginal damage is quite small. Small amounts of pollution are easily diluted in the environment, and the body can tolerate small quantities of substances. However, as the amount in the atmosphere increases, dilution is less effective and the body is less tolerant.

On the other hand, the marginal control costs, the cost incurred to control the damage, increase with the amount controlled. In Fig. 4.2 we use these two costs on the shapes of the relevant curves to derive the efficient allocation. A movement from right to left refers to greater control and less pollution emitted. The efficient allocation is represented by *Q′*, the point at which the damage caused by the marginal unit of pollution is exactly equal to the marginal cost of avoiding it.

Greater degrees of control (points to the left of *Q′*) are inefficient because the further increase in avoidance costs would exceed the reduction in damages. Hence, total costs would rise. Similarly, levels of control lower than *Q′* would result in a lower cost of control, but the increase in damage costs would be even larger, yielding an increase in total cost. Either increasing or decreasing the amount controlled causes an increase in total costs. Hence *Q′* must be efficient.

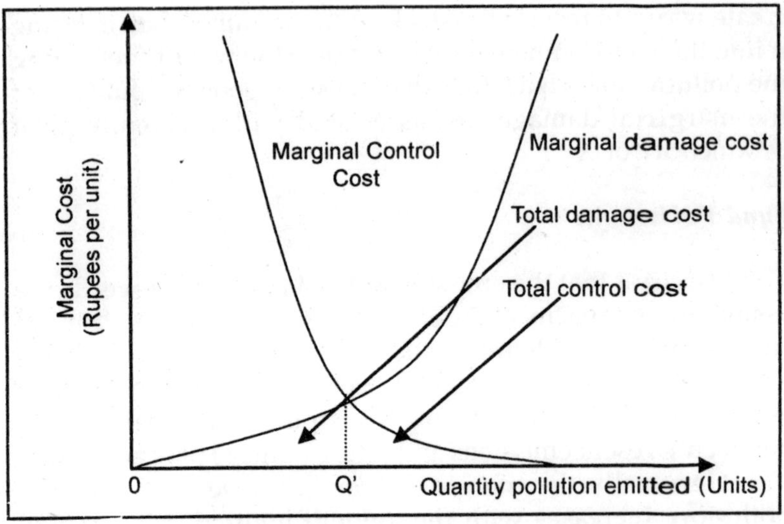

Fig. 4.2: Efficient Allocation of a Fund Pollutant

The diagram suggests that, under the condition presented, the optimal level of pollution is not zero. However, in some circumstances it may be zero or closer to zero. This situation occurs when the damage caused by even the first unit of pollution is so severe that it is higher than the marginal cost of controlling the last unit of pollution. This would be reflected in Fig. 4.2, as a leftward shift of the damage cost curve of sufficient magnitude that its intersection with the vertical axis would lie above the point where the marginal control cost curve intersects the vertical axis. This circumstance seems to characterize the treatment of highly dangerous radioactive pollutants such as uranium.

Market Allocation

Common property resources like air and water are misallocated by the market. Air and water resources have been over exploited as waste repositories. Since damage costs are externalities and control costs are not, what is cheapest for the firm is not always cheapest for society as a whole. The damage costs are not borne by the emitting source and hence, not considered by it, although they certainly are borne by society at large.

In the case of stock pollutants, the problem is particularly severe. Uncontrolled markets would lead to an excessive production of such commodities.

There are important differences between the inefficiencies associated with pollution control and that associated with the extraction or production of natural resources. For private property resources, the market forces provide automatic signals of impending scarcity. These forces may be understated (as when the vulnerability of imports is ignored), but they operate in the correct direction. Even when some resources are treated as common property (fisheries), the possibility for a private property alternative (fish farming) is enhanced. When private property and common property resources sell in the same market, the private property owner tends to ameliorate the excesses of those who exploit common properties. Efficient firms are rewarded with higher profits.

Regarding pollution no comparable automatic amelioration mechanism is evident. Because this cost is borne partially by innocent victims, rather than producers, it does not find its way into product prices. Firms which attempt to unilaterally control their pollution are placed at a competitive disadvantage; due to the added expense, their costs of production are higher than those of their less conscientious competitors. Not only does the unimpeded market fail to generate the efficient level of pollution control, it penalizes those firms which might attempt to control an efficient amount. Hence, the case for some sort of government intervention is particularly strong for pollution control.

Efficient Policy Responses

Efficiency is achieved when the marginal cost of control is equal to the marginal damage caused by the pollution for each emitter. One way to achieve this equilibrium would be to impose a legal limit on the amount of pollution allowed by each emitter. If the limit were chosen precisely at the level of pollution where marginal control cost equals marginal damage (Q' in Fig. 4.2), efficiency would have been achieved.

An alternative approach would be to internalize the marginal damage caused by each unit of emissions by means of a tax or charge on each unit of emissions. This per unit charge could either increase with the level of pollution or the tax rate could be constant as long as the rate were equal to the marginal social damage at the point where the marginal social damage and marginal control costs (*see* Fig. 4.2). Since the emitter is paying the marginal social damage when confronted by these fees, pollution costs would be internalized. The efficient choice would also be the cost-minimizing choice for the emitter.

Cost Effective Policies for Uniformly Mixed Fund Pollutants

Cost Effective Allocation

The damage caused by the mixed fund pollutants depends on the amount entering the atmosphere. In contrast to non-uniformly mixed pollutants, the damage caused by uniformly mixed pollutants is relatively insensitive to where the emissions are injected into the atmosphere. Thus, the policy can focus simply on controlling the total weight of emissions in a manner that minimizes the cost of control.

Assume that there are two emission sources currently emitting a total of 30 units of emissions. If the control authority determines that the environment can assimilate 15 units so that a reduction of 15 units is necessary. Fig. 4.3, is drawn by measuring the marginal cost of control for the first source from the left hand axis (MC_1) and the marginal cost of control for the second source from the right hand axis (MC_2). Notice that a total of 15 units reduction is achieved for every point on this graph; each point represents some different combination of reduction by the two sources. Drawn in this manner, Fig. 4.3 represents all possible allocations of the 15 units reduction between the two sources. The left hand axis represents an allocation of the entire reduction to the second source, while the right hand axis represents a situation in which the first source bears the entire responsibility. All points in between represent different degree of shared responsibility.

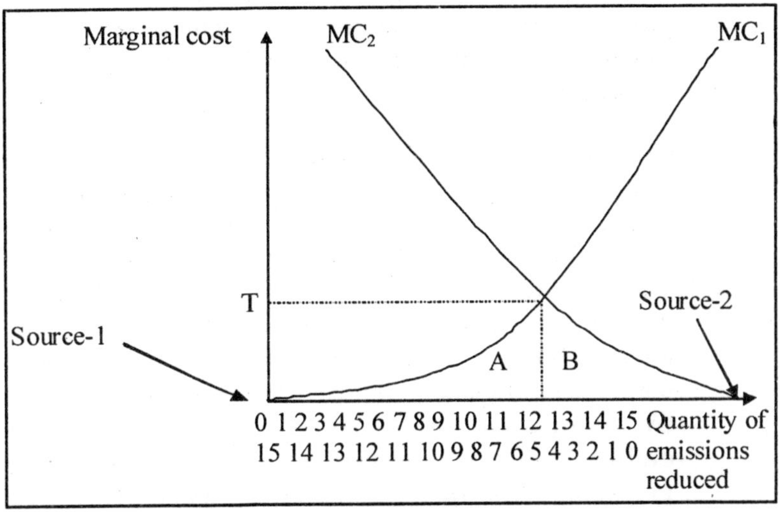

Fig. 4.3: Cost Effective Allocation of a Uniformly Mixed Pollutant

In the cost effective allocation, the first source cleans up 12 units, while the second source cleans up 3 units. The total variable cost of control for this particular assignment of the responsibility for the reduction is represented by area *A* plus *B*. Area *A* is the cost of control for the first source; area *B* the cost of control for the second. Any other allocation would result in a higher total control cost.

Figure 4.3 demonstrates one of the most important propositions in the economics of pollution control. The cost of achieving a given reduction in emissions will be minimized if and only if the marginal costs of control are equalized for all emitters. This is demonstrated by the fact that the marginal cost curves cross at the cost effective allocation.

Cost Effective Pollution Control Policies

This proposition can be used as a basis for choosing among the various policy instruments which the control authority might use to achieve this allocation sources have a large menu of options for controlling the amount of pollution they inject into the environment. The cheapest method of control will differ widely not only among industries but also among plants in the same industry. The selection of the cheapest methods requires detailed information on the possible control techniques and their associated costs.

(a) *Emission Standards*: In environmental economics this is referred to as the 'command and control' approach. An emission standard is a legal limit on the amount of the pollutant an individual source is allowed to emit.
(b) *Emission Charges:* An emission charge is a fee, collected by the government, levied on each unit of pollutant emitted into the air or water. The total payment any source would make to the government could be found by multiplying the fee times amount of pollution emitted. Emission charges reduce pollution because pollution costs the firm money. To save money, the source seeks ways to reduce its pollution.
(c) *Transferable Emission Permits:* Under this system, all sources are required to have permits to emit. Each permit specifies exactly how much the firm is allowed to emit. The permits are freely transferable; they can be bought and sold. The control authority issues exactly the number of permits needed to produce the desired emission level. Any emissions by a source in excess of those allowed by its permit would cause the source to face severe monetary sanctions.

Cost Effective Policies for Non-uniformity Mixed Surface Pollutants

For these pollutants the policy must be concerned not only with the weight of emission entering the atmosphere, but also with the location of emissions. Since the damage caused by non-uniformly mixed surface pollutants is related to their concentration levels in the air, soil, or water, it is natural that the cost-effective policies will focus on the attainment of ambient standards. Ambient standards are legal ceilings placed on the concentration level of specified pollutants in the air, soil or water. They represent the target concentration levels which are not to be exceeded. A cost effective policy results in the lowest cost allocation of control responsibility consistent with ensuring that the predetermined ambient standards are met at specified locations called receptor sites.

Single Receptor Case

In this simple case we desire to control pollution at only one receptor location. As given in Fig. 4.4, four sources individually inject (say 10 units of emission) at different points in time into a stream. The pollutant concentration is measured at receptor *R*. In general, the emissions from *A* or *B* would cause a larger rise in the recorded concentration than would those from *C* and *D*, even though the same amount was emitted from each source. This is because the emissions from *C* and *D* would be substantially diluted by the time they arrived at *R*, while those from *A* and *B* would arrive in a more concentrated form.

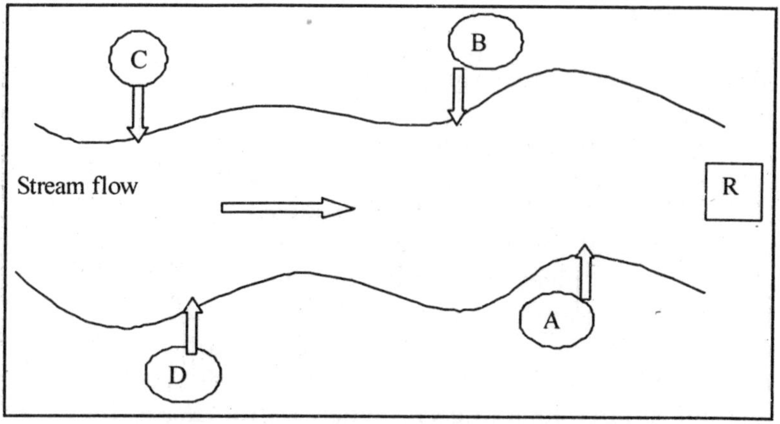

Fig. 4.4: Effect of Location on Local Pollutant Concentration

Since emissions are what can be controlled, but the concentrations at *R* are the policy target, our first task must be to relate the two by using a transfer coefficient. A transfer coefficient (a_i) captures the constant amount that the concentration at the receptor will rise if some 'i' emits one more unit of pollution. Using this definition and the knowledge that the a_i's are constant, we can relate the concentration level at R to emissions from all sources.

$$K_R = \sum_{i=1}^{I} a_i E_i + B \qquad \text{...(1)}$$

Where, K_R—Concentration at the receptor,
E_i—Emission level of the ith source,
I—Total number of sources in the region, and
B—Background concentration level (Resulting from natural sources or sources outside the control region).

This framework can be used to evaluate various policy approaches that the control authority might use. One of the most important policy approach is ambient charges. It is the charge used to produce a cost effective allocation of a non-uniformly mixed pollutant. This charge takes the form:

$$t_i = a_i F \qquad \text{...(2)}$$

Where, t_i—Per unit charge paid by the ith source on each unit emitted,
a_i— i^{th} source's transfer coefficient, and
F— Marginal cost of a unit of concentration reduction; which is the same for all sources.

In general sources will pay different charges when the objective is to meet an ambient standard at minimum cost because their transfer coefficients differ. An ambient permit entitles the owner to cause the concentration to rise at the receptor by a specified amount, rather than allowing the same amount of emissions to each owner. Using ΔK_R to represent this permitted rise and E to indicate the units of emissions allowed by each permit held by the ith source, we can see from Equation 1 that:

$$\frac{\Delta K_R}{a_i} = \Delta E_{Ri} \qquad ...(3)$$

The larger the transfer coefficient (that is, the closer the source is to the receptor), the smaller is the amount of emissions legitimized by a permit. Proximate sources must purchase more permits than distant sources to legitimize a given level of emissions. In this version of the permit system the sources pay the same price for each permit, but the amount of emissions allowed by each permit varies for location to location. The market automatically determines this common price, and the resulting allocation of permits is cost-effective. This cost effective system is called an 'ambient permit system' to differentiate it from the 'emission permit system', which is used to achieve a cost-effective allocation of control responsibility for uniformly mixed pollutants.

Many Receptor Case

The cost effective ambient charge paid by any source in the case of many receptors would be:

$$T_i = \sum_{j=1}^{J} a_{ij} F_j \qquad ...(4)$$

Where, T_i—Charge paid by the ith source for each unit of emissions,

a_{ij}—Transfer coefficient that translates emissions by source 'i' into concentration increases at the jth receptor,

J— Number of receptors, and

F_j— Monetary fee associated with the jth receptor.

Thus the source has to pay a charge that incorporates its effect on all receptors. The control authority could manipulate F_j for each receptor location until the desired concentration level is achieved at that receptor.

The extension of the ambient per unit system to the many receptor case requires that a separate permit market be created for each receptor. The price prevailing in each of these markets would reflect the difficulty of meeting the ambient standard at that receptor. All other things being equal, permit markets associated with receptors in heavily congested areas could be expected to sustain higher prices than those affected by a relatively few emitters.

Conclusion

There are many different types of pollutants, and different policy approaches are appropriate for each one. Stock pollutants pose the most serious inter-temporal problems. The efficient amount of a fund pollutant is defined as the amount which minimizes the sum of damage and control costs. Since pollution is an externality, markets will generally produce more than the efficient amount of both fund pollutants and stock pollutants. While policy instruments could in principle be defined to achieve an efficient level of pollution for every emitter, in practice it is very difficult because the amount of information required by the control authorities is unrealistically high. Policies to control non-uniformly mixed pollutants must take the location of the emission into account as well as the amount. The permit approach and the charge approach respond differently to growth in the number of sources, to inflation, to technological change, and to uncertainty.

REFERENCES

Baumol W.J. and W.E. Oates (1988), *The Theory of Environmental Policy*, Cambridge University Press, Cambridge.

Dales, J.H. (1968), *Pollution, Property and Prices*, Toronto University Press, Toronto.

Kneese, Allen V. and Charles L. Shultze (1975), *Pollution, Prices and Public Policy*, The Brookings Institution, Washington, DC.

OECD (1989), *Economic Instruments for Environmental Protection*, OECD, Paris.

Tietenberg, T.H. (1985), *Emissions Trading: An Exercise in Reforming Pollution Policy*, *Resources for the Future*, Washington DC.

5

Economic Development and the Environment

Introduction

We inhabit a world in which the human population has risen dramatically over the past century and will probably double during the present century. The material demands being made by the average individual have been increasing rapidly, though many human beings now alive are desperately poor; which necessitate economic growth, triggered by intensive resource consumption. However, the world's resource base is limited, and contains a complex, and interrelated set of ecosystems that are currently exhibiting signs of fragility. It is increasingly questioned whether the global economic system can continue to grow without undermining the natural systems, which are its ultimate foundation.

View of the 'Limits to Growth'

The *Limits to Growth* (Meadows, *et al.*) published in 1972, which was widely understood to claim that environmental limits would cause the collapse of the world economic system in the middle of the 21st century. However, it was a stimulus to the re-emergence of interest in natural resources on the part of economists. The *Limits to Growth* reported the results of a study in which a computer model of the world system, World3, was used to stimulate its future. World3 represented the world economy as a single economy, and included interconnections between that economy and its environment.

According to its creators, World3 was built to investigate five major trends of global concern—accelerating industrialization, rapid population growth, widespread malnutrition, depletion of non-renewable resources, and a deteriorating environment. These trends are all interconnected in many ways, and their development is measured in decades or centuries, rather than in months or years. With the model we are seeking to understand the causes of these trends, their interrelationships, and their implications as much as one hundred years in future (Meadows, *et al.*, 1972, p. 2).

It incorporated:

(a) A limit to the amount of land available for agriculture;
(b) A limit to the amount of agricultural output producible per unit of land in use;
(c) A limit to the amount of non-renewable resources available for extraction; and
(d) A limit to the ability of the environment to assimilate wastes arising in production and consumption, which limit falls as the level of pollution increases.

On the basis of a number of simulations using World3, the conclusions reached by the modelling team were as follows:

(i) If the present growth trends in world population, industrialization, pollution, food production and resource depletion continue unchanged, the limits to growth on this planet will be reached sometime within the next 100 years. The most probable result will be sudden and uncontrollable decline in both population and industrial capacity;
(ii) It is possible to alter these trends and to establish a condition of ecological and economic stability that is sustainable far into the future. The state of global equilibrium could be designed so that the basic material needs of each person on earth are satisfied and each person has an equal opportunity to realize his or her individual human potential;

(iii) If the world's population decide to strive for this second outcome rather than the first, the sooner they begin working to attain it, the greater will be their chances of success.

Another argument called 'Social limits to growth' was developed following the 'Limits to growth' (For instance, Hirsch, 1977). To this group the major propositions about the desirability of growth include:

(a) The desirability of growth financed by running down resources is limited by the cost imposed on future generations;
(b) The extinction or reduction in the number of sentient non-human species whose habitat disappears limits the desirability of growth financed by take over;
(c) The self-cancelling effects on welfare limit the desirability of aggregate growth; and
(d) The desirability of growth is limited by the corrosive effects on moral standards of the very attitudes that foster growth, such as glorification of self-interest and a scientific-technocratic world-view.

The last two of these propositions are called 'social limits to growth'. Once basic material needs are satisfied, further economic growth is associated with an increasing proportion of income being spent on positional goods. As a consequence, growth is a much less socially desirable objective than economists have usually thought.

Economic Growth and Environment: The Environmental Kuznets Curve

The World Development Report 1992 noted that 'The view that greater economic activity inevitably hurts the environment is based on static assumptions about technology, tastes and environmental investments.' For example, the per capita emissions of some pollutant into the environment (e) and per capita income (y), then the view that is being referred to can be represented as:

$$e = \alpha y \qquad ...(1)$$

So that 'e' increases linearly with 'y' as shown in Fig. 5.1. This is the sort of relationship that the creators of 'Limits to Growth' claimed.

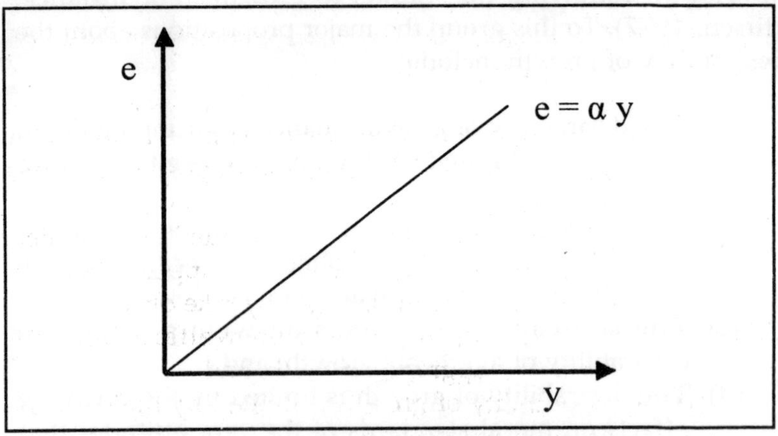

Fig. 5.1: Environmental Impact and Income: View of 'Limits to Growth' School

On the other hand, suppose that the coefficient α is itself a linear function of 'y':

$$\alpha = \beta_0 - \beta_1 y \qquad ...(2)$$

Then substituting Equation 2 into Equation 1 gives the relationship between 'e' and 'y' as:

$$e = \beta_0 y - \beta_1 y^2 \qquad ...(3)$$

For β_1, sufficiently small in relation to β_0, e/y relationship takes the form of an inverted U, as shown in Fig. 5.2. With this form of relationship, economic growth means higher emissions per capita until per capita income reaches the turning point, and thereafter actually reduce emissions per capita.

It has been hypothesized that a relationship like that shown in Fig. 5.2, holds for many forms of environmental degradation. Such a relationship is sometimes called an 'Environmental Kuznets Curve' (EKC), after Kuznets (1955), who hypothesized an inverted U for the relationship between a measure of inequality in the distribution of income and the level of income. If the EKC hypothesis held generally, it could imply that instead of being a threat to the environment as argued in the 'Limits to Growth', economic growth is the means to environmental improvement. That is, as countries develop economically, moving from lower to higher levels of per capita income, over all levels of environmental degradation will eventually fall.

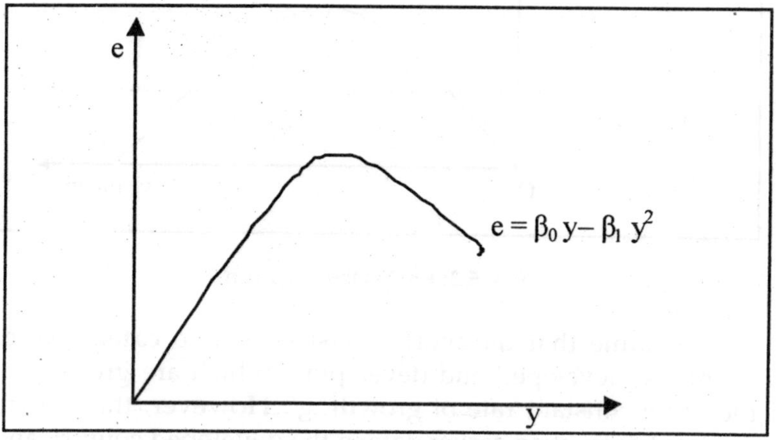

Fig. 5.2: Environmental Impact and Income: Kuznets Curve

Environmental Impact in the Long-run

The EKC implies that the magnitude of environmental impacts of economic activity will fall as income rises above some threshold level, when both these variable are measured in per capita terms. Some economists (For instance Common, 1995) examined the long-term implication of the EKC hypothesis. There are the following two possible outcomes of environmental impacts:

(a) Environmental impacts per unit of income eventually fall to zero as the level of income rises.

(b) Environmental impacts per unit income falling to some minimum level, say '*k*' as in Fig. 5.3; and thereafter remaining constant at that level as income continues to increase.

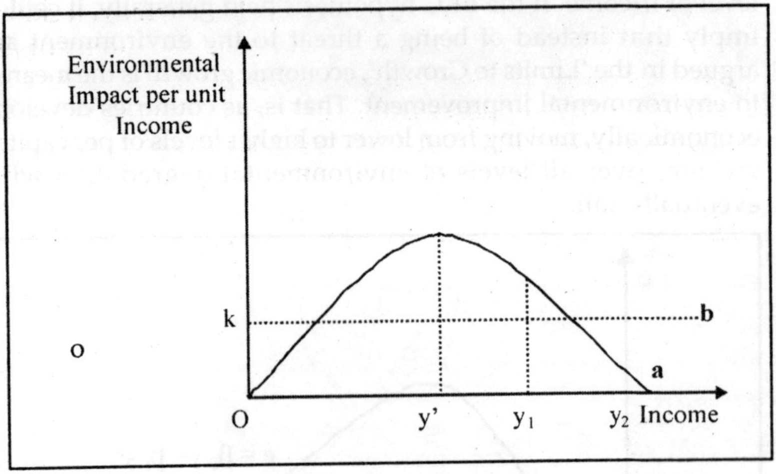

Fig. 5.3: EKC in the Long-run

Assume that the world consists of two categories of countries; developed and developing, which are growing at the same constant rate of growth 'g'. However, the growth process began at an earlier date in the developed country and so at any point in time its per capita income level is higher than in the developing country.

The above mentioned two cases (*a* and *b*) can be analyzed as follows. The highly optimistic version of EKC, '*a*' will be as given in the part-1 of Fig. 5.4. There we can see a dip in the central part of the curve; because for some period of time, income levels in the two countries will be such that the developed country is on the downward sloping portion of its EKC, while the developing country is still on the upward sloping part of its EKC. However, as time passes and growth continues, both countries will be at income levels where the EKC curves have a negative slope; together with the assumption of case '*a*' (impacts per unit income fall to zero). This implies that the total level of impacts will itself converge to zero as time becomes increasingly large.

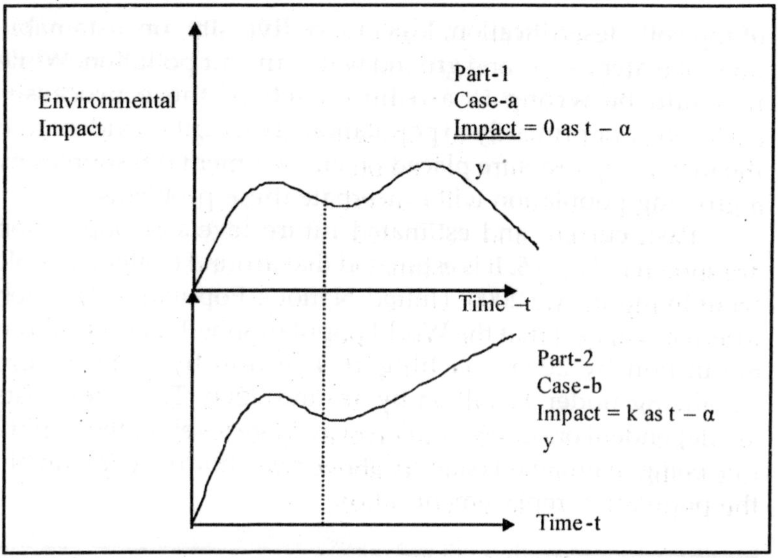

Fig. 5.4: Scenarios of Environmental Impacts

In case-b (part-2 of Fig. 5.4) no matter how large incomes be the ratio of environmental impacts to income can never fall below some fixed level *'k'*. As time passes, and both countries reach high income levels, the average of the impacts to income ratio for the two countries must converge on that constant value *'k'*. However, since we are assuming that each country is growing at a fixed rate *'g'*, the total level of impacts must itself eventually be increasing over time at the rate *'g'*. Even if environmental impacts per unit of income eventually fell to a tiny level, the total level of impacts would eventually grow in line with income.

Population Growth and the Environment

Human population growth, in conjunction with pressures for higher standards of living, increases the demands for agricultural land, energy and water resources, and intensifies the problems of managing and disposing of waste products. They are associated with a number of serious environmental changes including forest depletion, declining soil fertility, loss of top soil, desertification, loss of bio-diversity, unsustainable rates of water usage, and ground water and air pollution. While it would be wrong to attribute each of these processes exclusively or primarily to population growth, it is evident that the increasing pressure placed on environmental resources by a growing population will exacerbate these problems.

Past, current and estimated future levels of population are shown in Fig. 5.5. It is estimated that around 6 billion people were living in AD 2000. United Nations Population Division forecasts suggest that the World population will grow to about 8.3 billion by 2025, reaching 10.4 billion by 2100, before stabilizing under 11 billion by around 2200. These forecasts are dependent on an assumption of average levels of the fertility rate being maintained (slightly above two children per woman, the population replacement ratio).

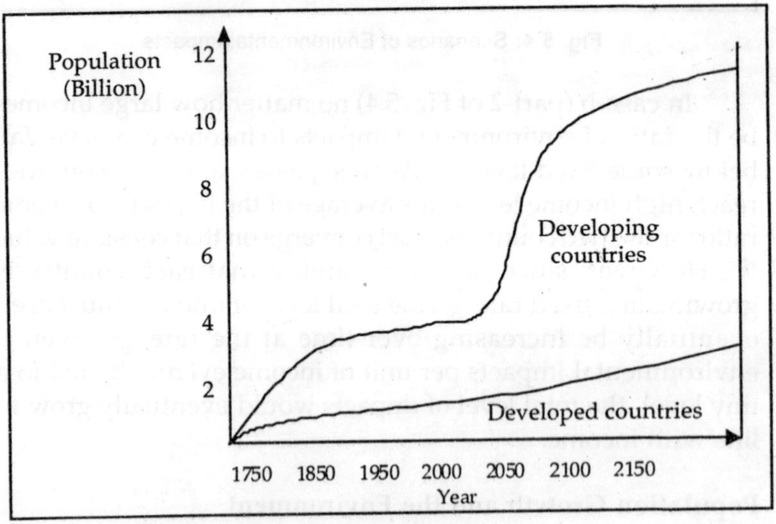

Fig. 5.5: Trend of World Population, 1750–2150

The linkage between population growth and the environment are complicated. Some of these linkages operate directly, others indirectly. Among these the following appears to be important.

(i) Higher levels of population place greater demands on non-renewable material resources and greater strain on renewable resource stocks, including world food resources;

(ii) Higher levels of population tend to be associated with greater volumes of material and energy throughput, increasing the likelihood that carrying capacities of environmental sinks will be exceeded;

(iii) Higher levels of population will tend to increase ecological pressures generally and promote changes in agricultural practices in particular that will reduce biological diversity; and

(iv) High rates of population growth may contribute to low and possible falling rates of real per capita incomes, which can exacerbate environmental pressures.

Continuing population increases will place increasing pressure on world agriculture and threatens the availability of adequate suppliers of food. Increasing affluence tends to change demand in the direction of meat and away from direct consumption of vegetables and grain. This imparts considerable physical inefficiency in food production, and causes prices to rise, reducing food access to lower-income families. At the same time there is limited availability of land to bring under cultivation. The scope for expanding the extensive margin of agriculture has become quite restricted. However, the most cost-effective method of obtaining output increases has been through expanding the intensive margin of agriculture. Furthermore, large productivity increases remained to be exploited through land irrigation. Increasing the intensive margin is also likely to become more difficult as a consequence of higher energy prices, leading to higher relative prices for inorganic fertilizers and other agriculture inputs.

However, future prospects offer some grounds for optimism. One of these is the likely future stabilization and the decline of global population that we discussed earlier in this chapter. Another derives from the application of new technologies such as bio-technology and precision farming.

Sustainable Development

Sustainable development would imply that the environmental capital stocks have to be held constant over time and their over exploitation can cause loss of plant and animal species and corresponding genetic resources, which would then limit options of future generation. There are certain ecological limitations beyond which exploitation of natural resources would not be sustainable. These limits determine the carrying capacity of the ecosystem or the extent to which natural resources could be exploited consistent with their sustained availability in the case of renewable resources.

There are considerable amount of divergence in the concept of sustainability as seen by economists, ecologists, and environmentalists. The identification of sustainable development requires:

(a) Good understanding of the physical, biological and social impact of human activities;
(b) Better estimates of the economic value of damage to the environment in order to design sound investment decisions; and
(c) Development of policy tools and strengthening of human resources and institutions to implement viable strategies and manage natural resources on a sustainable basis.

Origin and Development of the Concept of Sustainability

It was only in the early 1970s, for the first time, the attention of development economists was drawn by an MIT team of researchers in their Club of Rome Report, 'Limits to Growth' (we discussed earlier) to the likely grave consequences of natural resources depletion and degradation of ecology and environment. The UN Conference on Environment and Development held at Stockholm in 1972 gave further dimension on the ecological and environmental consequences of development. The discussion on this issue gained momentum with the World Commission on Environment and Development (1987) and the UN Conference on Environment and Development at Rio (1992). The World Bank brought to focus further the issue of sustainable development in its World Development Report 1992 and discussed the operational implication of the concept of sustainability.

Concepts of Sustainability

There are several points to note about the concept from the outset. Firstly, not all concepts are purely economic conceptualization. Secondly, the concepts are not necessarily mutually exclusive. Thirdly, some of the concepts view sustainability as a constraint on economic behaviour. Finally, concepts never explicitly specifies the duration of time over which sustainability is to operate.

The following are the important concepts of sustainability:

(a) A sustainable state is one in which utility (or consumption) is non-declining through time;
(b) A sustainable state is one in which resources are managed so as to maintain production opportunities for the future;
(c) A sustainable state is one in which the natural capital stock is non-declining through time;
(d) A sustainable state is one in which resources are managed so as to maintain a sustainable yield of resource services;
(e) A sustainable state is one which satisfies minimum conditions of ecosystem stability and resilience through time; and
(f) Sustainable development as capacity and consensus building.

Measuring Sustainable Development: Atkinson and Pearce Model

Atkinson and Pearce adopted a non-declining capital stock as the criterion for sustainability. The broad concept of capital used here includes physical and natural capital. In a world of changing population, the nation's per capita stock of capital is to be non-declining.

Atkinson and Pearce proposed two variants of the constant capital stock rule.

(i) A weak sustainability is achieved when the total capital stock (physical, human and natural) is non-declining through time. In this variant, development is sustainable even if some component (such as natural capital) is declining, provided the total capital stock is not falling. That is, the different elements of the capital stock are substitutes for one another. For example, if the loss of a particular ecosystem is compensated for by an increase in the stock of human knowledge.

(ii) The strong sustainability affords environmental (natural) capital at a special place. Sustainable development is attained if the nation's stock of environmental capital is non-declining.

Atkinson and Pearce developed a sustainability index and showed the results of a simple test for weak sustainability (Table 5.1).

$$\text{Sustainability Index } (Z) = (S/Y) - (\delta M/Y) - (\delta N/Y)$$

Where, S—Gross domestic savings,

Y—GDP,

δM—Value of depreciation of man-made capital,

δN—Value of depreciation of natural capital.

The test statistics, as given in Table 5.1, measures the nation's savings less than the depreciation of man-made and natural capital, each expressed as a proportion of GDP (Y). The index (Z) constitutes a measure of stabilization of a necessary condition for sustainable development. If Z is positive, the condition is satisfied, if Z is negative it is not. As given in the Table 5.1; out of 22 economies 8 failed the weak sustainability test. An economy is sustainable if it saves more than the depreciation on its man-made and natural capital. That is $Z \geq 0$.

Table 5.1: Testing for Sustainable Development—Atkinson and Pearce Index

Country	*S/Y*	*δM/Y*	*δN/Y*	*Z*
A. Sustainable Economies				
1. Brazil	20	7	10	+3
2. Costa Rica	26	3	8	+15
3. Czechoslovakia	30	10	7	+13
4. Finland	28	15	2	+11
5. Germany	26	12	4	+10
6. Hungary	26	10	5	+11
7. Japan	33	14	2	+17
8. Netherlands	25	10	1	+14
9. Poland	30	11	3	+10
10. USA	18	12	3	+3
11. Zimbabwe	24	10	5	+9
B. Marginally Sustainable				
1. Mexico	24	12	12	0
2. Philippines	15	11	4	0
3. UK	18	12	6	0
C. Unsustainable				
1. Burkina Faso	2	1	10	-9
2. Ethiopia	3	1	9	-7
3. Indonesia	20	5	17	-2
4. Madagascar	8	1	16	-9
5. Malawi	8	7	4	-3
6. Mali	-4	4	6	-14
7. Nigeria	15	3	17	-5
8. Papua New Guinea	15	9	7	-1

Source: Atkinson and Pearce (1993).

Environmental Accounting: The UNSTAT Satellite Accounting

The practical possibilities for environmental modifications to national income accounting conventions have been under active consideration by many individuals and institutions for a number of years. In the wake of the emergence of, and interest in, the idea of sustainable development, the UN's Statistical Division (USTAT) has proposed draft guidelines for new national income accounting conventions, the system of Integrated Environmental and Economic Accounting (SEEA). The essential idea is to measure the 'environmental cost' of economic activity in a period. Environmental cost (EC) is defined as the difference between the opening and closing value of the stock of environmental assets.

$$E_{ct} = \Sigma a_{it} V_{it} - \Sigma a_{it-1} V_{it-1} \quad ...(4)$$

Where the summation is over i =1, 2, ... , n assets, a_i represents the physical measure of the ith environmental asset, v_i the unit value assigned to the ith asset, and where t-1 refers to the start of the period and t to the end of the period.

For the ith asset $a_{it} v_{it} - a_{it-1} v_{it-1}$ is its depreciation over the period. Ec_t is the change in the balance sheet value of all 'n' environmental assets over the period, the depreciation of what is sometimes called 'natural capital'.

Environmental adjusted Net Domestic Product could then be defined as:

$$EDP_t = NDP_t - Ec_t = GDP_t - D_{Mt} - D_{NT} \quad ...(5)$$

Where *NDP* stands for Net Domestic Product, D_M for the depreciation of man-made reproducible capital, and D_N or *EC* for the depreciation of natural capital.

The UNSTAT proposals do not envisage replacing the publication of the standard GDP/NDP accounts with the publication of EDP accounts. They do envisage complementing the standard accounts with balance sheets for natural capital, from which users of the accounts could work out EDP. This would leave intact the current conventions for the measurement of GDP and NDP, so that adoption of the proposal would mean that figures on these constructs would continue to be available on a consistent basis with part data. The balance sheets for environmental assets are, therefore, referred to as 'satellite accounts'.

Conclusion

In future most environmental resources of production will not increase as rapidly as they have in the past. The effect of this decline on growth depends on the interplay among the law of diminishing marginal productivity, substitution possibilities and technological progress. Market imperfections frequently make sustainable development less likely. New sustainable forms of development are possible, but they will not automatically be adopted. Economics incentive policies can be used to manage the transition from current practices to these new forms of development.

REFERENCES

Beckerman, Wilfred (1974), *Two Cheers for the Affluent Society: A Spirited Defense of Economic Growth*, St. Martin's Press, New York.

Janson, Ann Mari, *et al.* (ed) (1994), *Investing in Natural Capital: The Ecological Economics Approach to Sustainability*, Island Press, Washington, DC.

Meadows, Donella, H., *et al.* (1972), *The Limits to Growth*, Universe Books, New York.

Sterner, Thomas (ed) (1994), *Economic Policies for Sustainable Development*, Kluwer Academic Publishers, Norwell.

World Commission on Environment and Development (WCED) (1987), *Our Common Future*, Oxford University Press, Oxford.

6

Environmental Policies

Introduction

One of the keys to understanding how society will cope with increasing resource scarcity and environmental damage lies in understanding how social institutions will react. The issue we are going to address in this chapter is "whether market systems with their emphasis on decentralized decision-making and democratic political systems, with their commitment to public participation and majority rule, equal to the challenges and the policy responses required to arrest environmental degradation."

On the positive side, markets have responded swiftly and automatically to deal with those resources experiencing higher prices. Demand has been reduced and substitution encouraged. Markets for recycling are growing and consumer habits are changing. No one has had to oversee these responses to make sure they occur. As long as property rights are well defined, the market system provides incentives for consumers and producers to respond to scarcity in a variety of useful ways. This characteristically rapid and smooth response illustrates none of the overshoot and collapse behaviour anticipated by the 'Limits to Growth' team.

As compelling as the evidence is for this point of view, it does not support the conclusion that, left to itself, the market would automatically choose a dynamically efficient or a sustainable path for the future. Market imperfections frequently make sustainable development less likely. The most serving imperfections of the market become evident in how it treats common property resources, such as the fish we eat, the air we breathe, and the water we drink. Left to its own devices, a market will over exploit common property resources, substantially lowering the net benefit received by future generation. Such over exploitation could, if not compensated for by sufficient increases in net benefits elsewhere in the economy, result in a violation of the sustainability criterion.

The need for government intervention is particularly acute in controlling environmental disasters like pollution. Uncontrolled markets not only produce too much pollution, but also tend to under-price commodities that contribute to pollution either when produced or consumed. Firms which unilaterally attempt to control their pollution run the risk of pricing themselves out of the market. Government intervention is needed to ensure that firms which neglect environmental damage in their operating decisions do not thereby gain a competitive edge.

One aspect of the policy process that does not seem to have handled well is the speed with which improvement has been sought. Public opinion polls world-wide shown that the world community supports environmental protection even when it raises costs and lowers employment. Policy-makers have reacted to this resolve by using tough legislation designed to force rapid technological development.

Rationale for Policy Instruments: Lessons from East Asia and Central America

Over the past quarter of a century, economic growth per capita in most part of the World and in particular in the southeast part of East Asia—Indonesia, Malaysia, Singapore, and Thailand—averaged 5 per cent a year. Socio-economic well-being improved enormously.

At the same time, environmental losses in East Asia have surpassed in many respects those of other regions. For example, 9 of the world's 15 cities with the highest levels of particulate air pollution are in this region. About 20 per cent of land covered by vegetation suffers from soil degradation owing to water-logging, erosion, and overgrazing at levels above world averages. Fifty to 75 per cent of coastlines and marine protected areas are classified as areas with highly threatened biodiversity, and the region has witnessed some of the highest deforestation rates in the world.

One lesson is that rapid growth can be a great ally of poverty reduction when supported by certain policy fundamentals. In East Asia these have included substantial and efficient investments in education, a relatively good income and asset distribution, a labour-intensive export orientation, and an emphasis on agricultural development. However, rapid growth has come at the expense of the environment. Rapid growth does not automatically improve the environment—environmental policies must also be put in place.

To be sure, many growth-inducing policies, such as clarifying property rights, investing in sanitation, improving education (especially for girls), and sound economic policies, help to improve resource use and contribute to a better environment. But in crucial areas, such as the control of pollution or sustainable forest use, environmental actions such as imposing taxes and standards, investing in technology, improving production methods, and recycling are necessary. Rapidly growing economies are learning this lesson the hard way and some are now taking corrective actions.

For a variety of economic and socio-political reasons, the Central American economies have grown slowly in recent decades, although their potential for sustainable development remains high. An exception is Costa Rica, a country with a strong record in promoting human development. But, more generally, the economies of Central America have been dominated by traditional exports, which have faced declining terms of trade; by a highly unequal income distribution; and by inadequate educational investments—all exacerbated by political instability. Costa Rica remains a notable exception. Because growth rates have been low, poverty levels have remained stubbornly high—as in other regions with slow growth. Environmental quality has deteriorated—there are large deforested areas, soil degradation, overfishing, and polluted water in coastal zones.

The experiences of East Asia and Central America show that both slow- and fast-growing economies can suffer from severe environmental degradation. The question then is whether, with the right priorities and policies, the environment can be protected irrespective of the pace of growth.

Growth *per se* is not to be blamed for environmental degradation, but, in some respects, rapid growth appears to make the problem worse. When the sources of environmental problems—underpriced resources (forests, water, or air), weak institutions, and unclear property rights—are not addressed adequately, rapid growth seems to aggravate them. However, growth and high incomes can mitigate environmental degradation and improve resource use if accompanied by environmental policies.

Grow First vs. *Clean up Later*

The human and ecological costs of environmental deterioration have been widely studied. In many instances, convincing evidence is available of the large social gains from environmental actions. And yet, environmental actions have been inadequate. The experience world-wide has emphasized a basic reason: the divergence between what is beneficial to society and what is beneficial for the private individual. When coupled with the lack of resources at low income levels, the pattern worldwide has been to grow first and clean up later.

Experience that calls this approach into question is accumulating. For one thing, it is a costly strategy socially and ecologically, and might threaten the sustainability of growth itself. Furthermore, new institutional arrangements, technologies, production methods, and targeted investments are beginning to offer opportunities to address growth and environmental protection in ways that are good for government finances as well as for private business.

The High Costs of Cleaning up Later

Ecological damage is often irreversible. Cleaning up later is not an option when terrestrial and aquatic biodiversity has been lost because of habitat destruction. For example, pollution and destructive fishing techniques have damaged a large proportion of coral reefs in some areas. As up to one-fourth of all marine species and one-fifth of known marine fish species live in coral reef ecosystems, the loss of reef habitats disproportionately threatens a high percentage of the ocean's plant and animal life. Complete reversal of this damage is unlikely; therefore, efforts need to focus on preserving global biological resources before they are damaged.

Environmental pollution causes considerable health costs, which are compounded when pollution control is postponed. Some of the evidence comes from widely publicized episodes—for example, mercury poisoning from a manufacturing firm in Minamata, Japan resulting in severe neurological afflictions ("Minamata Disease") for people in the area since the mid-1950s, or exposure to toxic materials causing acute illness or death as in the Bhopal, India tragedy of 1984. Other evidence, even if less visible, is widely prevalent, such as the steady health losses to children and adults from air pollution.

The cost is usually far less than the benefits to society of investing in pollution control. In this regard, an ounce of prevention is worth a pound of cure. It is usually cheaper to control pollution at its source through policy reforms, especially by removing subsidies, than by investing in pollution control later.

Strategies

Better Use of Resources

With proper concern for the environment, scarce resources can be put to high-return and sustainable uses. For example, in parts of Southeast Asia, uplands can be used for sustainable planting of fruit trees or other perennials rather than for planting maize or cassava for a few years and then abandoning cultivation as yields decline. Similarly, in areas of Latin America, forests can be protected for their higher social value rather than converted to ranches that generate negative returns. And in many cases, putting a resource to multiple uses generates a large net benefit. For example, management of tropical forests for multiple uses that include nontimber goods, water and soil conservation, biological diversity, and other environmental services, as well as timber, could generate higher social returns as well as revenue.

Bringing in Revenue

Applying pollution taxes, in addition to inducing lower emissions and better conservation of resources, can raise revenues that allow governments to scale back more distortionary forms of taxation. In Thailand, for example, a 10 per cent tax on the coal and lignite used in manufacturing could yield a return of 1 to 2 per cent of government revenue. The cost of such a tax is usually a fraction of the estimated health benefits it helps to produce.

Liberalization and Environmental Policy

Finally, there is the economy-wide link between a country's competitiveness and the environment. In one direction, trade liberalization without environmental policies makes the environment more vulnerable. The higher prices for forest resources resulting from trade liberalization can lead to excessive deforestation if property rights are unclear and logging rights fail to incorporate the resource costs. In the other direction, trade liberalization can increase the profitability of industries that have environmental safeguards in place.

Market Based Policy Instruments

Although the record is limited, innovative approaches in East Asia and Latin America offer the promise of growth with sustainable resource use. To take one example, a coalition of conservation and research organizations in El Salvador developed an eco-labelling initiative, ECO-OK, to give coffee farmers the incentives and information to produce coffee in an eco-friendly way. The programme simultaneously raises awareness and motivates consumers to seek products from socially and environmentally responsible farms. ECO-OK products meet environmental standards that protect rainforests, workers, and wildlife.

User Charges and Tradable Resource Rights

Experience with market-based instruments and regulations, notwithstanding the obstacles to their enforcement, illustrates the range of policies that are possible and widens the debate on options. In East Asia, considerable progress has been made in removing subsidies on gasoline, diesel, and kerosene. In Latin America, there are several examples of the application of market-based instruments (*see* Table 6.1). Some have been ineffective in achieving their full objectives as a result of institutional weaknesses such as under-funding, unclear jurisdiction, monitoring requirements, and legal design requirements. Nevertheless, there are some promising examples.

Resource User Charges

Brazil, Colombia, and Venezuela charge a forestry tax when tree harvesting is not compensated by equivalent reforestation. So far the taxes have been set at too low a level, and enforcement has been weak; nonetheless, the principle is sound.

Joint Implementation Agreements

Central America is relatively advanced in the creation of agreements for carbon sequestration through forest protection under Joint Implementation programmes. Costa Rica has just initiated such an agreement with Norway. The development of such agreements will depend in part on an emerging international consensus, but initial activities are promising.

Participation and Community Involvement

Where institutions are weak or enforcement is expensive, public participation and community involvement can be effective in

Table 6.1: Protecting the Environment: Application of Market-based Instruments in Latin America

	Credit Subsidies	*Tax/ Tariff Relief*	*Deposit-Refund Schemes*	*Waste Fees and Levies*	*Forestry Taxation*	*Pollution Charges*	*Ear-marked Renew-able Resource Taxes*	*Ear-marked Conven-tional Tax levy*	*Tradable Permits*	*Eco-labelling*	*Liability Insu-rance*
Barbados	*	*	*	*							
Bolivia			*	*	*				+	*	*
Brazil	*	*	*	*	*	*	*	*		*	*
Chile		*	*	*					*	*	
Colombia	*	*	*		*	*	*	*			*
Ecuador	*	*	*	*			*			*	
Jamaica		*	*	*		+					
Mexico	*		*	*		*		*	+	*	
Peru			*								
Trinidad and Tobago		*	*								*
Venezuela		*	*	*	*						

* In place.
+ Under introduction.

Source: Richard M. Huber, Jack Ruitenbeek, and Ronaldo Seroa da Motta, 1996, *"Market Based Instruments for Environmental Policy making in Latin America and the Caribbean,"* World Bank, Washington.

enforcing sustainable resource use and adapting local conditions to development needs. Traditional communities have known and used this approach for ages. It could be strengthened for today's market economy, as evidenced in Japan. The local government and resident groups in Japan negotiate with firms to arrive at a detailed written agreement on emissions levels. Between 1971 and 1991, the number of agreements increased from approximately 2,000 to 37,000. Once standards were agreed upon, they were effectively implemented. This consensual approach benefits local governments, residents, and companies alike.

Mainstreaming Environmental Concerns

A crucial approach involves mainstreaming environmental concerns in national plans and policies. This means that the environmental consequences of actions pursued by finance and planning, as well as environmental ministries are made explicit within core economic policies. In some countries innovative approaches to confront environmental problems are beginning to be applied. Mainstreaming them would mean that these options are put on the table at the time key fiscal, trade, and industrial policies are discussed. Their benefits and costs would be revealed, providing the basis to pursue the best approaches.

Inserting the environment into policy-making can produce much stronger results for economic growth and environmental sustainability than responding to individual environmental concerns along the way. Practical ways to do this are beginning to emerge, and there would be great benefit from disseminating them. More generally, integrating environmental awareness in education programmes, especially at the early stages, and influencing values and behaviour would be a fundamental step in mainstreaming environmental concerns.

Policy Choices

Tough questions remain with respect to both policy choices and the implementation of environmental actions. Win-win policy choices (for example, reducing energy subsidies to benefit both economic performance and the environment) should be relatively easy for the policy-maker to make. Pushing ahead with them should, therefore, be a high priority. But even in this case, there will be winners and losers from the changes, requiring the policymaker to manage the political economy of reforms.

Policy choices involving trade-offs to the policy-maker are more difficult to make, even if society would benefit on balance (for example, financial investments for pollution control that produce net gains in health and welfare). This difficulty is compounded if the benefits accrue later and especially if future benefits involve uncertainty, or if some of the benefits accrue to the rest of the world (for example, part of the gains from biodiversity from the protection of forests). Financial constraints make the decision hard to take even if it is socially beneficial.

Higher incomes eventually contribute to the demand for a more sustainable environment, especially in the so-called "brown" areas such as urban pollution. Higher incomes also provide the resources to help address the problem. However, this chain of events is particularly delayed in the case of the "green" dimensions of the environment, which faces severe deterioration in the early phases of rapid growth. And they also involve unacceptable thresholds of degradation, and irreversible losses, such as biodiversity. Protecting the "green" aspects during rapid growth remains a tough challenge.

Countries' institutional capacity to make, implement, and enforce difficult decisions is a key consideration. Even the best solutions require the support of well-functioning markets and property rights; where trade-offs are involved, additional measures to align the social and private benefits (through taxes, quotas, investments, etc.) are needed. When the benefits go beyond individual countries, financial and institutional arrangements across borders might be called for.

These dilemmas need to be recognized. Clearly, priorities have to be set, resource limits acknowledged, and systemic processes put in place to help make tough choices. There is a growing body of experience on how innovative approaches can help address trade-offs and institutional rigidities. Meanwhile, the evidence on the high costs of not taking these measures is mounting.

In the main, the experience of rapidly growing countries has been to grow first and clean up later. However, this neglect of the environment has resulted in irreversible losses and high cleanup costs. Current experiences and policies, even if limited, demonstrate that it is possible to protect the environment, promote growth, and enhance competitiveness at the same time. Most developing countries can benefit from both the positive and the negative lessons of rapid growth elsewhere. If they can take economic and environmental actions now, they could become the "green tigers" of the future.

International Environmental Cooperation

More than 170 international environmental treaties have been adopted to date. The past two decades have seen increasing attention being paid to environmental issues in the conduct of international relations. This reflects a growing awareness that the issues of environmental protection, liberalization of world trade, poverty and economic development, and North-South relationships are inextricably linked. From an examination of these agreements, it is possible to draw a number of tentative conclusions.

(i) International coordination of policy is easiest when an international political institution exists with the authority and power to construct, administer, and enforce a collective agreement.
(ii) International coordination of policy is easier the smaller is the number of parties affected and the more similar they are culturally.
(iii) International coordination of policy is easier the lower are the control costs of the intended programme.
(iv) International coordination of policy is easier the higher are the benefits of the intended programme.

(v) International coordination of policy is easier the less is the uncertainty about costs and benefits of the intended programme.

(vi) International coordination of policy is easier when it is relatively straight forward to achieve agreement about the appropriate international division of burdens of the intended programme.

The growth and increasing authority of international political and economic organization offers the prospect of creating vehicles for international coordination of behaviour. These organizations which play important roles in environmental policy include the Committee on International Development Institutions on the Environment (CIDIE), the European Union, the Organization for Economic Cooperation and Development (OECD), the World Bank, various NGOs, research institutions such as World Resource Institute, as well as multilateral development banks. Of greatest actual and potential impact seem to be the various branches of the UN.

UN environmental strategy makes no attempt to treat issues of environmental protection and environmental sustainability in isolation from issues of economic development, particularly in the poorer nations. Monitoring is the principal responsibility of the UN Commission on Sustainable Development (CSD), which works in close collaboration with NGOs. Coordination and integration of policy between various UN agencies is promoted with the assistance of two institutional mechanisms; the UN Administrative Committee on Coordination and the Inter-Agency Committee on Sustainable Development. Agenda 21 of the Rio summit also recommended the strengthening of the other UN organs dealing with environmental and development issues, particularly the UN's Environment Programme (UNEP) and the UN's Development Programme (UNDP).

Conclusion

One of the keys to understanding how society will cope with increasing resource scarcity and environmental damage lies in understanding how social institutions will react. Are market systems, with their emphasis on decentralized decision-making, and democratic political systems, with their commitment to public participation and majority rule, equal to the challenge? One aspect of the policy process that does not seem to have been handled well is the speed with which improvement has been sought. Public opinion polls world-wide have unambiguously shown that the general public supports environmental protection even when it raises costs and lowers employment. Policy makers have reacted to this resolve by writing very tough legislation designed to force rapid technological development. It seems clear that simple prescriptions such as 'leave it to the market' or 'more government intervention' simply do not bear up under a close scrutiny of the record. As we have seen in analysis of various environmental problems, the efficiency and sustainability criteria allow such distinctions to be drawn and they serve as a basis for policy reform.

REFERENCES

Baumol, W.J. and Oates, W.E. (1979), *Economics, Environmental Policy and the Quality of Life*, Prentice Hall, Englewood Cliffs, New Jersey.

Butlin, R. (ed.) (1981), *Economics of the Environment and Natural Resources Policy*, West View Press, Boulder, Colorado.

Daly, H.E. (1977), *The Steady State Economics*, W.H. Freeman, San Francisco.

Freeman, A.M. (1979), *The Benefits of Environmental Improvement: Theory and Practice*, John Hopkins University Press, Baltimore, Maryland.

Just, R.E., Hueth, D.L. and Schnitz, A. (1982), *Applied Welfare Economics and Public Policy*, Prentice Hall, Englewood Cliffs, New Jersey.

7

Valuing the Environment

Introduction

Environmental valuation is a very active and rapidly expanding field. The principal motivation for environmental valuation is to enable environmental impacts to be included in cost-benefit analysis. The basic strategy for environmental valuation is the 'commodification' of the services that the natural environment provides. Most of the environmental valuation literature is about services which flow to households rather than firms. The principles and lessons from practice that emerge in this context are of general applicability. By a household here we mean an entity that takes and acts upon decisions about consumption.

Dimension of Value

The natural environment provides mainly four categories of services for humans and their economic activities.

(a) Inputs or resources to production by firms (*R*),
(b) Sinks for the assimilation of wastes generated in production and consumption (*W*),
(c) Amenity services to households (*A*), and
(d) Life support services for firms and households (*I*).

The basic ideas concerning environmental valuation can be assessed as given in Table 7.1.

Table 7.1: Environmental Values of Forests (Output)

Output	*Services*	*Users*	*Divisibility*	*Excludability*	*Marketed*
1. Harvested timber	R	F	D	E	M
2. Standing timber	A	H	ND	NE	NM
3. Minerals	R	F	D	E	M
4. Flora	R, A, L	F, H	D, ND	E, NE	M, NM
5. Fauna	R, A, L	F, H	D, ND	E, NE	M, NM
6. Flood protection	L	F, H	ND	NE	NM
7. Water quality	W, A, R	F, H	D, ND	E, NE	NM
8. Soil protection	L, R	F	ND	NE	NM
9. Local climate	L	F, H	ND	NE	NM
10. Carbon fixation	W, L	F, H	ND	NE	NM

Notes: R—resource; A—amenity; L—life support; W—waste assimilation; F—firm; H—households; D—divisible; ND—non-divisible; E—excludability; NE—non-excludability; M—marketed; NM—non-marketed.

Environmental Cost Benefit Analysis (ECBA)

We know that cost benefit analysis is measured as:

$$NPV = \Sigma_t B_t - C_t/(1+r)^t \qquad ...(1)$$

And if NPV > 0 we accept the project.

In ECBA the benefits and costs include the value of environmental improvement and of environmental deterioration consequent upon among ahead with the project. In discussing ECBA it is convenient to keep ordinary benefits and costs, separate from environmental benefits and costs. Let *Bd* be the discounted value of the ordinary benefit and *Cd* represent the discounted value of the ordinary cost stream over the project life time. Then,

$$NPV = Bd - Cd - EC = NPV' - EC \qquad ...(2)$$

Where, *EC* is the stream of the net value of the projects' environmental impacts over the project's life time, and *NPV'* is what projects *NPV* would be if environmental impacts were ignored. In principle *EC* could be negative with *NPV* > *NPV'*. The net value of the environmental consequences of the project could, that is, be such as to strengthen, rather than weaken, the case for the project. However, we shall assume that *EC* is positive.

The ECBA decision rule is that the project should go ahead if:

$$NPV' = Bd - Cd > EC \qquad \text{...(3)}$$

The application of this criterion requires the identification and measurement of the impacts on the environment and then their valuation and aggregation to arrive at *EC*, which is a monetary measure of the environmental benefits of not going ahead with the project.

We can divide *EC* into four classes of benefit potentially accruing to individuals:

(a) *Use Value (UV)*: It arise from the actual and planned use of the environment.
(b) *Existence Value (EV)*: It arises from knowledge that the service exists and will continue to exist, independently of any actual or prospective use.
(c) *Option Value (OV)*: It relates to willingness to pay to guarantee the availability of the service for future use.
(d) *Quasi-Option Value (QOV)*: It relates to willingness to pay to avoid an irreversible commitment to development now, given the expenditure of future growth in knowledge relevant to the implications of development.

$$EC = UV + EV + OV + QOV \qquad \text{...(4)}$$

OV and *QOV* arise only when there is incomplete knowledge of future condition, where as *UV* and *EV* can exist where there is complete certainty about future conditions.

Environmental Valuation Techniques

There are different environmental valuation techniques and among them the most important are discussed under.

Travel Cost Method (TCM)

It was developed principally in papers by Clawson and Clawson and Knetsch. It was based on the simple idea that it ought to be possible to infer the values placed by visitors on environmental amenity services from the costs that they incurred in order to experience the services.

Consider a situation where some project threatens the amenity services currently provided by a protected area, for example, a national park, for which there is no access fee. Those responsible for deciding whether the project should go ahead are going to use ECBA, and wish to know the environmental cost to compare with the net development benefit. For the purpose of exposition, we shall assume that if the project goes ahead the value of the recreational amenity services from the area in question will go to zero.

In practical terms the first basic assumption for the TCM is that visit to the park are determined by a trip, or visit, generating function:

$$V_i = f(C_i, X_{1i}, X_{2i}, \ldots\ldots X_{Ni}) \qquad \ldots(5)$$

Where, V_i is visits from the ith origin or by the ith individual, C_i is the cost of visit from origin *i* or by individual *i*, and the *Xs* are other relevant variables. The second basic assumption is that the cost of a visit comprises both travel costs (*Ti*), varying with *i*, and admission price (*P*), constant across *i*, and that visitors treat travel costs and the price of admission as equivalent elements of the total cost of a visit. Visitors respond, that is, in exactly the same way to increases/decreases in total cost whether they are due to increases/decreases in travel cost or admission price, with $\partial V_i/\partial C_i < 0$. If we assume that the function is linear in costs, and suppress the role of other variables, this means that the trip generating equation to be estimated is

$$V_i = \alpha + \beta C_i + \varepsilon_i = \alpha + \beta(T_i + P) + \varepsilon_i \qquad \ldots(6)$$

Where ε_i is the stochastic component, or error terms, assumed to be normally and independently distributed, with zero expectation. Travel and the recreational amenity services of the park are being assumed to be weak complements and it is assumed that travel and access costs are behaviorally equivalent. That is β is assumed to be negative.

In the data for the case we are considering, *P* is zero. However, given the second assumption here, α and β can be estimated from data on V_i and T_i and used to figure the effects on visits of hypothetical changes in *P*. Note that this could be useful for figuring the effect on visits of the introduction of access charging, as well as for figuring a monetary measure of the utility of the recreational amenity with free access. Note also that Equation 6 is a Marshallian, uncompensated, demand function for visits. Given the assumption of zero expectation for the error term in Equation 6, if *P* varied the relationship between expected visits from origin *i* or by individual *i* and the price of access to the Park would be:

$$E(V_i) = \alpha + \beta P + T_i \quad ...(7)$$

Where, $E(V_i)$ is the expectation operator. The relationship between $E(V_i)$ and P is shown in Fig. 7.1 as the downward sloping straight line. There $E(V'_i)$ is visits when the access price is zero, and P'_i is the choke price that derives $E(V_i)$ to zero. Setting $E(V_i)$ equal to zero in Equation 7 and solving for the choke price gives:

$$P'_i = -(\alpha/\beta) - T_i \quad ...(8)$$

and for *P* equal to zero.

$$E(V'_i) = \alpha + \beta T_i \quad ...(9)$$

In the figure Marshallian consumers surplus for origin/ individual *i* at $P = 0$ is given by the area of the triangle $OE(V'_i)P'_i$. The area of a triangle is half base times height, which in this case is 0.5 times $OE(V'_i)$ times OP'_i, which using Equations 8 and 9 gives Marshallian consumers surplus:

$$MCS_i = -[E(V'_i)]^2/2\beta \quad ...(10)$$

Summing over *i*, to total consumer surplus when $P = 0$ is

$$MCS = -(1/2\beta)\ \Sigma_i[E(V_i)]^2 \quad ...(11)$$

In some applications of the TCM, surplus for $P = 0$ is calculated across i using the actual observed visits for each origin/individual, as in

$$MCS = -(1/2\beta)\,\Sigma_i\,V_i^2 \qquad \text{...(12)}$$

In either case, the crucial nature of the assumptions that visits respond in the same way to changes in P as to variations in travel cost is apparent. Given this assumption, the operational problem is to estimate α and β from data on V_i and T_i. The data is to be collected through primary survey or through secondary sources.

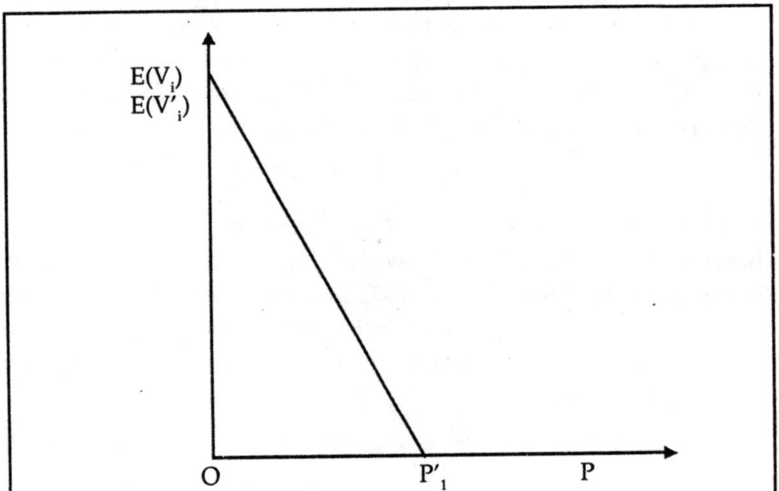

Fig. 7.1: Linear Trip Generating Function

Contingent Valuation Method (CVM)

The CVM is a direct method in that it involves asking a sample of the relevant population questions about their willingness to pay (WTP) or willingness to accept (WTA). It is called contingent valuation because the valuation is contingent on hypothetical scenario put to respondents. Its main use is to provide inputs to analyses of changes in the level of provision of public good/bad, and especially of environmental 'commodities' which have the characteristics on non-excludability and non-divisibility.

The CVM has two advantages over indirect methods.

(i) It can deal with both use and non-use values, whereas the indirect methods cover only the former, and involves weak complementarity assumptions.
(ii) In principle and unlike the indirect methods, CVM answers to WTP or WTA question go directly to the theoretically correct monetary measures of utility changes.

While the CVM can be used for use and non-use values, its actual use has mainly been in regard to the latter. Particularly, most CVM applications have concerned existence, or passive-use, values.

The steps involved in applying the CVM can be stated as follows:

(i) Creating a survey instrument for the elicitation of individuals' WTP/WTA. It includes the following three distinct, but related components.
  (a) Designing the hypothetical scenario.
  (b) Deciding whether to ask about WTP or WTA.
  (c) Creating a scenario about the means of payment or compensation.
(ii) Using the survey instrument with a sample of the population of interest.
(iii) Analyzing the responses to the survey. It can be seen as having two components.
  (a) Using the sample data on WTP/WTA to estimate average WTP/WTA for the population.
  (b) Assessing the survey results so as to judge the accuracy of this estimate.
(iv) Computing total WTP/WTA for the population of interest for use in an ECBA.
(v) Conducting sensitivity analysis.

Hedonic Pricing Method (HPM)

This is an indirect method, proposed in the early 1970s. The basic approach can be indicated in the context of atmospheric pollution, where the hedonic pricing technique has been widely used. While clean air is not a traded good, it is an attribute which seems to influence residential property prices. Evidence from revealed preferences suggests that, other things being equal, a positive relationship exists between the prices that people are willing to pay for housing and the quality of ambient air standards. Examination of property prices might, therefore, enable one to impute the value of clean air.

After collecting data regarding the determinants of rent, a representative sample of properties should be drawn, in such a way that properties in the sample are chosen from a variety of localities with differing levels of ambient air quality. Multiple regression analysis can be used to estimate the relationship between rents and all of the attributes relevant to rents. That estimated relationship can then be used to figure the relationship between rent and air pollution, holding all other determinants of rent constant. The estimated equation for the determination of rents is known as a 'hedonic pricing equation': the derived relationship between rent and pollution is often referred to as a 'rent-pollution function' or a 'rent gradient'.

The hedonic pricing method is a variant of the travel cost method, which seeks to use data on the attributes of recreational sites together with data on visitation rates and travel costs to value site attributes. The basic idea can be illustrated by considering just two sites which are the same in all respects, serve that one has some attribute that the other does not. The valuation of that attribute would then be inferred from the difference in the relationship between visitation and travel costs between the two sites.

Production Function Based Method

Environmental conditions are of relevance to production, and this is not just a matter of resource inputs to production as usually understood. Here we consider environmental valuation techniques based on environmental services or indicators, as arguments in production functions.

We can represent the basis for this technique as the production function:

$$Q = f(L, K, E) \qquad ...(13)$$

Where, L and K have the usual meanings, and E is environmental indicators, and we have,

$$\partial Q/\partial L > 0, \partial Q/\partial K > 0, \partial Q/\partial E > 0$$

Consider a river fishery, where E is water quality. Suppose that some policy to improve water quality is under consideration. If we knew the algebraic form of the production function and the parameter values, we could use that information to map some change in water quality (ΔE), into a change in harvest (ΔQ), for constant levels of L and K. If we could then convert ΔQ into a monetary measure we would have valued the environmental quality change as it affects production. If E was also an argument in utility functions, we would have to estimate the value of ΔE in consumption, as well as production, by one of the techniques already discussed (This is known as 'dose-response' valuation technique).

To convert ΔQ to a monetary measure it is necessary only to multiply it by the unit price of Q, in this case caught fish, to get the change in revenue. Ellis and Fisher (1987) show how this should be done using measure of changes in the sum of producer and consumer surplus, and give illustrative calculations for a case where E is wetland acreage and Q is the harvest of blue crabs.

Two closely related techniques that have been used for environmental valuation in relation to production are 'avoided cost' and 'averting expenditure'. Write the production function as:

$$Q = f(L, K; E, A) \qquad ...(14)$$

Where,

$$\partial Q/\partial L > 0, \partial Q/\partial K > 0, \partial Q/\partial E < 0, \partial Q/\partial A > 0$$

In this case increases in the environmental indicator *E* reduce output for given levels of input of *L*, *Q* and *A*, which some 'averting' input. We are now considering a factory for the production of computer components, where clean air is important. *E* is ambient air quality, where the factory is located, and *A* is inputs of air-filtration service. According to the averting expenditure approach, air quality deterioration would be valued in terms of increases in expenditure on *A*. According to avoided cost approach, air quality improvement would be valued in terms of reduced expenditure on *A*.

Averting expenditure and avoided cost approaches to valuations for households can also be derived from a household production function.

Environmental Valuation, Ethics and Social Choice

The original motivation for the work that economists have done on environmental valuation was to enable the natural environment to be accounted for in cost-benefit analysis. In working through the enormous literature on environmental valuation methodology that has appeared in the past few decades, it is easy to end up immersed in technical detail and losing sight of what it is all for. There can also be a tendency to overlook the relevance of some of the criticism of environmental valuation as practiced by economists that has been made by non-economists and by some economists. Much of the criticism is of ECBA, and the ethical foundations of welfare economics, rather than of environmental valuation *per se*, though often developed in the valuation context.

Ethics are relevant in two ways. First, ethics as the study of morally correct behaviour has been used to argue that ECBA is the wrong way for society to make decisions with environmental implications. This argument has focused particularly on decisions which have implications for those environmental services that economists treat as being covered by existence or on-use values, especially life-support services (As we have seen existence values are the domain of CVM). The second way in which ethics will concern us is that it has been suggested that the ethical attitudes held by individuals will influence their responses about existence values in CVM surveys, with implications for the usefulness of the survey results in ECBA.

Conclusion

The original and still the principal motivation for environmental valuation was to enable environmental impacts to be included in cost-benefit analysis. The basic strategy for environmental valuation as discussed in the introductory part of this chapter is the commodification of the services that the natural environment provides. The services are used by households and firms and are treated as arguments in utility and production functions, respectively. The standard theories for consumers and producers behaviour can then be used to derive methods for assigning values to environmental services.

REFERENCES

Freeman, A.M. (1993), *The Measurement of Environmental and Resource Values, Resources for the Future,* Washington D.C.

Hanley, N. (1989), 'Problems in Valuing Environmental Improvements from Agricultural Policy Changes: The Case of Nitrate Pollution', *Discussion paper No.89/1,* Economics Department, University of Stirling.

Hansman, J.A. (ed) (1993), *Contingent Valuation: A Critical Assessment,* North Holland, Amsterdam.

Pearce, D.W. and Moran, D. (1994), *The Economic Value of Biodiversity,* Earth Scan, London.

Turner, R.K. and Bateman, I. (1990), *A Critical Review of Monetary Assessment Methods and Techniques,* Environmental Appraisal Group, University of East Anglia.

Vaze, P. (ed.) (1998), *UK Environmental Accounts: 1998,* The Stationery Office, London.

PART II
AGRICULTURAL ECONOMICS

8

Introduction to Agricultural Economics

Introduction

Agricultural economics is the part of economics that surveys agriculture in its many facets and forms. The agricultural economist is concerned with the entire food and fibre system, from the inputs used in production all the way through the production, processing, distribution and consumption chain.

The food and fibre system is related to almost every facet of our economy and our environment. As a result, the study of agricultural economics necessarily encompasses a great deal more than just the activities of the farmer or rancher. Since the food and fibre system is an important part of our natural environment, agricultural economists deal with issues of resource conservation, pollution control and water management. They also study the agri-business sector as purchasers, processors and distributors of food and fibre products. Thus the scope of agricultural economics is very broad and quite diverse. The common issue is how the gifts of sunlight, soil and water are converted into food—the staff of life.

Economics is that particular social science that deals with the allocation of scarce resources among an unlimited number of competing alternative uses. Scarcity creates the need for a system to allocate the available resources among some of those potential users. Agricultural economics is the social science that deals with the allocation of scarce resources among those competing alternative uses found in the production, processing, distribution and consumption of food and fibre. Agricultural economics involves the application of economics to agriculture, and as such it is defined as, 'An applied social science that deals with how producers, consumers and societies use scarce resources in the production, processing, marketing and consumption of food and fibre products.'

Basic Skills of the Agricultural Economists

The study of agricultural economics provides us with an opportunity to explore phenomena common to everyday life from the perspective of an analytical scientist. Just as artists or novelists try to explore human behaviour through their chosen media, agricultural economists observe the behaviour of man as an economic creature and try to develop rules for behaviour that will help every participant in economic society to achieve their goals. Thus, the role of the agricultural economist is to devise rules for making decisions in an ever changing, uncertain economic and agriculture environment. These rules can be used to make production, consumption, marketing and financial decisions. By studying the logic of these managerial rules, we can learn how to adjust managerial decisions to the changing environment in which our economic and agricultural activity occurs.

The application of economics to agriculture in a developing economy is more complex and as such the role of the agricultural economists at various levels also differs.

Role at Microeconomic Level

Agricultural economists at the micro level are concerned with issues related to resource use in the production, processing, distribution and consumption of products in the food and fibre system. Production economists examine resource demand by businesses and their supply response. Market economists focus on the flow of food and fibre through market channels to its final destination and the determination of prices at each stage. Financial economists are concerned with issues related to the financing of businesses and the supply of capital to these firms.

Resource economists focus on the use and preservation of the nation's natural resources. Other economists are interested in the formation of government programmes for specific commodities that will support the incomes of farmers and provide food and fibre products to low income consumers.

Role at Macroeconomic Level

Agricultural economists involved at the macro level are interested in how agriculture and agri-business affect domestic and world economies and how the events taking place in other sectors affect these firms and *vice versa*. For example, agricultural economists employed by the Indian Agriculture Ministry will evaluate how changes in monetary policy affect the price of food. Macroeconomists with a research interest may use computer-based models to analyze the direct and indirect effects that specific monetary or fiscal policy proposals would have on the farm business sector. Macroeconomists employed by multinational food companies examine foreign trade relationships for food and fibre products. Others address issues in the area of international development.

Food and Fibre Industry

The term agriculture means different things to different people. Some might think solely of farmers and ranchers when they use this term, others might think of agri-business firms. In recent years, many agricultural economists have referred to the food and fibre industry when describing the agricultural scene. The food and fibre industry includes farmers, ranchers and agri-businesses.

The food and fibre system—from the farmer to the consumer—is one of the largest sectors in the developing economies. The system includes all economic activities supporting farm production, such as machinery repair and fertilizer production, food processing and manufacturing, transportation, and wholesale and retail distribution of food and apparel products. As the Fig. 8.1 suggests, the food and fibre system encompasses the activities of the farm input supply sector, the farm sector, the processing and manufacturing sector, and the wholesale and retail trade sector.

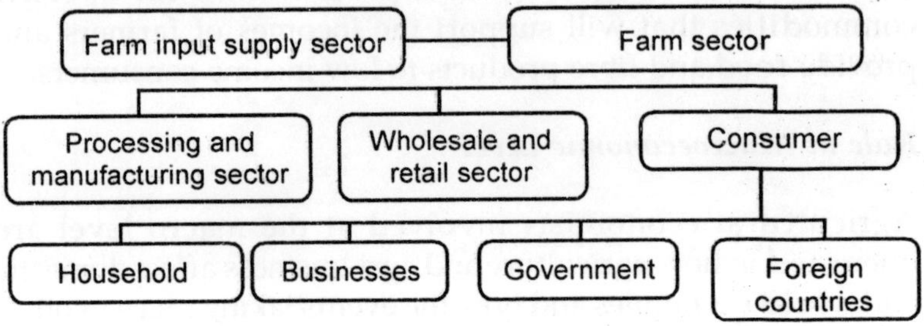

Fig. 8.1: Food and Fibre Industry System

Choice Making and Opportunity Cost

Resource scarcity forces consumers and producers to make choices. These choices have a time dimension. The choices one makes also have an associated opportunity cost. It is one of the more powerful concepts in economics. All economic resources have value. Sometimes that value is determined in a market place where the user of a resource pays the prevailing price for the use of the resources. On the other occasions, resources are used that have economic value, but those resources are not purchased in the open market. In the latter case, economists use the principle of opportunity cost to determine the economic value of a resource even though there is no manifest market value of that resource.

Opportunity cost is the economic value of a resource in its highest value alternative use. That is, if a resource is being used in one economic activity, then that resource has given up the opportunity of being used in another economic activity. What are the earnings forgone in that other activity? That is the opportunity cost of the resource. For example, an agri-business firm considering the purchase of a new computer system must also consider the income it could receive by using this money for another purpose. The bottom line expressed in economic terms is whether the economic benefits exceed the costs, including foregone income. By focusing the use of our resources on a specific task, we are engaging in specialization. Societies may find it to their advantage to specialize in the production of coffee, wheat, teff, etc.

REFERENCES

Drummon, H. Evan (2001), *Agricultural Economics*, Prentice Hall, New Jersey.

Friedman, M. (1974), *Essays in Positive Economics*, University of Chicago Press, Chicago.

Penson, John B. *et al.* (2002), *Introduction to Agricultural Economics*, Prentice Hall, New Jersey.

9

Role of Agriculture in Economic Development

Introduction

Over the past two centuries there have been major changes in the roles attributed to agriculture in economic development. As the 19th century began agriculture was viewed as a major impediment to progress by the two greatest economists of the era—Malthus and Ricardo. The combination of a limited supply of land and diminishing returns to the application of labour and capital to land were deemed to limit the improvement of welfare. These were the conditions prevailed in a developed country like England.

In his 'Principles of Economics,' Alfred Marshall argued that even when there exists diminishing return in cultivation; it may be possible for an increase in the population to cause a more than proportionate increase in the means of subsistence. To him, 'even in agriculture the tendencies to increasing and diminishing returns appear pretty well balanced, sometimes the one, sometimes the other being the stronger.' Several studies have shown that for 1900-1982, that the real price of cereals declined by 0.8 per cent annually, all food by 0.3 per cent, and all agricultural product by 0.8 per cent.

The growth stage theories (e.g. Eugene Rostow) call our attention to significant changes in variables and parameters as economic growth occurs. However, the assumption that there are clearly defined stages in the transition from primarily agricultural to primarily industrial economies cannot be supported empirically or, for that matter, theoretically. The process is one of continuous adjustment and change without artificial breaks or turning points. This is not to say that the adjustments occur without interruption or at a constant pace but rather that changes occur through product and factor markets that determine agriculture's relationship to the economy as a whole.

Dual Sector Models

The dual sector models (Social dualism, technological dualism, financial dualism, etc.) of the 1950s and 1960s represented retrogression from the neo-classical modifications of the Ricardian model of agriculture in economic development. The neo-classical modifications included the emphasis upon the role of productivity change in agriculture as an offset to the effects of diminishing returns and recognition of the low income elasticity of demand for food.

Some implications of the dual sector models were interpreted as assigning to agriculture in the developing countries a negative or static role in economic growth. These implications were translated into policy frameworks that were disastrous in the role assigned to agriculture in the growth of developing countries and which adversely affected the welfare of farm people in most developing countries, and, consequently, had adverse effects upon economic growth overall. The assumption that the value of the marginal product of labour in agriculture was zero over a wide range of employment gave intellectual support to the conclusion that agriculture's primary contribution to economic growth was to provide a costless supply of labour to support the growth of industry and the development of cities.

Another unfortunate development was the proposition that the long run trends in real agricultural prices were adverse and investment in agriculture was not an appropriate use of the limited resources of developing countries. This view provided additional intellectual support for import substitution policies that stressed industrial development at the expense of agriculture. During the 20th century the overall trend in real prices of agricultural products in international markets has been a declining one. But declining real product prices does not mean that investment in agriculture would yield substandard returns or that real wages in agriculture must lag behind real wages elsewhere. Productivity improvements can and have more than offset the consequences of declining real prices for grains and other crop products in most countries. Where there have been increases in real per capita incomes and factor markets have functioned well, the real return to labour in agriculture have increased over time.

The model of economic growth and the role of agriculture presented by Colin Clark have served policy makers and the farmers of the developing world for better than the inferences based on the dual sector models. In Clark's model, the transformation of an economy with rising real incomes from one with most of the employment in agriculture to an economy emphasizing industry and service sectors was quite explicable—the increase in productivity in agriculture combined with income elasticities of demand for farm output that were both less than unity and declining as real per capita incomes increase make possible the transfer of labour from agriculture to the rest of the economy, where productivity is also increasing, while equating the supply and demand for farm products at constant or even declining real prices.

Agricultural Price and Income Policies

There is an enormous body of evidence to support the conclusion that policy makers in both the developing and developed countries have misunderstood the role of agriculture in economic development and how factor and product markets function. It has now been well established that during recent decades that there is an inverse relationship between real per capita incomes and the degree of protection of agriculture. This means, other things constant, that the lower a country's real per capita income, the higher the level of taxation of agricultural output and the higher the per capita incomes, the higher the level of subsidization.

The industrial economies have subsidized their agriculture, especially since the early 1960s. The policies followed by the European Economic Community, Japan and the US have had a significant negative effect upon the international market prices for agricultural products. Consequently the discrimination against developing country agriculture was even greater. Nominal rate of protection being zero, agriculture in the developing countries would have been adversely affected if they produced any of the temperate zone agricultural products.

Agriculture's Contribution to Economic Growth

The contribution of agriculture to economic development lies in the following:

Providing More Food to the Rapidly Expanding Population

In LDCs, food production dominates the agriculture sector. When output expands with increased productivity it increases the incomes of the farmers. Rise in per capita income leads to substantial rise in the demand for food. In such economies, the income elasticity of demand for food is very high. Moreover, the increase in the growth rate of population due to a rapid decline in the mortality rates and slow reduction in fertility rates tends to raise further the demand for food.

Increasing the Demand for Industrial Products and thus Necessitating the Expansion of the Secondary and Tertiary Sectors

A rise in rural purchasing power, as a result of the increased agricultural surplus, is a great stimulus to industrial development. Moreover, the demand for such inputs as fertilizers, better tools, implements, tractors, irrigational facilities, etc. will lead to the grater expansion of the industrial sector. Besides, the means of transport and communications will expand when the agricultural surplus is to be transported to urban areas and manufactured goods to the rural areas. Prof. Simon Kuznets called it as 'market contribution' of agriculture.

Providing Additional Foreign Exchange Earnings for the Import of Capital Goods for Development through Increased Agricultural Exports

Underdeveloped countries mostly specialize in the production of a few agricultural goods for exports. As output and productivity of the exportable goods expand, their exports increase and result in larger foreign exchange earnings. Foreign exchange earnings can be used to build the efficiency of other industries and help the establishment of new industries by importing scarce raw materials, machines, etc. Kuznets called it the 'product contribution' of agriculture.

Increasing Rural Incomes to be Mobilized by the State

When agriculture grows faster, in countries where agriculture dominates, the taxation of agriculture in one form or another is essential for mobilizing agricultural surplus in order to accelerate economic development. Kuznets called it as the 'factor contribution' of agriculture, where there is a transfer of resources to other sectors, these resources being productive factors.

Providing Productive Employment

As agricultural productivity and farm income increase, non-farm rural employment expands and diversifies. It include textiles, furniture, tools, handicrafts, leather and metal working, transport, marketing, repair works, construction, etc.

Improving the Welfare of the Rural People

Increase in rural incomes as result of the agricultural surplus tends to improve rural welfare. Peasants start consuming more food especially of a higher nutritional value and they build better houses fitted with modern amenities. They also set the services of schools, health centres, irrigation, banking, transport, communication, etc.

Agriculture as a Declining Industry

Agriculture's important contribution to economic growth was the transfer of labour to the non-farm sector. Governmental contributions universally fail to accept the transfer of labour from farms to non-agricultural jobs as essential for the economic health of the farm population. Instead it seems to be assumed that any decline in the farm population is as indication that policies have failed. If the labour transfer occurs slowly relative to the shifts in the demand for and supply of labour to agriculture, the incomes of farm families will grow more slowly than incomes in the rest of the economy.

There has been and is a reluctance of policy makers in industrial countries to accept the declining relative importance of the agriculture and the transfer of labour out of agriculture that is inevitably associated with economic growth. Some farm price and income policies, such those of European Economic Community, attempt to limit the decline in farm employment and thus slow down the transfer of labour from the rural to urban areas. The evidence is very clear that such policies fail to achieve that result. Data for all the major industrial countries for the past three decades do not show a negative relationship between the level of protection and the rate of decline of farm employment. The countries with high rates of protection, such as Japan and members of the European Community, have had more rapid declines in farm employment since 1960 than the countries with the lowest rates of protection, such as Australia, Canada, New Zealand and the US.

Governments have seldom adopted measures to facilitate the adjustment of rural areas to what economic growth requires. Basically it amounts to providing the necessary infrastructure in rural areas—roads, schools, communications, medical facilities, marketing structures, electricity, etc.

The experience of all the market economies has been that a large part of the adjustment of the farm population to economic growth has been through part-time farming—the combining of farm and non-farm employment in the same household and often for the same persons. As commercial as the agriculture of the US is thought to be, in most recent years 60 per cent or more of the incomes of farm families have come from non-farm activities; hardly more than a quarter of all farms are full-time farms in the sense that more than half of their family incomes come from farm operations. In Japan and Taiwan as well as in Germany an even larger fraction of farms are part-time. Part-time farming has permitted the majority of people living on farms in industrial countries to share in the increasing incomes created by economic growth. If there had not been significant growth of non-farm jobs in rural areas permitting the development of part-time farming, there would far fewer farm households or there would be many more farm households with low levels of income. The primary alternatives to part-time farming were either a greater migration to the cities or the damming up of more poor people in the countryside.

Alternative Organizations of Agriculture

The organization of farm resources is an important aspect of the economic transition. The alternatives range from maintaining the large farm organizations, perhaps under the guise of joint stock companies, to creating much smaller farming cooperatives to family farms. The issue of the ownership of farm lands is as much a political as an economic issue. With appropriate policies, legal and institutional arrangements an efficient agriculture could exist under numerous different tenure arrangements—the term under which a farmer or a farm organization obtains access to the use of land. It can be by ownership, by a use right or by a variety of rental arrangements.

In the US where any tenure arrangements is possible, the most numerous form of organization is that of the family farm and of the family farms, part-ownership. In this case the farm operator family owns part of the land and rents the other part. It is important that the dark shadows of the past not prevail to either make land rental illegal or to encumber it with so many conditions that it is not a viable alternative. If land rental is to be consistent with efficient use of agricultural resources, there must be competition in the land rental market.

The success of the agricultural and rural reforms in China since 1978 show that not everything has to be perfect for rural people to make major contributions to economic development. What the example shows is that if the governmental restrains on the behaviour of farm people are gradually relaxed and markets are permitted to develop and grow in significance, farm people will respond by working harder and more productively than under the old restrictive regime of the communes. But it was not only the form of farm organization that rural people found repressive. Very important was the many restraints on what farm people were permitted to do. At the beginning of the reform period, almost all forms of individual or private non-farm activities were prohibited, such as selling directly to urban residents, engaging in production of handicrafts or simple manufacture, or buying and selling with the intent to make a profit. Individuals were not allowed to own the means of production, such as a tractor or truck. As these restraints were gradually lifted over the first half of the 1980s, all forms of rural productive activity expanded at rapid rates. Agricultural output grew at an unprecedented rate of 7 per cent annually from 1979 to 1984 and rural industrial output has grown much more rapidly than the output of large and heavily subsidized urban state enterprises.

Economic Instability and Agriculture

Changes in economy-wide variables have major effects on the economic state of agriculture. These effects can be such as to increase greatly the variability and uncertainty faced by farm people. It is not only national macro-economic policies that are important. The increased importance of international trade, combined with the integration of capital markets, has meant that many of the changes in macro-economic variables within a country originate from outside the country and are thus beyond the control of that country.

There are other macro-economic variables that negated some of the desired effects of national agricultural policies. Changes in exchange rates of currency will affect the domestic agriculture. The overvaluation of US dollar in 1950s and 1960s negatively affected the American agriculture. The changes in interest costs were so great in a number of countries that the stabilizing effects of direct price and income policies were significantly offset. In the US and in Australia, for most years during the 1970s real interest rates were negative and the rapid increases in farm land prices reflected the effect of such low interest rates as well as the expectations concerning the level of farm prices.

During the 1970s the macro-economic setting was far more important than the farm price and income policies in all the industrial economies, with the possible exception of Japan, where the farm policies were quite effective in isolating agriculture from the swings in the macro-economic variables.

Importance of Agriculture

Numerous statistics can be presented which suggest the importance of agriculture. But there is no one measure of the importance of agriculture's contribution to the total economy.

There are those who take the extreme position that the prosperity of the whole economy hinges upon the prosperity of agriculture, and that depressed farm income leads to overall depressed economic conditions. This is true in highly agrarian societies. However, as countries develop the effect of agriculture on economic condition of the total economy becomes less.

The percentage of a nation's resources employed in agriculture depends to a large extent upon the efficiency with which agriculture is organized. As nations develop, the productivity of labour in agriculture increases and labour is generally transferred from agriculture to other sectors. In highly developed countries the percentage of labour force employed in agriculture is smaller than that in less developed countries (*see*, Fig. 9.1).

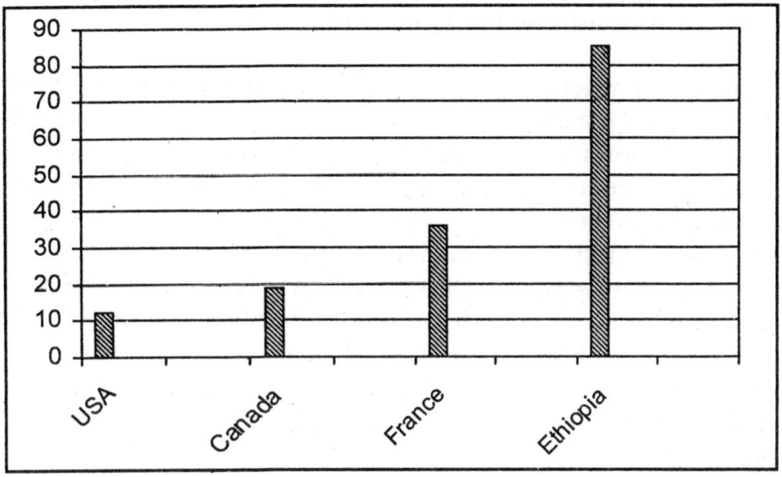

Fig. 9.1: Percentage of Agricultural Labour Force in Selected Countries (Middle of the 20th Century)

Total number of employed persons engaged in agricultural production is a better measure of the magnitude of agriculture's position relative to the total economy than is farm population. Because many people living on farm, gain their livelihood from non-farm jobs.

The nature of agricultural production changes over time. For this reason, it is difficult to compare the importance of agriculture in different countries, or even in the same country, at two different time periods. Part of the reduction in farm population due to development has been the result of shifting processing jobs formerly done on farms to non-farm parts of the economy.

The share of national income going to agriculture also is often used as a measure of the importance of agriculture. In developed countries the national income originating from agriculture is comparatively less than that in the developing world. In the US only less than 5 per cent of the national income is originated from the agriculture sector, whereas it is more than 60 per cent in Ethiopia.

Firms in Agriculture and Other Industries

A farm is a particular business firm which combines resources in the production of agricultural products. On a farm, the farm manager combines producing units or enterprises, such as cows, chickens, cotton, corn, etc. into an overall business. Each enterprise, however, is a part of the farm firm. The firm is a decision-making unit or managerial unit of production.

Since the firm is a decision-making unit in the production of commodities, it is both a buyer and seller. There are two general types of information which may be gained from the study of the firm as an individual economic unit. First, by studying the firm and analyzing the conditions which confront producers, it is possible to indicate the course of action profitable for producers to take. That is, by study of the firm, we may be able to provide the producer with information which would be useful in his decisions regarding the use of his resources. Thus, we may be able to indicate means by which individual firms can get greater return for the use of resources which they control.

Another major reason for studying individual agricultural firms is to predict the consequences of changes in economic conditions upon the production of the firm, and, in turn, upon the aggregate amount of products which will be available for consumption. Hence, the firm is studied in order to point out or determine changes in resource use which might be profitable from the stand point of the individual producers and to increase our knowledge of the effects of changes in economic conditions on the amount of production at the industry level. When individual firms increase production from a given amount of resources, society gains in that a greater quantity of product is available for distribution among the people.

Decision-making

From the economic view-point, decisions are viewed as being pursued in such a way as to maximize some objective subject to the resources available. There are four basic elements involved in making economic decisions.

(a) Decision Maker

In making choices, someone, say the manager or farmer must accept the responsibility for appraising the alternatives and choosing between them. He studies the alternative courses of action known to him, evaluates them, and decides which courses of action he will pursue. The decision-maker also has to accept the risks involved in making unprofitable decisions.

(b) Objectives of Decision

There are many possible reasons why people enter a business or engage in farming. In the most general sense, people engage in business with a view of maximizing their satisfaction. This satisfaction may come from some combinations of many objectives of lesser importance. Some contend that people enter a business for the purpose of obtaining net revenue. Economic analysis can be used to determine what action would be profitable to a producer.

(c) Conditions Facing Decision-makers

Each decision is made in a particular situation. Some of the existing conditions can be changed by the decision-maker, and some can't. For example, a farmer has limited quantities of resources to use in the production of alternative farm products. Within the limits of his freedom, he can choose the uses to which he will put these resources. The problem with which he is confronted is to allocate or divide the resources over which he has control among the many possible uses for them in such a manner as to maximize the attainment of his objectives. In making decisions, the farmer must recognize that there are some conditions over which he has little control but which are likely to influence his choices.

(d) The Measuring Stick

The last element of the decision-making framework pertains to the manner in which the resources that are controllable by the decision-maker are related to the objectives which he pursues. This 'measuring stick' provides the guides or standards by which the decision-maker is able to appraise the different uses of his resources. In economic analysis efficiency provides the measuring stick for evaluating choices.

Conclusion

In this chapter we reviewed the importance of agriculture in developing countries with a discussion on the dual sector model and the need for suitable agriculture price and income policies. The contribution of agriculture to economic development lies in providing more food to the increasing population, increasing the demand for industrial products and thus necessitates the expansion of the secondary and tertiary sectors, providing additional foreign exchange through increased agricultural exports, increasing rural incomes to be mobilized by the state, providing productive employment, and improving the welfare of the rural people.

REFERENCES

Boserup, E. (1965), *The Conditions of Agricultural Growth*, Aldine, Chicago.

Dorner, P. (1972), *Land Reform and Economic Development*, Penguin, Harmonds Worth.

Griffin, K.B. (1974), *The Political Economy of Agrarian Change: An Essay on the Green Revolution*, Harvard University Press, Mass.

Hayami, Y. (1992), 'Agricultural Innovation, Economic Growth and Equity: A Critique of Michael Lipton,' *South East Asian Journal of Agricultural Economics*, 1 (June).

Mellor, J.W. (1966), *The Economics of Agricultural Development*, Cornell University Press, Ithaca, NY.

10

Farm Production Decisions

Introduction

One distinguishing feature of agricultural production is that it always involves biological processes. This has many important implications for the application of economic theory to the study of agricultural production, marketing, and pricing. Agricultural production, crop production particularly, requires environmental inputs such as sunlight, water, heat, and time that are often beyond the control of farmers. The control of production quality and yields is often far from complete. In addition, crop production requires land, so the production activities are spread thinly over millions of acres.

Production activities involve the growth of animals and plants, and the length of time between the application of inputs and the garnering of output might take anywhere from six weeks in the case of broilers to several years in the case of tree fruits. Crop production also typically takes place on an annual cycle. The result is that agricultural production involves heterogeneous outputs produced in small lots, often on a seasonal basis, scattered hither and yon over wide geographic areas.

Production Function

The production function for any commodity is an equation, table, or graph showing the quantity of the commodity that can be produced per unit of time for each of a set of alternative inputs, when the best production techniques are used. A simple agricultural production function is obtained by using various alternative quantities of labour per unit of time to farm as fixed amount of land and recording the resulting alternative outputs of the commodity per unit of time.

Table 10.1 shows a short-run production function for wheat. Land is measured in hectares, labour in worker-years, and total products (*TP*) in tones per year. All units of land, labour or wheat are assumed to be homogenous or of the same quality. The average product of labour (AP_L) is obtained by dividing each quantity of *TP* by the corresponding quantity of labour; land being the same. The marginal product of labour (MP_L) is obtained by the differences between the successive quantities of *TP*.

Table 10.1: Production Function of Wheat

Land	*Labour*	*TP*	AP_L	MP_L
1	0	0	0	—
1	1	3	3	3
1	2	8	4	5
1	3	12	4	4
1	4	15	3.75	3
1	5	17	3.40	2
1	6	17	2.83	0
1	7	16	2.28	–1
1	8	13	1.63	–3

It is interesting for a farmer to know that wheat can be produced by combining land, seed wheat, nitrogen, phosphoric acid, potassium oxide, machinery, equipment and labour. However, this information would not be very useful unless the farmer know something about the manner in which these inputs must be combined in order to produce wheat. That is, he must know how and when to prepare the land, apply the fertilizer, and sow the seed. Otherwise it is possible to combine these inputs without getting wheat.

When a farmer is considering the question of how much nitrogen to use in wheat production he may consider the other inputs as given or fixed in specified kind and quantities. In this case, we have:

$Y_1 = f(X_1/X_2, X_3, \ldots\ldots\ldots, X_n)$

That is, the amount of Y_1 (wheat) depends upon the amount of X_1 (nitrogen), given the amount of other inputs (X_2, X_3, ..., X_n), which might be land, seed wheat, labour, rainfall, temperature, etc. The vertical line indicates that input X_1 is variable and others are fixed in quantity.

The manner in which the amount of wheat varies as the amount of nitrogen varies depends upon the amount of nitrogen used. It is possible that there is a constant relationship between application of nitrogen and the amount of wheat produced. In this case the production function may be in the following form:

$Y_1 = a + bX_1$

For example, if farmers expand one unit of wheat for each two units of nitrogen applied, then the linear relationship is as follows:

$Y_1 = a + 0.5\ X_1$

Where, the '*a*' indicates the yield of wheat without applying nitrogen, and the 0.5 indicates that Y_1 increases by 0.5 unit for every increase of one unit of nitrogen.

Cobb-Douglas Production Function

The Cobb-Douglas is the most widely used production function in empirical works. The function is expressed by

$Q = AL^{\alpha}K^{\beta}$

Where, Q is output and L and K are inputs of labour and capital respectively. A, α, and β are positive parameters determined in each case by the data. The greater the value of A, the more advanced is the technology. The parameter α measures the percentage increase in Q resulting from a 1% increase in L, while holding K constant. Similarly, β measures the percentage increase in Q resulting from a 1 per cent increase in K while holding L constant. Thus, α and β are the output elasticity of L and K respectively. If $\alpha + \beta = 1$, there are constant returns to scale, if $\alpha + \beta > 1$, there are increasing returns to scale, and if $\alpha + \beta < 1$, there are decreasing returns to scale.

Irrational Production in Agriculture

By using the data in Table 10.1, we can show the TP, AP and MP as follows:

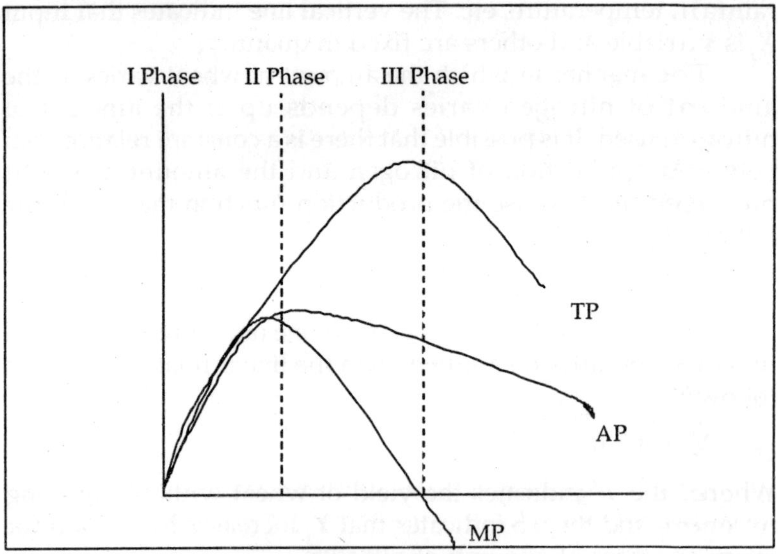

Fig. 10.1: Production Function

The input-output relation showing TP, AP, and MP can be divided in three Phases in such a manner that we can isolate the portion of the production function in which production is most profitable. In Fig. 10.1, phase-I of the production function goes to the level of input at which the maximum AP is obtained. In this phase, the AP is increasing and MP is greater than AP. Here it will always be profitable for the producer to continue to add inputs as long as the AP is increasing. For example, in a situation in which one input, say land, is free and another input, say labour, is expensive and limited. Under this situation it pays to limit the quantity of land used in relation to the quantity of labour used, even though land is free.

In the III phase, the total product is decreasing. Hence, in the III phase, the MP or the amount of product added by additional units of input is negative. Since additional quantities of input reduce total output in the III phase, it is not profitable to operate with a combination of resources existing in this phase. The point at which MP becomes zero represents the maximum quantity of variable input which will ever be profitable to use in combination with other inputs. For example, if labour are free and land expensive, it would be profitable to add labour up to the point, when the return from land is at a maximum. At this point, the MP of an additional unit of labour is zero. If labour is added beyond this point, the MP is negative, and it does not pay to operate in this region.

Thus, the phase-I and phase-III set the limits to the phase in which it is profitable to operate. Therefore, phase-II is the region in which production is most profitable. In phase-II, TP is increasing; MP is decreasing, is positive, and is less than the AP; and the AP is decreasing. This is the phase of rational production. But at the same time it should be emphasized that this region is one of diminishing returns; both AP and MP are decreasing.

In agriculture, producers do not have perfect knowledge of production relations. Because of this imperfect knowledge, it is possible to observe that producers combine resources in such proportions that they operate in phase-I or III of the production function. For example, in the production of many crops insufficient time is used to reach phase-II. Adding more time would increase the AP from use of the time.

On the other hand, evidence of production in phase-III is often noted. For example, during the later summer, we can see in tropical developing countries too many cattle on a given quantity of pasture, resulting in over-grazing of pastures and less production than could have been obtained with fewer cattle.

Application of Input-Output Analysis

Economic decisions by farmers frequently fall in the category of problems concerning the most profitable level of application of one input, given the level of other inputs, in the production of one commodity.

Under many soil and climatic conditions, the amount of agricultural commodity a farmer can expect to produce depends on the amount of inputs including fertilizers used per unit of land. In determining how much fertilizer to apply, the farmer must compare the added revenue which would be received from the application of fertilizer with the additional cost. He estimates the additional revenue expects to receive by multiplying the additional amount of the agricultural commodity expected to be harvested by the price he might reasonably expect to receive for his agro-products. Additional costs include expenditures for additional fertilizer, expenses involved in the application of the fertilizer, and expenses involved in harvesting and marketing the additional agro-products. If the farmer is to make decision consisted with maximization of net revenue, it is necessary for him to know how each of these items varies with the level of application of fertilizer.

The amount of fertilizer application varied in different fields depending upon the inputs, including weather. Experiments in US shows, under dry weather and wet weather conditions, diminishing returns are in evidence (Fig. 10.2). The difference in dry weather yield and good weather yield increases as the law of fertilizer application increases.

Weather conditions are important in determining the increase in yield resulting from the application of fertilizer. However, the farmer can't control weather conditions.

The quantity of an input most profitable to use in the production of a commodity is expected to change as the price of the input and the price of the commodity changes. The extent to which the most profitable level of application of an input varies depends on the shape of the production function and on the price of the input in relation to the price of the product.

Application of Cost Functions

Cost analyses are often helpful to farmers and processors in making decisions. Among other uses, cost analysis can be used to determine whether an enterprise is profitable, what size of the plant should be constructed, and what level of output is necessary before it pays to purchase some machine.

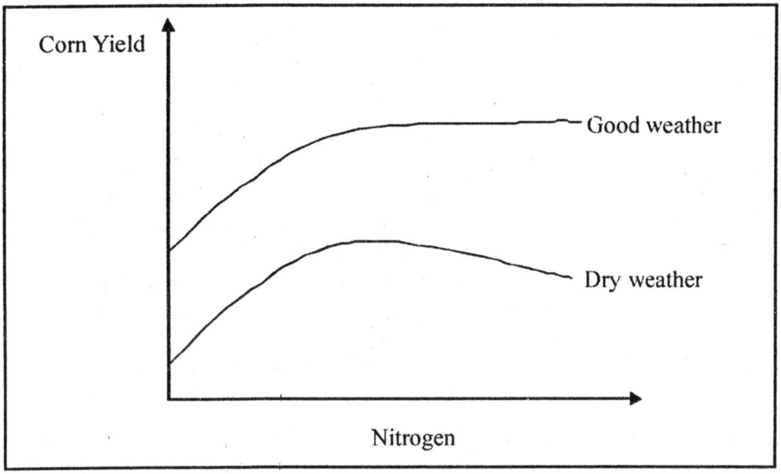

Fig. 10.2: Response of Corn to Nitrogen, USA

The low price of grains at harvest and the higher price later provide and incentive for grain producers to consider the possibility of increasing their net revenue by storing grains for sale at the later date. However, costs are associated with storage of grain. It may even be necessary to dry the grain artificially before it can be safely stored. Such variable costs include expenditures for cleaning bins, labour, hauling to bins, electricity, insect control, fuel for grain moving equipment, grain insurance, and loss in weight or shrinkage during storage. A farmer contemplating storage, and who does not already own storage facilities, must consider all costs, which include the costs of adding such facilities. To such farmers, all costs of storage are variable. He must include as variable costs the cost of interest on investment, property taxes, annual repairs, insurance and depreciation.

The volume of grains which is dried and stored has a large effect on the total costs. Therefore, the volume stored affects the farmer's decision as to whether to build drying and storage facilities and store grain on his farm or to sell at the time of harvest.

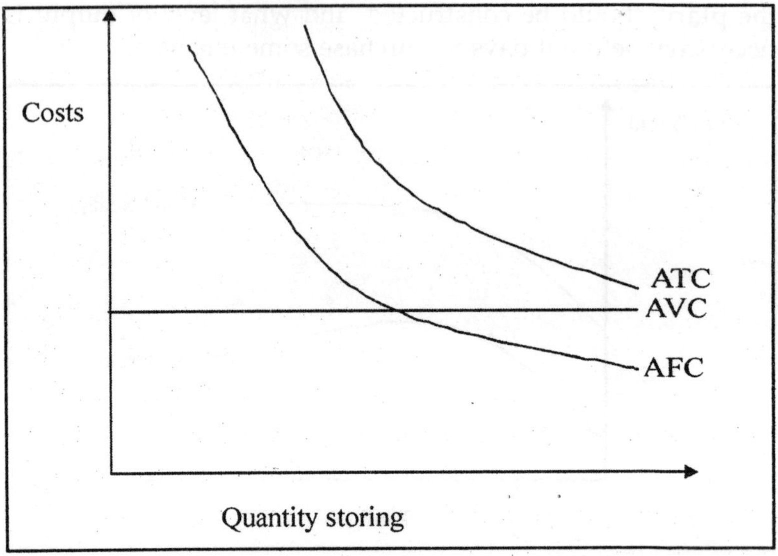

Fig. 10.3: Costs of Storage

Farmers have an additional alternative in storing grain. They can store grain in commercial facilities. When this is possible, a farmer may find that commercial storage is most profitable for small volumes, whereas on-farm storage result in more net revenue if the farmer has large volumes to store. A farmer may find that commercial storage is cheaper than on-farm storage for any volume stored unless on-farm facilities are already available. In any case, all available alternatives must be weighed by a farmer before making his decision.

Family Farm Model

The economic agents visualized in economic theory have limited affinity with their real-world counterparts. To make theory conform more realistically to agriculture, we define a family farm as a farm in which the family or household supplies labour, equity capital, and management.

The following are the major assumptions of the family farm model:

(i) No distraction between managerial labour and labour used to plant crops, feed animals, milk cows, etc.
(ii) The authority for decision may be diffused throughout the entire family.
(iii) Once a household organizes a farm (enters farming) all the family labour is fixed in farming.
(iv) The family farm is free to hire labour; hired labour and family labour are not perfect substitutes.

The definition of profit in short-run model is as follows:

$$\pi = TR - TVC - TFC \quad ...(1)$$

Where, π is profit, *TR*—total revenue, *TVC*—total variable cost, and *TFC*—total fixed cost. Total revenue is calculated by multiplying price times output. Total variable cost equals the sum of the products of variable input quantities times their respective prices.

$$QR = TR - TVC \quad ...(2)$$

Where, *QR* is the quasi-rent. Since quasi-rent is the net return over variable cost; it can be interpreted as the amount of money available to remunerate the fixed factors, that is, as the potential return to fixed equity capital and fixed family labour.

Equation (1) can be written as

$$\pi = QR - TFC \quad ....(3)$$

TFC is break up into components, one attributed to fixed capital and the other to family labour. The fixed cost of capital is denoted by CC (cost of capital). The fixed cost of family labour is denoted by TE (transfer earnings).

A household entering farming means the family labour will be fixed in the farm business. Taking family labour as the 'residential claimant', the return to family labour (RFL), is defined as:

$$RFL = TR - TVC - CC \quad ...(4)$$

Box 10.1: Definition and Illustration of Cost of Capital

If a household has $ 100 at the beginning of the current year (Year-1), but owns no other assets. The household plans to retire at the end of some future year, year-T (Say 20 years). The $ 100 could be invested in a money market fund at an annual rate of interest given by 'i' (Say 5%). How much money would be available at the end of year T?

The formula is: $M_T = M_0 (1+i)^T$ .... (A)

Where, M_0 is the initial amount of money invested at the beginning of year1 and M_T is the amount to be withdrawn at the end of year T

Answer

$$M_0 = \$ 100$$
$$i = 5\% = 0.05$$
$$T = 20$$
$$M_{20} = 100 (1 + 0.05)^{20}$$
$$= \$ 265.33$$

If the household has the alternative of purchasing a farm complete with land and machinery. The farm would be operated entirely by hired labour. At the end of each year, the household receives quasi-rent (QR), which is deposited in the money market fund. How much money will have accumulated in the money market fund under the investment option at the end of year T?

Let QR_t—the quasi-rent to be invested in the money market fund at the end of each year 't' (t = 1,2,3,........T) and will be constant for all 't'. At the end of period T, the household would have:

$$QR (1 + i)^{T-1} + QR (1 + i)^{T-2} + QR (1 + i)^{T-3} + \ldots\ldots\ldots\ldots$$

$$+ QR (1 + i)^{T-T} + S = QR \sum_{t=1}^{T} (1 + i)^{T-t} + S \qquad \ldots(B)$$

Where, S—the salvage value or the price of the farm assets at the end of year T.

$$\text{That is, } M_T = CC \sum_{t=1}^{T} (1+ i)^{T-t} + S \qquad \ldots. (C)$$

From Equation C, we get;

$$CC = \frac{M_T - S}{\sum\limits_{t=1(1+i)}^{T} T-t} \qquad \ldots (D)$$

Equation D defines CC, the opportunity cost of capital tied up in the fixed plant. In general, CC equals user cost of capital. That is, the implicit valuation of the flow of services provided by fixed factors over many years. In real world situation, it reflects the interest rate, depreciation, and other factors as well. Aside from considerations of risk, an entrepreneur would by the plant if the resulting wealth at the end of year T were lager than M_T.

Household's transfer earnings (*TE*) is defined as the minimum *RFL* that would prompt the household to enter farming. For a household that is already established in farming, *TE* is the minimum *RFL* that would keep them in farming.

The household decision regarding entering farming is as follows:

(a) If *RFL* > *TE*, the household enters farming.
(b) If *RFL* < *TE*, the household does not enter farming.
(c) If *RFL* = *TE*, the household is indifferent between farming and next best alternative career. Here the farmer is said to be a marginal farmer.

That is, profit is given by:

$$\pi = TR - TVC - CC - TE \qquad ...(5)$$

$$\pi = TR - TVC - TFC \qquad ...(6)$$

Where, *TFC* equals the sum of *CC* and *TE*. Now the farmers' choices regarding entering the farming are as follows:

(a) If $\pi > 0$, the household enters the farm industry. The returns to the family's resources in farming exceed the return in the non-farm sector.
(b) If $\pi < 0$, the household stays out of farming.

Although *CC* is based on opportunity cost of capital, *TE* is not based on the opportunity money cost of labour. Rather, *TE* is based on opportunity cost of labour when both money and work satisfaction are taken into account.

Fig. 10.4 shows the short-run cost curves for a family farm; giving curves for average fixed cost (*AFC*), average variable cost (*AVC*), average total cost (*ATC*), and marginal cost (*MC*). Fixed cost is divided into two components: average cost of capital (*ACC*), defined as *CC* divided by output, and average transfer earnings (*ATE*) defined as *TE* divided by output. The *AFC* curve is found by summing vertically *ACC* and *ATE*. *ATC* is found by summing vertically *AVC* and *AFC*.

In Fig. 10.4, at 'Po' price total revenue (Poqo) equals the sum of total variable cost (AVCoqo), cost of capital (ACCoqo), and the transfer earnings (ATEoqo). Profit equals zero and the returns to family labour (RFL) equal TE.

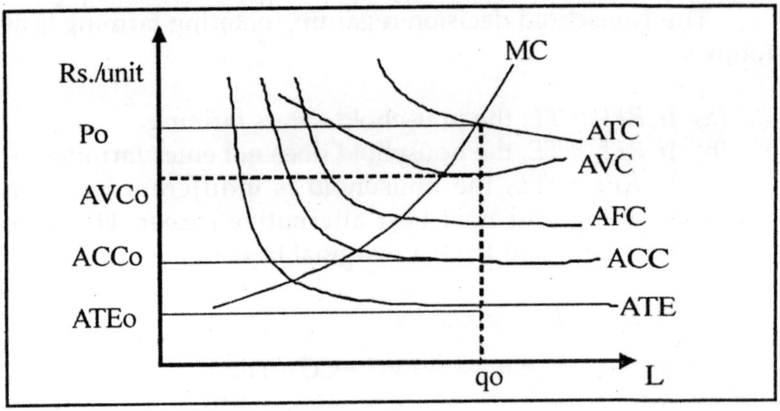

Fig. 10.4: Cost Curves of Family Labour

The supply function of farm operations as a function that shows how many households would be willing in the long run to organize and operate farms (enter or stay in farming) at alternative level of returns to family labour (RFL). If transfer earnings equal 'TEo' for all households, then the farm operator's supply function is perfectly elastic. If the supply function for all farm inputs, including that for farm operators are perfectly elastic, then the long run supply function for farm output will also be elastic.

Farm Output and Input Pricing

Consider a farm choosing land *'a'* and other inputs *'k'* in the production of output. For simplicity, we will consider only the single-output case. Let *'p'* denote the expected output price, *'J'* be the price of input *'k'*, and *'R'* be the rental price of land. Assume that output and output price are independently distributed random variables and that the farmer is risk neutral. Then the farmer makes decisions by maximizing expected profit.

$$\pi\ (p, J, R, TFC) = \text{Max}_{k,a}\ [pf\ (k,a) - J'k - Ra - TFC] \quad ...(7)$$

Where, $f(k,a)$ denotes expected output, 'pf' is expected revenue, 'Ra' is the rental cost of land. $J'k$ is the cost of inputs other than land, and TFC denotes total fixed cost.

Assuming that the farm chooses to produce and to use positive amounts of inputs (that is, quasi-rent is not negative), the first-order conditions associated with the maximization problem are:

$$P\frac{\partial f}{\partial k} = J \quad ...(8a)$$

$$P\frac{\partial f}{\partial a} = R \quad ...(8b)$$

The expression 8 states that, at the optimum for a producing farmer, the expected marginal value product (left hand side of the equation 8) equals the input cost (right-hand side of equation 8).

Let $k'(p, J, R)$ and $a'(p, J, R)$ denote the optimal input choices for 'k' and 'a' corresponding to equations 7 and 8.

The optimal supply function is given by

$$q'\ (p, J, R) = f(\ k', a')$$

Equation 7 is rewritten as:

$$\pi\ (p, J, R, TFC) = \text{Max}_q\ [pq - C\ (J, R, q) - TFC] \quad ...(9a)$$

where, 'q' denotes expected output and

$$C\ (J, R, q) = \text{Min}_{q,a}\ [J'k + Ra{:}q = f(k,a)] \quad ...(9b)$$

is the cost function characterizing the input choices that minimize the cost of producing a given expected output level 'q'. Denote by $k^c\ (J, R, q)$ and $a^c\ (J, R, q)$ the corresponding cost minimizing input demand function. The equivalence of equations 7 and 9 implies the following.

$$k'\ (p, J, R) = k^c\ [J, R, q'\ (p, J, R)] \quad ...(10a)$$
$$a'\ (p, J, R) = a^c\ [J, R, q'\ (p, J, R)] \quad ...(10b)$$

Expression 10 indicates that the cost minimization problem (10b) is fully consistent with the profit maximization problem (equation 7).

Assume that the land is necessary input such that $f(k,0) = 0$ for any $k \geq 0$. Define quasi-rent (ϕ) as total revenue (pq) minus total variable cost [$C(J, R, q)$]. Then the farmer would decide to produce only if $\phi(p, J, R) > 0$. Indeed if $\phi(p, J, R) < 0$, then the farmer would be better off producing nothing. In this case $\phi = 0$ and $\pi = -TFC$.

Analysis of Farm Programmes: Direct Payment Programme

In a direct payment programme, the government announces a target price p' for a farm commodity, say food, and makes direct payments to farmers to assure that the real prices they receive will not fall below p'. That is, the farmer's output is sold at the market price p. If the market price equals or exceeds the target price p', the government does nothing. If the market price falls below p', the government sends a check to the farmer equalling $(p' - p)\,q$, where 'q' equals the farmer's output. The direct payment per unit of output equals $(p' - p)$.

In real world applications, it is important that the direct payment be based on the market price, an average for the nation, say, as opposed to the actual search for the highest price.

In Fig. 10.5, DD is demand curve and SS supply curve. Intersection of the curves give the competitive price 'Pc' and the competitive output 'Qc.' For any market price less than the target price Po', farmers receive a per unit direct payment that brings the price they effectively receive up to Po'. For all such market prices the effective farm price equals Po', and in the aggregate, farmers produce 'Qg'. For market prices in excess of Po', the market price becomes the effective price. Thus the supply curve that shows how much farmers would be willing to produce at alternative market prices is given by the curve SSg, kinked at Po'. The new equilibrium price 'Pg' and output 'Qg' are given by the intersection of DD and SSg.

In equilibrium buyers are able to buy what they want at the marker price 'Pg'; farmers sell as much as desired at the effective farm price Po'. Market participants are in equilibrium because they could not further their goals by changing their decisions. The farmer receives a government check equal to

(Po′ – Pg)q, with the direct payment per unit equaling (Po′ – Pg). Government expenditure equals (Po′ – Pg) Qg.

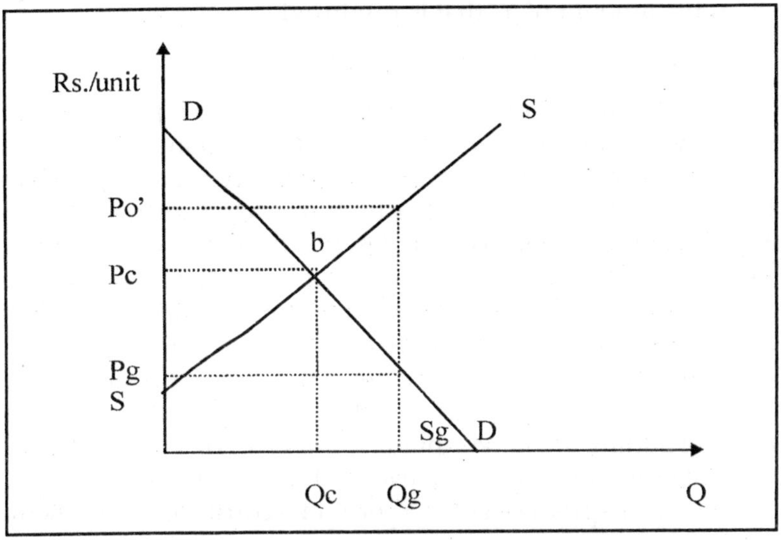

Fig. 10.5: Equilibrium under Direct Payment Programme

Product Choices and Production Possibilities

A common problem faced by the farmers or producers is to decide how to allocate the resources he owns, rents, or borrows to the alternative products, which can be produced. It involves choices between the number of cows and sheep, the acres of teff and wheat, or coffee and tea, etc. A producer wishes to obtain maximum satisfaction from the use of his resources. Farmers usually wish to know how much revenue will have to be given up to have some combination of enterprises other than that which would give maximum net revenue. When a farmer states that he prefer chickens to cows, it means that, if chicken yield the same or greater net revenue from his resources than cows, he will choose chickens.

A producer is interested in the effect that producing more of one product has on the production of alternative products. For example, he is producing two products, Y_1 and Y_2 using the same resource X_1. The amount of X_1 that can be used to produce Y_1 depends upon the amount of X_1 used in producing Y_2. Therefore, the amount of Y_1 that can be produced depends upon the amount of Y_2 that is produced.

That is, $Y_1 = f(Y_2)$

The relationship existing between any two products can be shown graphically by considering the amount of resources used as constant. In this way it can be shown, what happens to the quantity of each product as resources are transferred from Y_1 to Y_2, or the reverse. We can describe the effect of producing more Y_1 on the production of Y_2 by 'production possibilities' or 'iso-resource relationships'. It shows the maximum amounts of one product (Y_1) which can be produced for particular levels of another product (Y_2) from a given quantity of resources.

Two separate product functions in Table 10.2 show the effect of adding the same input X_1 to either Y_1 or Y_2. The graphic presentation of the data is shown in Figure 10.6. The input X_1 can be used to produce either Y_1 or Y_2 or a combination of them.

Table 10.2: Production Functions

Input (X_1)	*Output* (Y_1)	*Output* (Y_2)
0	0	0
5	7	11
10	13	20
15	18	28
20	22	35
25	25	41
30	27	46

If only 30 units of X_1 are available to the producer for production of Y_1 and Y_2, we can determine various combinations of the two products in such a manner that a maximum of one is obtained for any level of the other (Table 10.2). If the producer uses all 30 units of X_1 in the production of Y_2, he obtains 46 units of Y_2 but does not get any Y_1. He can shift 5 units of X_1 to the production of Y_1. In doing so, he receives 7 units of Y_1, but only 25 units of X_1 are available to produce Y_2. He can produce only 41 units of Y_2 with these 25 units of X_1.

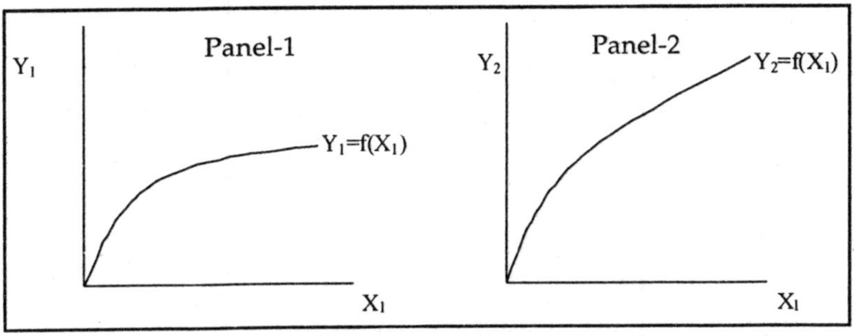

Fig. 10.6: Production Function (X_1 and Y_2) Panel-1
Production Function (X_1 and Y_2) Panel-2

The data are shown as production possibilities curve in Fig. 10.7. Commodity Y_1 on the X-axis and Y_2 on the Y-axis. The way in which two products can be substituted for each other is important from an economic stand point. There are as many production possibilities curves as there are input levels.

Table 10.3: Possible Product Combination for 30 Units of Input

Units of X_1 Used in the Production of		*Output*		*Marginal Rate of Substitution ($\Delta Y_2/\Delta Y_1$)*
Y_1	Y_2	Y_1	Y_2	
0	30	0	46	—
5	25	7	41	–5/7
10	20	13	35	–6/6
15	15	18	28	–7/5
20	10	22	20	–8/4
25	5	25	11	–9/3
30	0	27	0	–11/2

The maximum net revenue obtainable with a given amount of inputs is where the physical rate of substitution between two products is equal to the rate at which the products exchange in the market, or where $\Delta Y_2/\Delta Y_1 = P_{Y1}/P_{Y2}$

If, as inputs are transferred from Y_2 to Y_1, $P_{Y1}\Delta Y_1 > P_{Y2}\Delta Y_2$, more inputs should be added to produce Y_1 and less Y_2 should be produced. On the other hand, if $P_{Y1}\Delta Y_1 < P_{Y2}\Delta Y_2$, adding inputs to the production of Y_2 will be profitable.

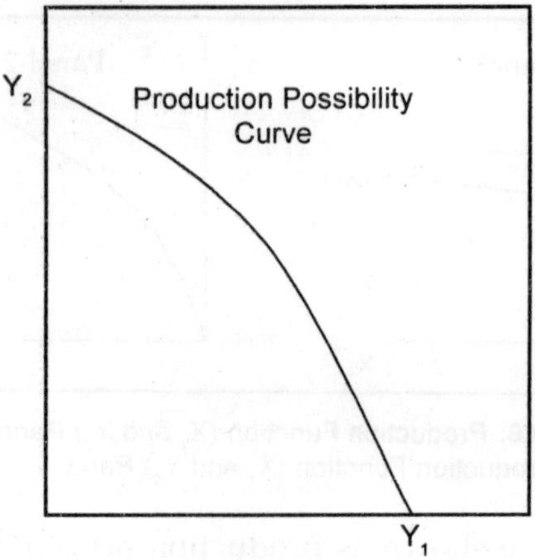

Fig. 10.7: Production Possibility

Farm Organization and Budgets

Net revenues farmers getting vary widely from farm to farm. Differences in net revenues of farm families result from differences in kinds and quantities of resources, which they own and differences in the use which they make of these resources. Farmers can compare the costs of different methods of performing operations or they can compare net revenues from producing different kinds of products. In order to make these comparisons, farmers must have information in regard to the consequences of alternative choices. Construction of enterprise budgets is one method by which producer can compare directly the revenues and costs of alternative enterprises.

A budget is a plan or a record of what one might expect to obtain from particular production practices. An enterprise budget consists of a statement of expected revenues and expenses from the products of a particular product. Development of a budget requires information pertaining to the amount of product which should be expected from particular quantities of inputs and information in regard to the expected prices of the product and of the inputs.

We can express the enterprise budget in the following equation form.

If $Y_1 = f(X_1, X_2, \ldots\ldots\ldots, X_n)$

Then Net Revenue $= Y_1P_{Y1} - (X_1P_{X1} + X_2P_{X2} + \ldots\ldots\ldots\ldots + X_nP_{Yn})$

An enterprise budget is shown in Table 10.4 for cotton production. It shows the amount of cotton which might be expected over the long run from particular levels of application of fertilizers and other inputs.

Table 10.4: Sample Enterprise Budget for Cotton Production (1 Acre)

Particulars		*Price ($)*	*Units*	*Quantity*	*Amount ($)*
I.	IncomeYield				
a.	Lint	0.315	Pounds	625	196.88
b.	Seed	0.031	Pounds	1060	32.86
	Total				229.74
II.	Expenses				
a.	Seed	2.75	Bushels	1	2.75
b.	Fertilizers	0.275	Pounds	190	15.25
c.	Pesticides	0.26	Pounds	60	15.60
d.	Others (Labour)	0.05	Hours	45.5	58.66
	Total				92.26
	Net Revenue				229.74 – 92.26 = 137.48

The items which should be included in an enterprise budget are those variable inputs which are used in the production of the particular commodity under consideration. In the enterprise budget shown in Table 10.4, only the variable expenses are charged to the cotton enterprise. No charge was made for the fixed expenses of land, equipment, and family labour. On the same manner, if a farmer has more than one crop on the farm, he would not charge all of the combine expenses to one crop. Such expenses are put in the category of fixed cost and are not relevant in influencing the farmer's production decisions as to choice of enterprises.

A farmer can construct budgets for each enterprise he wishes to consider on his farm. He needs to obtain information as to the amount of inputs and information as to input and output prices. A farmer can tell from the construction of a budget whether he could obtain positive net revenue from the production of a commodity.

Land Tenure Arrangements

Land tenure refers to the possession of rights to the use of land. People hold varying kinds of rights in the use of land and are said to belong in different tenure classes. Although it is difficult to rank tenure classes according to the degree of rights which are held, it is generally recognized that the owner-operator without debt has the most freedom of action with respect to the use of his inputs. At the other end of this scale of rights in land are found the hired farm labourers and share-croppers. Between these two extremes are share tenants, cash tenants, mortgaged owners, part-owners, and numerous combinations of these groupings.

There are many different types of tenure arrangements in agriculture economy world-wide. These arrangements influence the efficiency with which inputs are used. They also affect the degree of uncertainty encountered in the operation of a farm. Although innumerable breakdowns are possible, most tenure arrangements can be plced in one of the following.

Owners

This group includes those who have title to all of the land they operate. This is known as ownership in fee simple. It entitles the owner to sell or use his land as he sees fit within the limits of the law. Owners as a group generally have more freedom in their production plans than any other tenure class. However, in order to obtain ownership many owners have had to be satisfied with relatively small farms because of the small amount of capital available to them. Many farmers are capable of managing larger farms than they are able to buy. Also, where there owners have a large debt, they may have to adjust their production so that their short-term income will be sufficient to meet living expenses plus payments on their debt obligations. This may mean that a farming pattern will be necessary which will not yield the greatest long-term income for the family. For this reason, we may find that ownership does not always guarantee the most efficient organization of resources.

Part-Owner

This group includes those farmers who own some land and rent additional land in order to enlarge their farming units. Part-owners have, on the average, large farms in terms of acres and in value of land and building than do owner-operators or tenants. Renting additional land is a way of gaining control of larger quantities of resources without increasing risk by going further into debt. With the relatively high capital requirements needed for efficient farming, many farmers have found this form of tenure to be very satisfactory.

Tenants

Tenants are those farmers who rent all of the land they operate. Several different tenant categories exist. Share-croppers, for example, are tenants who pay a particular type of rent, a share of the crop. The basic function of tenancy is to allow two or more people to combine their inputs into a single producing unit. Unfortunately, conflicts between land lord and tenant can arise with leasing arrangements.

Supply of Individual Farm Products

Production of agricultural products varies substantially overtime. Some of the changes in quantities of commodities produced likely result from changes in uncontrollable conditions such as weather. On the other hand, many changes in production result from changes in relative prices and costs. In some years there are fairly definite cycles of production of agricultural products. A possible explanation of the cyclical behaviour is demonstrated by the 'Cobweb' theorem of production.

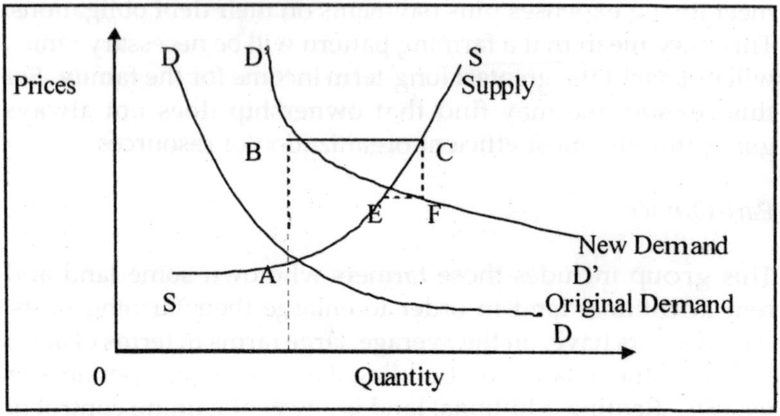

Fig. 10.8: Cobweb Behaviour in Agriculture Production

According to the Cobweb theorem, producers of a commodity expect the price in the next period of production to be the same as the current price and make production plans accordingly. As shown in Fig. 10.8, the industry is in equilibrium at A, that is, the consumers are willing to purchase the same quantity that the producers are willing to supply. The original demand curve DD shows the maximum quantities of the good that consumers are willing to purchase at alternative prices. If the demand shifts D'D' because people's preferences change so that they are willing to buy more of the good at all prices. Now the consumers are willing to pay the price at B for the same output for which they originally were willing to pay the price at A. In planning their production, producers consider the current price at B as the future price and make plans to increase their production to C accordingly. When production has been increased, however, it is necessary to take a lower price for the product than was anticipated. Consumers are willing to pay a price equal to that at F for the new output. In view of this, producers plan to decrease their production in the next time period to the amount at E. In some cases, this process continues until an equilibrium level of output at the intersection of the supply curve and the new demand curve is reached. In other case, equilibrium is never reached, and has a continuous fluctuation in prices and production.

Conclusion

The purpose of this chapter is to illustrate the various physical relationships that exist between inputs and outputs with which agricultural economists must be familiar. No rational farmer would want to produce beyond the point at which the marginal physical product equals zero, because further input use would cause the level of output to fall. Application of input-output analysis reveals that the extent to which the most profitable level of application of an input varies depends on the shape of the production function and on the price of the input in relation to the price of the product. The family farm model shows that the supply function for all farm inputs, including that for farm operators are perfectly elastic, then the long-run supply function for farm output will also be elastic.

REFERENCES

Antle, John M. and Daniel A. Samner (1996), *The Economics of Agriculture: Selected Papers of D. Gale Johnson*, University of Chicago Press, Chicago.

Barnum, H.N. and Squine, L. (1979), 'An Econometric Application of the Theory of the Farm-Households,' *The Journal of Development Economics*, Vol. 6, March.

Drummon, Evan H. and John W. Goodwin (2001), *Agricultural Economics*, Prentice Hall, New Jersey.

Helmberger, Peter G. and Jean Paul Chavas (1996), *The Economics of Agricultural Prices*, Prentice Hall, New Jersey.

Pim, A. (1946), *Colonial Agricultural Production*, Royal Institute of International Affairs, London.

Schultz, T.W. (1953), *The Economic Organization of Agriculture*, McGraw Hill, New York.

11

Land Economics and Land Utilization

Introduction

Land economics deals with the economic relationship between man and land. It deals with man's economic use of the surface resources of the earth and with the physical and biological, economic, and institutional factors that affect, condition and control his use of these resources. Leonard A. Salter has defined it as, 'a social science that deals with those problems in which social conduct is strategically affected by the physical, locational or property attributes of whole surface units.' Land economics involves a wide variety of economic relationships; but it is always concerned with problems and situations in which land, its use, or its control, is regarded as a factor of strategic or limiting importance.

The broad scope of land economics is illustrated by the physical and biological, the economic, and the institutional factors that affect man in his use of land resources. The physical and biological framework is concerned with the natural environment in which man finds himself and with the nature and characteristics of the various resources with which he must work. The economic framework is concerned with the operation of our price system as it affects each individual in his attempt to make profitable use of his land resource base. This framework deals with man's tendency to maximize his returns. The institutional framework is concerned with the role of man's cultural environment and the influence of the forces of social and collective action on his behaviour. Together with the level of technology, these three factors set the stage within which man's use of land takes place at any given time.

Origin and Development of Land Economics

Land economics had its beginnings in the later decades of the 19th century. It was first recognized as a collegiate course in 1892, when Richard T. Ely started his seminar on 'Landed Property' at the University of Wisconsin, USA. The topics covered under land economics include the following:

(i) Topics connected with terminology,
(ii) Problems of historical nature, *e.g.* History of land utilization,
(iii) Other theoretical questions,
(iv) Conservation topics,
(v) Socialization of Land-Public policy, and private and public land ownership and control,
(vi) Taxation and other public revenues from land,
(vii) Relation of land to the human element, *e.g.*; agricultural labour, farm tenancy, etc.,
(viii) Substitutes for free land (New opportunities), and
(ix) Contemporary land policies (Actual and Proposed), *e.g.* enlargement of land ownership, land reforms, etc.

Development of land economics shows a close connection with public issues. Before First World War the existence of tenancy and the availability of land for settlement took precedence. After the land boom following the war, attention shifted from tenancy to land valuation and ownership and to the burden of land debts and taxes that the boom had fostered. Also with the decline in the demand for agricultural products, studies of land abandonment and of agricultural decadence replaced work on land settlement. Because the overwhelming importance of these problems, the idea developed that land utilization research was a basis for community organization and planning.

Methodological Orientations in Land Economics

Methodclogical orientations in land economics will be classified into three periods.

(i) Before 1900

Four streams of thought originated before 1900, which are of special significance to the orientation of land economics.

(a) The socio-political philosophy underlying our family farm ideology and associated agrarianism;
(b) The classical and neo-classical doctrines about land;
(c) History as a methodological orientation to social science; and
(d) Empiricism as a method of science.

(ii) 1900 to 1946

Land economists in the period tended to be anti-theoretic, whether they are followers of the German historical school or of the empiricism founded by Bacon. During the period, methods of statistical inferences were developed; but largely unnoticed by land economists. Some analyses of land prices by correlation and regression were performed in the period; however, land economists mainly used the historical method or the tabular analysis, so characteristic of farm management research in the period.

(iii) Since 1946

Increased use of econometrics, operational and other mathematical and statistical techniques in land economists' research have added the methodological diversity of land economists. Major methodological orientations in land economics included shift from description to analysis, from ordinal to cardinal measurement and identification, from normative to positive characterization of data, and from applied to basic studies.

Land Utilization

Our natural resource environment, or land as the economists call it, is necessary for human survival. It provides us with standing room, with living space, with food, and with the vast array of raw materials we use in the satisfaction of our wants. Land can be used for several purposes and according to the use to which it is put may be classified as agricultural land, forestry, land used for habitation, commerce, transport, recreational purposes, and land remaining as barren, waste, deserts, etc. Agricultural land is further classified as cropped area, pastures, and fallow lands. Allocation of land among alternative uses is a complex economic problem, especially in developing countries, where population pressure is very high and per capita availability is very low.

The pattern of land use of a country at any particular time is determined by the physical, economic and institutional framework taken together. That is, the existing land use pattern in any country has been evolved as a result of the action and interaction of various factors such as the physical characteristics of land, the institutional framework, the structure of other resources (capital, labour, etc.) available and the factors of the region in relation to other aspects of economic development. Further land use in any society is determined to a great extent by the relative importance of its produce in sustaining the population.

Principles of Land Utilization

Land utilization is determined by various factors, which can be brought together to form certain principles.

(i) principle of Maximization: It is based on the assumption that people attempt to maximize the utilization of land in an earnest possible manner. The use of land is also determined by the cost involved and the incurred profit.

(ii) Equi-marginal principle: The transfer of land from one use to another will occur until the rate of achievement from transference equals the rate of loss from withdrawal.

(iii) Diminishing Marginal Rate of Substitution: With the increasing amount of production and consumption, the increment of satisfaction diminishes for any type of land utilization.

(iv) Diminishing Marginal Productivity: According to Malthus, the growth of population surpassed food production and food supply and this principle is known as the 'Diminishing Physical returns'.

(v) Specialization: This principle of land utilization shows that each and every crop cannot be produced with the same amount of benefit and the same level of production.

(vi) First Choice: Certain lands are more suited for the production of only certain particular crops and so these crops should be the first choice for the use of such lands.

(vii) Mapping and Search for Alternative Better Utilization: Mapping the use of land through field to field survey, data analysis, cartographic analysis of maps and statistical analysis are the fundamental issues of this principle.

(viii) Optimization of the Quality of Land Use in Relation to Environment: The optimization of the use of land should be searched in similar environment with favourable ecological conditions and in the same environment in which maximum production could be achieved with better infrastructure facilities.

(ix) Increasing the Efficiency and Capability of Land: This principle is to increase the efficiency and capability of land after knowing the shortcoming through land use and classification.

(x) Fixation of Cropping System Around Human Habitation for Least Effort and Low Travel Cost: Man tries to set things at accessible points with less cost, and time involved in travelling. Hence the desire to see the presence of almost all categories of land use gives rise to competition in between the varying objectives of the use of land.

(xi) Conservation of Land for Future Judicious Use: Conservation means the reduction of the rate of exhaustion of productive capacity of land resources in order to bring more and more land under intensive use.

Determinants of Land Utilization

The demand for land is a derived type of demand. Very few people seek land for its own sake. Instead, they want it because of what it produces. The products of land vary from the food we eat; the clothes we wear, and the materials we use in our daily life to the scenery we enjoy and the prestige and other satisfaction with land ownership. The overall demand for land resources finds its roots in the needs and aspirations of individuals who make up society. Up to a certain point, they are all primarily concerned with the physical need to secure sufficient food and other materials to sustain life. Beyond this point, their demand for land and its products is influenced largely by technological development, custom and tradition, their educational and cultural backgrounds, their incomes and spending power, individual tastes and personal goals, and by the changing attitudes that come with economic development. Each of these factors will determine the land utilization pattern in a country, which will change according to the variations in above factors.

However, the most important determinants of land use changes are the following:

(i) Population growth,
(ii) Economic development, and
(iii) Urbanization.

Distribution of Population in Relation to Land Resources

With the beginning of the agricultural revolution, the some what static population situation that had prevailed began to change. The increase in food production paved the way for an upward trend in population. This trend was accelerated by the industrial and sanitary-medical revolutions of the next two centuries. Increasing trade and commerce, the settlement of new areas, the trend towards industrialization and higher productivity per man, and the success with which modern medical science tackled the problem of high mortality rates—all added up to new incentives for population increase. World population growth is given in Fig. 11.1.

Many world problems involving the derived demand for land are directly related to the distribution of population with respect to land resources. Our total population is not scattered evenly between areas and it is not distributed in accordance with the population carrying capacity of the land resources found in various areas. This means that some of the world's people are better endowed with food and other land resources than others. And it also means that some areas are approaching the limits of their population carrying capacity, while others are capable of supplying high levels of living for some what larger population than they now have.

The relationship between population numbers and land resources is stated quantitatively in terms of population density or number of persons per square kilometre, and qualitatively in terms of per capita availability of land resources (man-land ratio). Man-land ratio may be applied in various ways. They are frequently used in a very specific sense to describe the areas of crop land per farmer, the average arable crop land equivalent per person, or the average per capita supplies of food or energy resources found in given areas. They may be used to indicate that some populations are primarily dependent upon local agricultural resources, which others have strong industrial and trade ties to large hinter land areas.

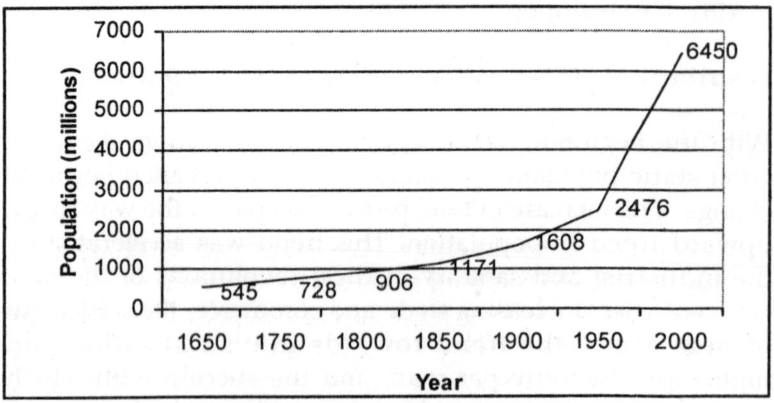

Fig. 11.1: World Population Growth

Land in Economic Growth

The economic growth of a country consists of increases in national income. The income is viewed as a stream that has its origin in the productive services rendered by resources. These resources consist of stocks, and the augmentation of these stocks is an essential part of the process of economic growth. However, land is a resource that cannot be readily augmented. We think of the stock of land as being virtually fixed. There is a negative correlation between economic development and land based economic activities in the theories and models that developed over the years. Thus it can be seen that economic growth and economic activities which concentrate on land resources are changing, and more clearly the importance of land related economic activities are declining, that is, the primary sector activities, including agriculture and allied sectors.

Demand for Land and Competition

With increasing population growth and development oriented economic activities, the area needs of almost every type of land use are bound to increase. The problem of meeting these additional land requirements would be greatly simplified if each use could expand without impinging upon lands needed or used for other purposes. Unfortunately, the fixed nature of the World's land resource base makes this an idle dream. Accordingly, each new upward spurt in the demand for land may be expected to contribute further to the competition and conflicts between various land uses.

One major form of competition between land uses comes with the encroachment on residential, recreational, and other consumption uses on areas used for production purposes. Much of the sprawling outward growth of our cities has come at the expense of areas once used for agriculture. Most cities experience continual competition between commercial, industrial, traditional, and other uses for the control of particular sites. This same situation exists in agriculture when various crops and livestock enterprises compete for the use of certain fields and when various individuals compete against other for the privilege of owning or operating particular farms.

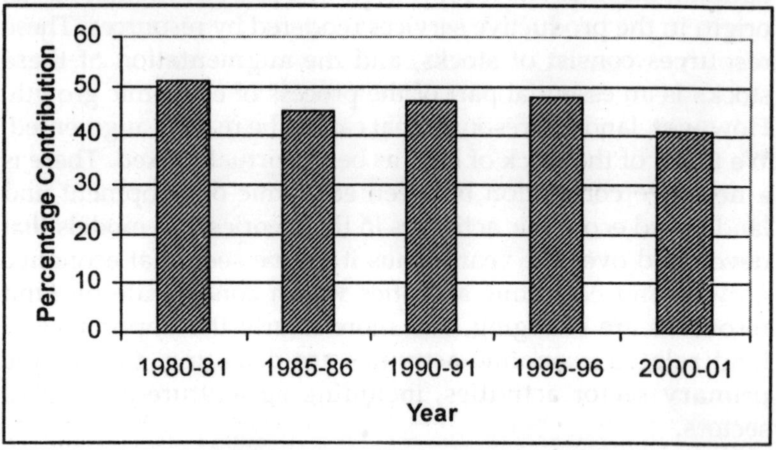

Fig. 11.2: Percentage Contribution of Agriculture to GDP in Ethiopia

Expanding urban are not only types of land use that infringe upon agricultural areas. Oil drilling and open pit mining operation, recreational uses, and new highway and air-port developments often bite into the nation's stock of productive farm lands. Crop land in its turn tends to outbid and displace lower types of uses. Arable grazing lands may plough for crop use and forested on cut over areas may be cleared for farming. Irrigation often converts grazing or waste areas into farm land; and drainage projects often favour the cultivation of land areas that may have value for wild life purposes.

Under market conditions, the control of land resources normally goes to the highest bidders. These bidders are then free to put their lands to those uses which offer the highest returns. In most cases, these uses coincide with—or at least are not contrary to the long-run welfare of society. However, quite often, operations find it profitable to either exploit their land resources or to shift them to uses not compatible with the long-run interests of society.

Exploitative practices and the encroachment of consumption uses on lands that could be held for long-run production purposes are often tolerated by society, particularly when it enjoys a plentiful supply of land resources. But as society faces the problem of increasing competition for the use of its limited resources, it sometimes finds it necessary to assign higher priorities to some uses than to others.

Urbanization and Land Uses

The most costly use of land in modern times is its use in the urban sector. Prior to the 19th century most part of the demand for land had come from agricultural uses. The industrial revolution and the concomitant urbanization added a new dimension to the demand for land. More and more land is being demanded for urban uses.

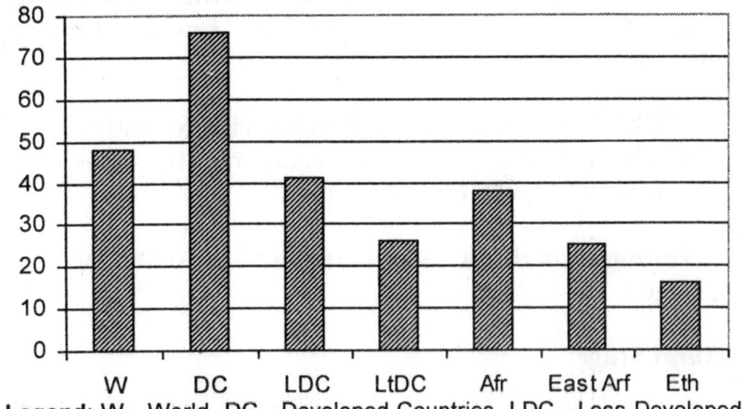

Legend: W—World, DC—Developed Countries, LDC—Less Developed Countries, LtDC—Least Developed Countries, Afr—Africa, East Afr—East Africa, Eth—Ethiopia

Fig. 11.3: Urban Population (Per cent), 2001

Urbanization is an unique interaction between economic and geographic factors, resulting complete change of a land area. Urbanization involves; concentration of people at population densities higher than those associated with agricultural population, population shift from agricultural to non-agricultural, and land use shift from agricultural to non-agricultural.

Land use pattern around an urban place is determined by the extend of influence of the city exert over its neighbouring outskirts, which varies from one landscape to another. The influence of an urban centre on its surrounding rural land scape is mainly through changing economic structure of the neighbourhoods.

Model of Transformation of Agricultural Land (Rural-Urban Fringe Model)

The influence of urbanization on land use can be best explained with the help of the rural-urban fringe. It is an area, where the transition of land use occurs from rural to urban uses, due to the socio-economic pressures from urban centres. The changes taking place in the fringe villages have two fundamental aspects:

(i) Changes in land uses within the village; and
(ii) Changes in the social and economic life-styles of the original people of the village.

The model of this transformation consists of the following five stages:

(i) Rural Stage

The characteristics of this stage are the following:

(a) Unaffected by the presence of the city,
(b) No daily movement of people from the village to the city for employment or for sale of farm products, and
(c) Occasional visits occur for medical facilities, purchase of agricultural equipments, etc.

(ii) Stage of Agricultural Land Use Change

The characteristics of this stage are the following:

(a) Village becomes the vegetable farm and milk shed of the city,
(b) Commercialization of agriculture in the village,
(c) Improvement of transportation facilities,
(d) People's awareness and direct contact with the city increases, and
(e) Social and economic transformation of the village.

(iii) Stage of Occupational Change

The characteristics of this stage are the following:

(a) Village population responds to the employment opportunities in the city,
(b) More and more children are sent to schools within and outside the village,
(c) Occupational change progresses and finally, at least one member working in the city,
(d) Some enterprising village families venture into business in the city, and
(e) Quantum jump in terms of the spatial mobility of the village population.

(iv) Stage of Urban Land Use Growth

The characteristics of this stage are the following:

(a) Land belonging to farmers in the villages are purchased by real estate agents (from the city) and developed into residential colonies or industrial sites,
(b) Land values in the village tends to increase,
(c) As more and more of the agricultural lands of the village are acquired for urban uses, the farmers in the village are compelled by circumstances to give up farming altogether, and

(d) Farming as an occupation sees a progressive decrease in importance and the way of life in the village is increasingly urbanized.

(v) Urban Village Stage

The characteristics of this stage are the following:

(a) All lands that was in agricultural use is taken up for urban uses,
(b) With the increasing pressure of population on the city, the poorer sections are compelled to seek dwelling space within the village in slums,
(c) Population comprises original dwellers and new comers, and
(d) Only urban land uses.

The rural-urban fringe offers the greatest challenge to the land use planners; since all obnoxious land uses are pushed towards the fringe villages from the city.

Conclusion

Land can be used for several purposes and according to the use to which it is put may be classified as agricultural land, forestry and land used for sites, land used for industries, commerce and for transport, recreational purposes and other land remaining as barren, waste, deserts, etc. The pattern of land use of a country at any particular time is determined by the physical, economic and institutional framework taken together. Land economics deals with the economic relationship between man and land. Agricultural land use pattern is determined by the extent of influence an urban centre exerts over its neighbouring outskirts. Proper development and utilization of land in rural-urban fringe requires the preparation of a detailed physical plan for land use.

REFERENCES

Acherman, Joseph, *et al.* (1962), *Land Economics Research*, John Hopkins Press, Baltimore.

Mandal, R.B. (1982), *Land Utilization: Theory and Practice*, Concept Publishing Company, New Delhi.

Nair, Reji. D. (2003), *Land Economics: Issues in Land Use*, Centre for Studies in Development Strategy, Thiruvananthapuram.

Salter, A. Leonard (1967), *A Critical Review of Research in Land Economics*, The University of Wisconsin Press, London.

Vink, A.P.A. (1967), *Land Use in Advancing Agriculture*, Springer-Verlag, New York.

12

Agricultural Policy

Introduction

Policy is defined as a deliberate course of action, as contrasted with a haphazard type of activity followed by a public body, private firm, family or individual. Policy generally implies wisdom in managing affairs, based on a definitive plan or programme created through a process of thought and reason. It is a universal activity of rational individuals, families and firms, political movements, organized groups, governments, and agencies of government.

Elements of Policy

Policy involves planning based on certain beliefs, values and goals, taking into account the resources that may be available for reaching the goals, and the benefits and costs of using one plan or another. The basic elements of policy involve the following:

(a) Goals that may be established,
(b) Means that may be used to reach these goals,
(c) Implements such as agents or agencies that activate and control the means, and
(d) Constraints that are applied to the plan or programme.

The basic concept of policy is that of deliberate action or activity involving these four elements.

Agricultural Policy

Agricultural policy, which is regarded as an important area of public policy, is defined as a course of public action directed primarily but not exclusively towards the farm and agribusiness sectors of society. It involves the full range of public decisions that influence individuals and firms to decide what products shall be produced, how they shall be produced, and for whom.

Agricultural policy applies to two broad sets of markets.

(i) *Agricultural Input Markets*: Through which the resources and commodities used in farming are made available for production. Policy in the input markets applies to the use of land and other natural resources, agricultural credit, industrial products used by agriculture, and the human resources employed in all sectors of agriculture.
(ii) *Agricultural Product Markets*: Through which farm products are marketed and processed for consumption at home and abroad. Policy in the product markets involve a broad range of laws, government rules and regulations that apply to these markets.

Need for Agricultural Policy

Agricultural policy is required mainly due to the following reasons:

(a) Increasing the productivity of agriculture is essential for meeting the growing world demand for food, and governments are widely and deeply involved in helping almost all sectors of agriculture to increase their productivity.
(b) Economic stability is important and is the responsibility of government.
(c) The government policy greatly influences income distribution.

Purpose of Studying Agricultural Policy

Because of the importance of agricultural policy in influencing our lives, study of agricultural policy is of great importance to policy makers. The two parts of policy study involve vision and analysis of possible policy choices. Vision and analysis are both important, and we study policy to broaden and sharpen our vision, and to improve our competence in analysis.

Beliefs and Values Underlying Agricultural Policy

Studying policy will help us understand what consequences one policy choice or another may have, and from this we can decide whether the result is good or not. The beliefs are balanced by certain concepts of justice and equity, those applied to the distribution of resources being quite important for agricultural policy. The governments play a positive role in seeing that resources are made available to individuals and families in just and fair manner. Government involvement with agriculture comes from the concepts of justice and equity, and beliefs concerning what are beneficial and worthwhile.

The following are the important beliefs and values underlying agricultural policy:

- *(i) Democratic Creed*: Among the democratic creed the following are important:
  - (a) All persons, no matter how wise or good, are of equal worth and dignity, and
  - (b) No person, again no matter how wise or good, is wise or good though to have dictatorial power over another.
- *(ii) Enterprise Creed:* This is based on the following value judgments:
  - (a) Members of a family bear a mutual responsibility to each other, the mainstream of which flows at least initially from parents to their children, and then branches out in various ways.

(b) The primary function of the governments is to prevent the lazy from pressing governments, businesses, or other institutions and individuals into sharing the burden of their imprudence.

(c) Within the general laws of the State, proprietors deserve exclusive rights to prescribe the rules under which they operate.

(d) It is a prime function of government to prevent any one individual or institution, including the government itself, from infringing on the managerial freedom of proprietors.

(iii) Creed of Self-integrity: Within a democratic state, the creed of self-integrity deals specifically with the status of dissent, and this has played and continues to play a crucial role in making agricultural policy.

Goals of Agricultural Policy

Goals of agricultural policy are defined as the ends of objectives towards which activity may be directed. Means are the ways in which goals are achieved. Values are the standards or preferences, based on beliefs that guide behaviour. A clear cut distinction among values, goals and means is difficult to arrive at. Yet it is essential to have definable goals that can be described in terms of productivity, stability, income distribution and welfare.

(i) Productivity and Development

In agriculture, it means having more quantity food, more goods produced jointly with food, under given level of resource use. The productivity goal is quite evident in public investment in research and agricultural education and extension programmes. Education increases the productivity of people, and provides for broad advances in science and technology. This has made modern agriculture a high-technology, capital-intensive industry. Changes in agriculture are still rapid, and productivity continues to rise.

(ii) Stability

Much of agricultural policy is aimed at increasing stability; it include price supports and storage programmes, trade agreements, supplementary payments to farmers, crop insurance, credit programmes, and others. Variability in both prices and crop yields is a major cause of instability in agriculture, and well-designed policy can do much to counter act or offset this variability.

(iii) Income Distribution

The goal of income distribution involved the following two aspects:

(a) The compensation levels of income between farm and non-farm families, with the lower average income of farm families often invoked as a justification for aid to agriculture.
(b) The skewness in income distribution among farm families, which is greater than among people employed in other sectors.

The policy goals are based to stabilize agricultural income, and farmers tend to gain in the short-run from programmes that raise and stabilize their prices and incomes.

(iv) Welfare of Farmers

Attainment of welfare depends on productivity and equity in distribution, along with liberty and justice. Maintaining individual freedom is one of the important considerations in deciding how far to go with a production control or income support programme.

Generally policy cannot be directed towards the maximization of any particular goal. Rather it is a process for maximizing the general welfare, which involves innumerable compromises among wide variety of goods.

Economic Organization of Agriculture

Agriculture has been defined as an industry covering the organization of resources, such as land and minerals, capital in wide variety of forms, and management and labour, for the production and marketing of food and fibre. It is organized in three major economic sectors, such as farming, agribusiness, and publicly supported sector of research, education, and service.

(i) Farm Sector

Farming includes ranching, and is subdivided for policy analysis into two separate but interrelated economies: crops and livestock. The crops economy uses a variety of resources to produce primary products from the soil. The livestock economy uses feedstuffs and bulky raw materials from the crops economy, combined with other resources, to produce animal products, including poultry and poultry products. Since it uses the commodities from the crops economy to produce other finished and semi-finished commodities, it may be viewed as a secondary economy within agriculture; just like milling wheat, crushing soybeans, of processing fruits and vegetables.

(ii) Agribusiness Sector

Agribusiness is also divided into two separate economies for purposes of policy analysis: the farm input supply economy and the marketing processing economy. The farm input supply economy includes the farm machinery and equipment industry, the commercial fertilizer industry, the pesticide industry, and the commercial feed and seed industries. The agricultural marketing and processing economy embraces the loan and complicated system of assembling, transforming, storing, conveying, and distributing the commodities produced in the crops and livestock economies through to retail levels.

(iii) Publicly Supported Sector

Agriculture production depends on a large number of services that are in large part publicly supported. This includes agricultural research and education, market regulation, transportation and communication facilities, food inspection and grading, and a number of other services.

Economic Transformation of Agriculture

In the long history of human race, the development of agriculture has been spurred by necessity and deliberate design, rather than accident of technology. Traditionally, shortages of food have been met by people increasing their efforts to get more food. Stages of hunting and gathering have given way to growing crops and domesticating animals. For the interpretation of transformation of agriculture, it is expedient to concentrate on three economies—the crops, livestock, and marketing economies—and on the two economic models of traditional and the industrial models of agriculture.

(i) Traditional Model

The traditional model may be visualized in its most primitive stage as consisting almost entirely of land and labour. Markets do not exist, or are poorly developed, and almost all efforts are directed towards survival. For some three to four million years on the earth the human race survived this way. Then 10 to 15 thousand years ago agriculture began to be transformed slowly to more advanced stages. But, until just few decades ago, land and labour were the major resources in farm production. Then, with innovations of modern technology, under the pressures of war and its aftermath, agriculture was transformed more swiftly, into what we now call the industrial model.

(ii) Industrial Model

The industrial model of agriculture emphasizes commodities from the scientifically advanced agribusiness farm input industries, and education and training of labour. The industrial model is essentially dynamic, rather than static because, in its pure form, all resources may be produced to order. If perfect divisibility of resources is assumed, then there will be neither increasing nor decreasing returns to scale. Farm firms will appear in a wide variety of sizes and types, rather than in a uniform standard size or type, as in the traditional family farm. Agribusiness firms will also vary widely in size and type, depending on experience, and in factors such as financing, managerial goals and expertise, and the timing of business decisions.

In 1964, Theodore Shultz, the first agricultural economist who got the Nobel Prize, developed the thesis that transforming traditional agriculture into the more productive industrial model requires prices farm inputs and products to be set at levels that make it profitable for the necessary investments to be made. But this alone may not be sufficient. Advances in science and technology that reduce the real prices of industrial inputs are crucial, as are investments in human resources, or human capital, to reduce the real cost of organizing and managing.

Characteristics Important for Policy

Agriculture is unique among the major industries because of the combination of economic, physical, and biological factors that determine supply. The biological nature of production in the crop and livestock economies, set against relatively stable domestic but less stable export demand, leads to both random and cyclical fluctuations in price. Inelastic supply and demand for total output in the short-run exaggerate these price fluctuations; and lags in production, in respect to price signals result in the Cobweb models of alternating cyclical fluctuations in output and price, which fit many agricultural situations.

The current policy emphasis on farm price supports and production controls, farm income payments, storage programmes, and other measures has its foundation in the biology of agricultural production and in the economics of the markets served by agriculture. The biology of cultivating crops and raising animals is a high-risk operation in terms of both output and price. The risks and uncertainties of disease, pests, and unfavourable weather fall most heavily on the individual farmer. This burden accounts for measures taken by individual operators to avoid risk or reduce their uncertainty, through the use of pesticides to protect crops and livestock, diversification to reduce effects of both price and output variations, and use of hail and all risk crop insurance, for example. Risks also extend beyond the farm into the food processing and marketing system. Food firms go to considerable expense to protect themselves from product spoilage and loss, and to avoid losses related to changes in markets.

(i) Land as a Factor in the Crops Economy

The crops economy is essentially land based, as nearly all plant life requires soil, in which roots are anchored and from which nutrient-laden water is absorbed for growth. The crucial economic role of land is one of the distinguishing characteristics of agriculture, and it often accounts for the dominance of the crops economy in policy making.

(ii) Geographic Orientation

The extensive nationwide geographic orientation of agriculture leads to regional specialization based on comparative advantage. The broad geographic orientation develops a political strength for agriculture that far exceeds what might be assumed solely on the basis of the number of people in farming.

(iii) Large Numbers of Independent Producers

Geographic scatter and the absence of pronounced technical or internal economies of large scale, particularly in the crops economy, account for the large number of farm firms, a factor that influences policy and is characteristic of agriculture.

(iv) Economic Structure as a Policy Issue

Determining what goals shall be pursued in respect to the economic structure of agriculture has long been an important policy issue.

(v) Effects of Inflation and Deflation

The effects of policies favouring large-scale industrial agriculture were greatly strengthened by the long-term inflations. It provides opportunities for windfall gains which could be exploited to best advantage by wealthy investors, corporations, and large scale firms. The declining real prices for farm products made the situation more difficult for the family farmer who was depending mainly on cash income from farming.

(vi) General Issue for Policy

The general policy issue is what kind of economic structure and income distribution is wanted for agriculture. The rise of new political groups—consumer, special interest, and others—has already expanded the agenda for agricultural policy, and will generate new issues in the future.

Market for Policy Analysis

The growth of agricultural markets depends on population growth and its distribution; real income or per capita purchasing power and its distribution; and the terms of trade. By the last it meant the value of the domestic currency relative to other currencies, and the conditions of trade; that is, whether free or not. In addition, changes in tastes and in programmes designed to improve nutritional standards are influential and government subsidies, such as food stamps and foreign aid programmes, contribute in a supplementary way.

In the early periods of development in all countries the domestic markets absorb the lion's portion of farm output in terms of both volume and quantity. In most of the developing countries expanding populations created a growing pressure on local food-producing capacity. The slow growth in the domestic market with unstable prices for farm products tends to imply increasingly inefficient use of agriculture resources especially in developing countries. The emphasis on dietary improvements and other health-related activities that have started momentum in developing countries have not resulted in an increase in the total food demanded by the average consumer.

Domestic demand will probably increase in accordance with population growth, neither much faster nor much slower, except in so far as farm products displace industrial materials. Since the rate of population increase is decreasing in developed countries, with largest increases in older-age groups, population growth will play a progressively smaller role. Increases in real income among more affluent consumers will have a limited effect because of the low income elasticity of demand for food.

Slow growth of the domestic market for total farm output may be projected as a basis for planning and policy-making. This leaves the export market as the major factor for future growth in the demand for total agricultural output.

The overview of markets for policy analysis is not one of overwhelming population growth such as existed in the past in the world agriculture, nor is it one of great resource stringency; however, it is a major issue of concern for the developing world. It is rather a view of some countries developing increasingly large food export potentials, and some others developing larger and larger food deficits, which means increasing demands for imports only if there is more trade and economic development in these countries.

Supply and Demand for Policy Analysis

The theory of supply and demand as applied to agricultural policy seeks to provide an explanation of the level and fluctuations of prices in agricultural input and product markets.

This consists of an analysis of the factors determining the quantities of commodities supplied and the quantities demanded under given conditions.

In visualizing agricultural supply, if there is a change in physical or biological conditions, such as the weather, the supply schedule will change. The basic determinants of agricultural supply include the following:

(a) The technology of production,
(b) Prices of resources used in production,
(c) Prices of products that may be substituted for the given products in production,
(d) Expectations concerning the prices of the agro-products,
(e) The number of sellers in a market, and
(f) The government policies regarding taxes and subsidies.

A change in any of these determinants will cause the supply change.

The most important determinants of demand for agriculture products include the following:

(a) Population growth,
(b) Per capita income,
(c) Prices of other goods,
(d) Advertising,
(e) Taxes and subsidies, and
(f) Sociological and demographic factors.

Generally the agricultural supply function is very inelastic in the short run, while the supply of individual commodities tends to be more elastic, especially where commodities can be most easily substituted for one another in the agricultural production process. A general implication for the policy is that the aggregate production function will respond rather slowly to either very high or very low agricultural prices. Strong increases in demand from poor crops in other countries may result in relatively high prices for two or three years or longer, while good weather, or rapid introduction of new production technologies, in the absence of equivalent demand increases, can result in relatively low product prices. In the absence of farm commodity policies these may last for several years. These are also depends upon the elasticity of demand.

If the elasticity of demand for food is – 0.237; it indicates that a 10 per cent increase or decrease in price will result in a 2.37 percentage change in the opposite direction in quantity demanded. Or a 2.37 per cent change in quantity supplied will result in a 10 per cent change in price in the opposite direction. The quantity demanded or supplied is measured in terms of index numbers weighted by value. Therefore, in cases of general price increases, low value commodities may be substituted for high-value commodities, and with general price decreases, the reverse substitution may be made.

In the export markets the demand for agricultural products is not as elastic as it was earlier due to heavy restrictions imposed by most of the countries. Under these circumstances, the elasticity of price transmission, which is the importing country's price response to the price received by exporters, would be less than one. Under a free-trade model, if there were perfect price transmission, it would be one; where protection was complete, so that the exporters' price was not reflected at all in the importing country, it would be zero. Where elasticity of price transmission was zero, the elasticity of export demand would be zero, or near zero, depending on the policy of the importing country. Here the real elasticity of export demand faced by the agriculture exporting countries could vary from high elasticity when trade was relatively free to nearly zero elasticity when export prices were not transmitted to those of the importing country.

Government Intervention

Government intervention in agriculture required to improve farm economic conditions has taken many forms.

(i) Adjusting Production to Market: One approach to improving farm economic conditions is to reduce the number of resources employed to produce a product plagued by surplus conditions. This is achieved by the government's renting whole farms or by paying farmers not to produce the product by requiring them to set aside part of the land normally used to plant this crop in order to qualify for farm Programme benefits. With less land planted to this crop, supply will decline and market price will rise. If the demand curve is inelastic, farm revenue will increase.

(ii) Price and Income Support Payments: Another general approach by government to improve farm economic conditions is to directly support farm prices and government purchases of surplus commodities. If the level of production rises during the year, the government can step in and buy excess supply at the announced price floor. Alternative approach is to support farm incomes through direct transfer payments from the government to farmers.

(iii) Foreign Trade Enhancements: A third approach to improving farm economic conditions involves the link between agriculture and foreign markets. There are essentially two general ways in which such enhancements can improve farm economic conditions. First, the government can institute tariffs, or a tax on imports, which make imported agricultural products more expensive to domestic consumers, or institute quotas, which limit the quantity of a particular good that can be imported. Both actions protect producers in the domestic agricultural sector. Second, the government can enhance the attractiveness of agricultural products in foreign markets by subsidizing their purchase, thereby stimulating the export demand.

(iv) Other Forms of Intervention: The governments' world-wide has used a variety of other approaches to enhance economic conditions in agriculture. These approaches include credit subsidies to farm borrowers who cannot otherwise qualify for credit, and loan guarantees for loans made to farmers and ranchers by commercial banks and other non-governmental lenders.

Rationale for Government Intervention

The rationale typically adviced for governmental intervention in the agricultural sector of an economy is the need to:

(i) Support/protect an infant industry,
(ii) Curb market powers of imperfect competitors when necessary to promote social good,
(iii) Provide for food security,
(iv) Provide for consumer health and safety, and
(v) Provide for environmental quality.

Tariffs, a form of tax on imported goods that raises their price to domestic consumers, and import quotas are typically used to shield an infant industry from foreign competition. Many governments intervene in their food and fiber industry to ensure an adequate food supply from domestic sources. Although it is an important issue in all countries, some nations drain off resources from other potential uses in an effort to meet their food needs internally.

In some countries the Environmental Protection Agencies are charged with the responsibility of monitoring the use of the nation's resources, including land (soil erosion), water (pollution), labour (occupational safety) and air (pollution). Thus the farm sector and the rest of the nation's food and fibre industry are heavily influenced by government intervention.

Conclusion

Agricultural policy deals with purposeful or deliberate government actions that are designed to bring about results that are consistent with a societal concept of what ought to be. Developmental agricultural policies are those actions that seek to improve the infrastructure that supports the food industry. Agricultural price and income support policies seek to maintain prices and incomes at higher levels than a free market would provide. There are two reasons agricultural policy issues are so potent: first, policy issues inherently deal with what ought to be rather than what is, and secondly, agricultural policy issues are so important that agriculture and food security are so vital in developing countries.

REFERENCES

Halcrow, Harold G. (1984), *Agricultural Policy Analysis*, McGraw Hill Book Company, New York.

Johnston, B.F. and Kilby, P. (1973), *Agriculture and Structural Transformation: Economic Strategies in Late Developing Countries*, Oxford University Press, New York.

Krueger, A.O. and Schiff, M. and Valdes, A. (eds) (1991), *Political Economy of Agricultural Pricing Policies*, John Hopkins University Press, Baltimore.

Schultz, T.W. (1964), *Transforming Traditional Agriculture*, Yale University Press, New Haven.

Von, Brunn. J., *et al.* (1993), *Aid to Agriculture: Reversing the Decline*, International Food Policy Research Institute, Washington, D.C.

13

Food Production and Security

Introduction

Food security is sometimes equated at national level with 'food self-sufficiency'. Some nations with food production deficits enjoy considerable national food security. They import to satisfy their population's food consumption needs. The volume and nature of these countries' exports, which produce the income to pay for food imports, allow some food-deficit nations to enjoy considerable food security (for example, Japan). Such security probably will continue as long as the political economy of producing nations encourages food exports (for example, USA). On the other hand, some countries have national food self-sufficiency but export so much food that many of their own citizens go hungry (for example, Brazil). Some nations neither produce enough food nor have an import capability to satisfy consumption needs. In such countries chronic hunger is abundant. Thus national food security is not to be understood simply as national food self-sufficiency but whether people, on the whole, are able to consume a minimum diet, the production sources of which are reasonably secure.

People secure in their food entitlements consume what is necessary to enjoy a vigorous life. As many as 750 miilion people in developing countries consume but 90 per cent of that amount, and it is estimated that 340 million of these are 'acutely undernourished;' eating but 80 per cent or less of a minimum nutritional standard. For millions of people, life's daily routines reflect a constant worry about and search for ways to provide sufficient food for themselves and their families. Frequently, neither worry nor effort produces satisfaction. Nutrition related disease and early death result; malnutrition both takes and denigrates human life.

Economic Development and Food Supply

As a society moves towards economic development, we expect to see a population surge with a high rate of natural increase. Because of this, developing countries must increase food production rapidly at least to maintain the amount of food available on a per capita basis.

Quantity

The demographic pressure on the food system in developing countries is not the only source of strain. With development come rapidly expanding incomes, which combined with very high income elasticities, produce even higher rates of growth in food demand. However, developed countries have very low income elasticities because most consumers already have more than enough to eat. If incomes rise, the consumer does not consume more food. On the other hand, in developing countries additional income is immediately converted into additional spending on food. Some studies have shown that the income elasticity for protein sources in developing countries exceeds one. That is a 10 per cent increase in incomes would result in increased spending on protein sources in excess of 10 per cent. Table 13.1 illustrates the difference between the rate of growth of food demand in a developed country and a developing country.

Table 13.1: Hypothetical Growth Rates of Food Consumption

Country	*Rate of Growth of Population (%)*	*Rate of Growth of Income (%)*	*Income Elasticity*	*Rate of Growth of Food Consumption (%)*
1. Developed country	0.5	3.0	0.1	0.8
2. Developing country	3.5	3.0	1.0	6.5

Quality

Not only does the quantity of food demanded increase with the development process, but also the quality of food increases dramatically. As incomes increase, consumers move away from traditional food sources such as wheat, rice, and teff and towards protein sources such as meat, dairy products, and eggs. Most studies have shown that the income elasticities for these protein sources in developing countries are well above one, so even as total food demand is growing rapidly, the demand for these protein sources is growing even more rapidly.

Processing and Marketing

As development progresses and incomes rise, the typical diet moves away from wheat, teff, and starches and towards meat, milk, and eggs. Take note of the marketing demands associated with these two sets of food products. Teff, wheat, and starches require very little processing and can be easily stored for long periods of time. By comparison, meat and dairy products require substantial processing and must be refrigerated. In addition, as incomes increase, the quantity of marketing services included in food increases rapidly as the consumer shifts away from raw agricultural ingredients and towards food products that are already prepared.

So while food demand increases rapidly in developing countries, the demand for food marketing services increases even more rapidly making food marketing one of the engines of economic growth. One of the keys to facilitating and accelerating the development process is for government to provide the infrastructure that encourages the rapid expansion of food marketing.

Patterns of Growth in Food Production

There has been a sustained increase in world output of agricultural products since 1960. Most of the major groups of countries and geographical areas of the world have participated in this increase. The rise in food production is not confined to the advanced industrial economies as shown in Fig. 13.1. The decline is associated not with a bias against food production for domestic consumption and in favour of cash crop production for export, but with a generally poor economic performance as reflected in negative growth per capita of GDP, investment, exports, manufacturing, and agriculture.

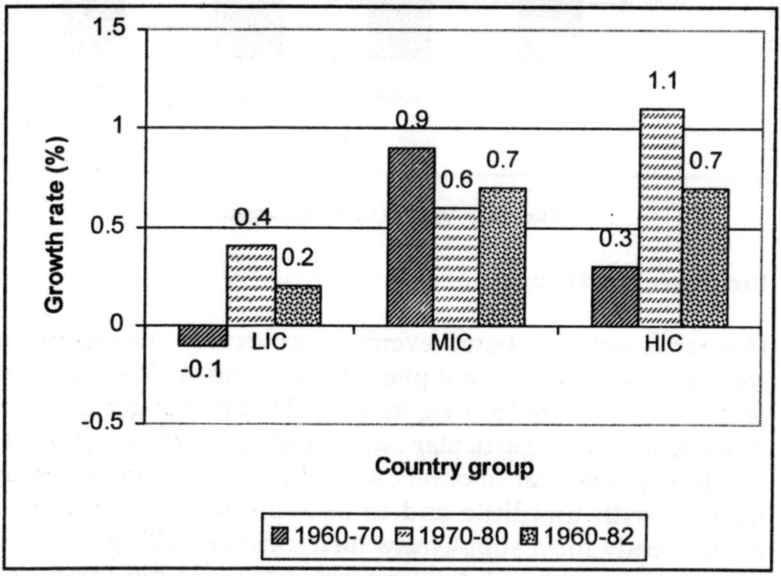

Fig. 13.1: Per Capita Agricultural Product Growth

In recent years food output per person world-wide have been reversed with unanticipated abruptness. Since 1984, the growth in grain production slowed, falling behind that of population (as Malthus has predicted). From 1984 to 1993 world grain output per person fell by 11 per cent. If population grows and farmers can't increase grain output by more than 12 million tonnes per year, per capita supplies will continue to diminish, dropping from the historical high of 346 kg in 1984 to 248 kg by 2030.

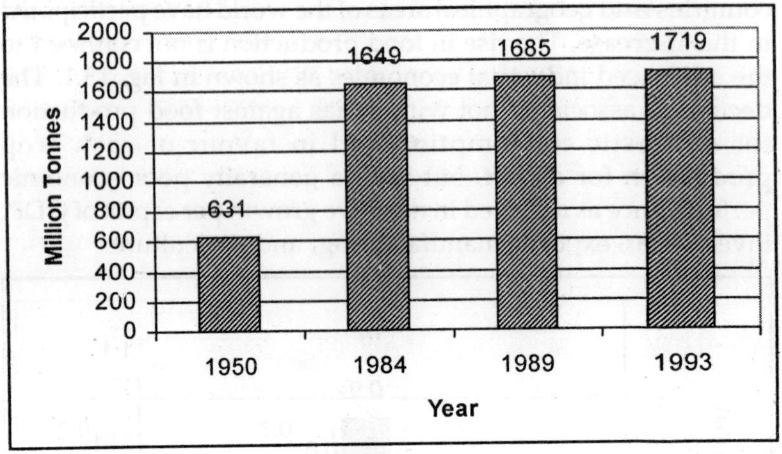

Fig. 13.2: World Grain Production

Incidence of Hunger

Hunger is not distributed evenly or randomly throughout a society; it is largely a rural phenomenon and within the rural areas is concentrated among the poor. That is, hunger tends to be associated with particular classes and occupational groups, landless agricultural labourers, small tenant cultivators, deficit farmers with tool little and to be self-sufficient and who consequently must supplement their incomes with part-time, off-farm jobs, pastoralists living on or beyond the fringes of the arable land, and fisher people and petty artisans supplying traditional goods and services in traditional ways.

The fundamental cause of hunger is the poverty of specific groups of people, not a general shortage of food. This relationship is governed by what the Nobel laureate Amartya Sen calls 'entitlement systems,' that is, the set of relations embodied in a society's laws, customs, and conventions that determines the ability of people to command access to food. Entitlement to food is through the application of labour, trade, production, return on assets, or through transfer or gift. Unfortunately, the bundle of entitlements of many people is not large enough to permit adequate nutrition.

The ownership of land, livestock, and other productive assets, as well as jewellery and other forms of savings, are part of the entitlement system. Indeed, the extent to which a household can transform assets into food often determines whether starvation occurs. One of the most common features of famine conditions is distress sales of assets by already poor households. In periods of drought, land owning cultivators of small holdings, for instance, starve partly because their reduced output leads to a decline in cash income and hence in market purchasing power, and partly because distress sales lead to a fall in the price of land and consequently in the rate at which their assets can be transformed into food. An analogous situation faces the pastoralists. A drought causes a reduction in the number of livestock. More important, however, it forces herdsmen to sell their animals and this, in turn, leads to a sharp fall in the price of cattle and hence in the value of the herdsmen's assets. The pastoralists, hit by drought, are decimated by the market mechanism. The pastoralists' assets decline in quantity and in unit value; their ability to command grain in the market vanishes, and they starve.

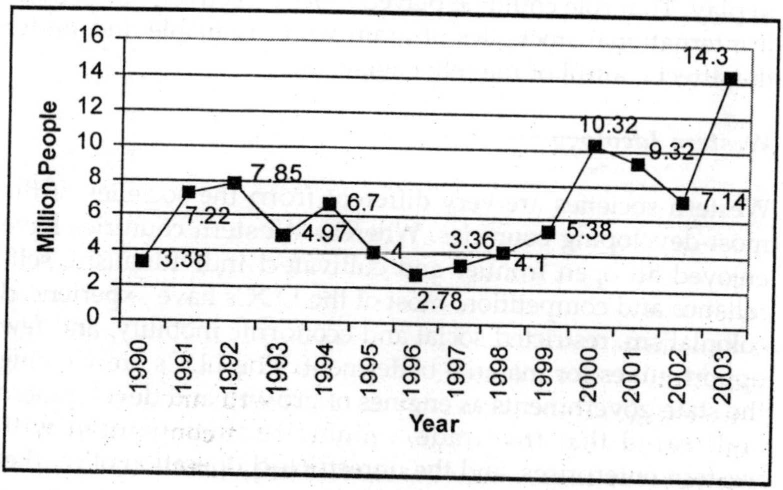

Fig. 13.3: Population Affected by Famines in Ethiopia

International Linkages

In a world of sovereign nation-states, the government of each country must assume the larger part of the responsibility for ensuring that everyone under its administrative authority has enough to eat. This responsibility is an inescapable consequence of the way the world is presently organized. Indeed, if a government is consistently unable to guarantee its own people enough to eat, it is doubtful that the minimum condition for statehood exists. This does not imply that hunger is exclusively a national phenomenon or solely a national responsibility. Clearly, there are international forces at work that affect the geography of hunger.

Studies have shown that foreign aid, whether loans or grants has done little on average to accelerate the long run growth of the LDCs. It has done even less to reduce inequality in the distribution of income within the recipient countries and consequently has had no discernible impact on reducing the incidence of hunger and malnutrition. In short run, during famine conditions, emergency relief and obviously has a role to play. That role could be played more effectively, moreover, if international stockpiles of grain were available and under the direct control of the relief agencies.

Western Ideology

Western societies are very different from the societies of the most developing countries. Whereas Western countries have enjoyed an open frontier and cultivated individualism, self-reliance and competition, most of the LDCs have experienced colonialism, restricted social and economic mobility, and few opportunities for material betterment. The LDCs are viewing the state governments as engines of growth and development and feared that free trade, uninhibited competition with western enterprises, and the unrestricted operation of market forces would result in neo-colonialism.

Transfer of Technology

The importing of western agricultural technology into inegalitarian and socially divided LDCs often has accentuated inequality and occasionally has further impoverished the weakest sections of the rural population. For example, the introduction of mechanical farming methods in Arsi province in Ethiopia, under a Swedish aid programme resulted in the eviction of more than 5000 tenant households between 1967 and 1975. Even the Green Revolution (agricultural revolution) has proved to be less green than was once hoped; certainly it has not made revolution of a different hue less likely. Perhaps the most avidly promoted western agricultural technology in the LDCs is large multi-purpose dams. In fact, the very first loan ever made by the World Bank to an LDC was to China in 1948 for a dam. However, there are plenty of signs that large dams have produced very low economic returns, have damaged forestry and fisheries, have caused widespread salination of the soil, and have inflicted much hardship on ordinary people.

Food Security Challenges in the World

Two problems are at the crux of the world's food security: chronic food insecurity in most developing countries and widespread fluctuations in annual food production in many developed and developing countries. The first is a long-term problem of aggregate food supply in developing countries, a problem that requires increasing current rates of food production growth through out the LDCs. The second problem is more a short-term fluctuation in annual food production that have particularly negative impact on the poor.

In recent years the growth of world food production has been accompanied by a steadily increasing degree of production variability: between the periods 1960-61 to 1970-71 and 1971-72 to 1982-83, the coefficient of variation of total world cereal production increased from 2.8 per cent to 3.4 per cent. At the same time the impact of rising degree of price variability can also be neglected. Although international grain prices were relatively stable in the 1950s and 1960s, since 1971 they have become highly variable. The coefficient for export prices was more than eight times as high in the 1970s as it was in the 1960s.

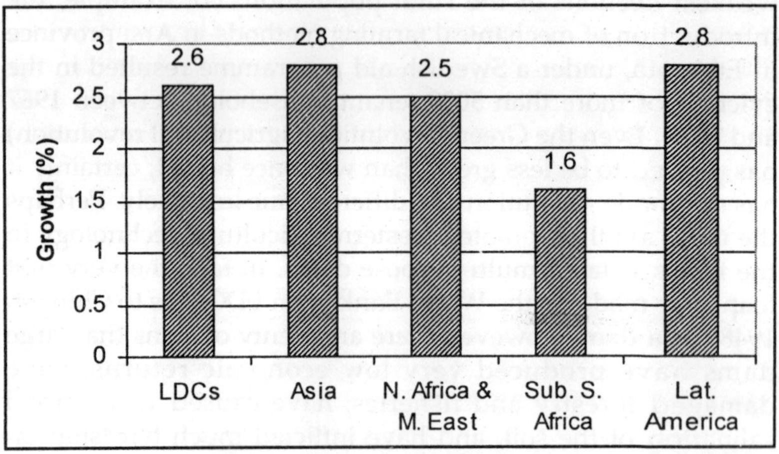

Fig. 13.4: Annual Food Production Growth, 1961-80

The poor suffer either through a reduction in their purchasing power from higher prices or through a reduction in their employment opportunities. As food prices rise, the wealthier classes try to maintain their food consumption by reducing their consumption of those very labour-intensive goods and services that provide employment for the poor. A decline in food production therefore not only reduces the food supplies available to the poor, but may also reduce their ability to procure those supplies at higher prices.

Food Needs and the Developing World

In order to ease the burden on the poor, it is necessary to accelerate current rates of food production growth throughout the LDCs. This is because of the tremendous world need for food, if the poor are to prosper, as well as the critical role that the food production sector must assume in any equitable pattern of economic growth. In some developing countries the initial benefits of a faster rate of food production growth may well tend to benefit the surplus producing peasant cultivator and not the poorest rural people.

In most LDCs food production growth requires more attention to crop yields. Through out the world, even in Africa, the rate of growth of the cropped area has declined sharply in recent years. This indicates that an ever-increasing proportion of the food needed to feed the world must come from increased yields per unit of land. In the last few decades increased crop yields have become the main source of food production growth in the developing world. Increases in yields require prolonged and continuous technological change in agriculture. Depending on the situation, improvements in agricultural technology (such as HYVs of seeds, fertilizers, and pesticides) produce yields two to four times higher than those achieved by traditional means.

In general, the new seed/fertilizer inputs commonly associated with the Green Revolution can't succeed without considerable state intervention in agriculture. The state needs to come in and establish those types of rural institutions and services that the private sector will not undertake. Most LDCs would have to wait a very long time for the private sector to build efficient agricultural research and technical education systems, or even irrigation and fertilizer distribution systems in the countryside. All of this focuses attention on the need for a high level of public investment in the basic building blocks of agricultural development: irrigation, input facilities, rural roads, and especially agricultural research systems.

The level of public investment is not the only factor determining agricultural success in the LDCs. Certainly such factors as the character of land distribution, the quality of human capital stock, and other socio-economic factors also plays leading role. But the public investment in agriculture is clearly an important factor, if for no other reason than that the common pattern in many developing countries is to under-invest in the rural sector. For example, in Africa, governments have typically spent very little on agriculture. During the period 1978-80 the median annual expenditure on agriculture in 15 African countries was only 7.4 per cent of the total government budgets. During the same time foreign donors have generally paid less attention to African agriculture than have national governments. As a result, most African countries today suffer from a poorly developed rural infrastructure, little research on food crops, and poorly developed input delivery systems.

Food Marketing

The food marketing system refers to all the activities and services that occur between the producers/providers of food and food stuffs and the consumer. Food marketing deals with how the product of a wheat farmer in a village and a bread manufacturer in a city and a bakery owner in another city are connected. There is another marketing system that is important for agriculture and that is the input or farm service marketing system that sells inputs such as fertilizers and chemicals to farmers. Firms engaged in farm service marketing, agricultural production, and food marketing are known collectively as agri-business.

Food marketing produces utility—utility for which the ultimate consumer is willing to pay. The four utilities that are produced are time, place, form, and possession.

(i) *Time*: The agribusiness firms that stored the wheat or the flour created a time utility, allowing production and consumption to occur at different points of time. Since storage is not a free good, the consumer will ultimately pay for the time utility that is created.

(ii) *Place*: Moving the product to the consumer creates place utility and adds to the value of the good as perceived by the consumer.

(iii) *Form:* The conversion or production processes create form utility; they change the form of the product into something that the consumer wants. In doing so, they add utility to the product—additional utility that the consumer is willing to pay for.

(iv) *Possession:* When the marketing system changes the possession of the product to the consumer, the utility of the consumer increases. It is the expected increase of possession utility that encouraged the consumer to exchange some currencies for the right to claim possession.

The food marketing system and the competition within that system create choices for the consumer. A dynamic, vibrant food marketing system provides consumers with abundant choices. The food marketing firm that can give the potential customer what he wants (form), when he wants it (time), where he wants it (place), and at the lowest price (possession) is the firm that will make the sale and prosper.

Approaches to the Study of Food Marketing

Food marketing is a very complex system with literally millions of interactions. Mainly there are four approaches to the study of food marketing.

(i) Functional

In this approach to the study of the food marketing system, the complexity of the system is divided into specific tasks that must be performed and each task is studied independently. Transportation and storage are two of the more important functions.

(ii) Institutional

This approach emphasizes the role of different participants in the food marketing chain and their relationships to one another. The institutional approach also examines the role of governmental and regulatory agencies in the food marketing system.

(iii) Market Levels

This analysis follows food through the marketing system as it moves from stage to stage. This is akin to studying each link of a chain to evaluate its contribution to the chain. The analysis looks at different steps in the process and evaluates the contributions to the creation of utility at each of these steps.

(iv) Commodity

In this approach the entire marketing chain of a single product is examined. All aspects, functional and institutional, of the marketing of a specific commodity are studied in an integrated fashion.

Food Marketing Bill

The food marketing system produces utility or value by changing some characteristics of a product as it moves from the farm to the consumer. Each of these productive activities has a cost that must ultimately be paid for by the consumer. The sum of all these costs is called the food marketing bill.

When a consumer checks out at a super market and pays Rs. 1000 for several bags of food, what is that consumer buying? Basically two things are being purchased: the farm value of the agricultural commodity and the food marketing services that have been added to the value of the food as it moved through the marketing chain. As shown in Fig. 11.5 the vast majority of what the consumer purchases is marketing services as opposed to farm value. Of the total Rs. 564 million spent on farm food in the model food marketing bill only 120 million or 21 per cent is for the agricultural product itself. Nearly four times as much is spent on marketing services—those additional utilities that are added to food products.

The component parts of the food marketing bill as shown in Fig. 11.5 reveal that virtually half of it is labour, including everything from the driver of the truck to the butcher to the cashier at the super market. The other part of the food marketing bill is a collection of various different expenses, the largest of which is packaging—a necessary utility that is usually added by the processor. The 'other' category included expenses such as advertising, depreciation, interest, rent, repairs, and taxes.

Food Market Levels

The study of food market levels examine the different middlemen that a typical product will move through. Some foods will move through many different levels, while others will take a more direct approach. In some instances the roles of several different middlemen may be combined into a single firm or activity.

(i) Assemblers

The first post-harvest activity is assembly, in which a small quantity of output from a large number of producers is brought together in large enough volume to enter into the processing chain.

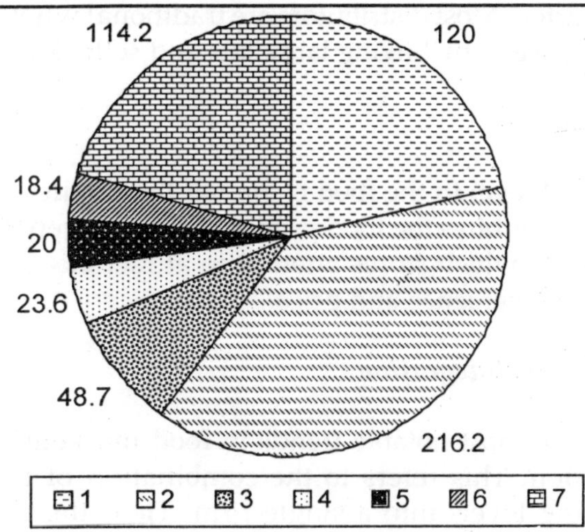

Legend: 1. Farm value, 2. Labour, 3. Packaging, 4. Transportation, 5. Power, 6. Profits, 7. Others

Fig. 13.5: Model Food Marketing Bill

(ii) Commodity Processors

Commodity processors are firms that buy raw agricultural commodities such as wheat and process them into ingredients for retail food products. These are the companies that buy wheat by the train load and produce flour for sale to the bakeries.

(iii) Food Processors

Food processors are manufacturers of final food products. These firms buy both raw agricultural products from assemblers and processed ingredients from commodity processors and convert them into finished food products ready for the consumers.

(iv) Distributors

Distributors are the mirror image of assemblers. They buy from the food processors by the carload and sell to many retailers by the carton. Most distributors are traditional wholesalers who earn their keep by buying large lots and selling small lots.

(v) Retailers

At the last level in the food chain fall the retailer from whom the customer buys the food product. It is a fiercely competitive business in which stores attempt to attract customers on the basis of convenience and price.

(vi) Vertical Integration

One of the most notable trends in food marketing is vertical integration. This refers to the combination of two or more marketing levels into a single firm. Then the coordination between the levels is accomplished by management directive rather than through markets sending price signals.

(vii) Industrialization

Another trend in the food marketing business has been given the name of industrialization. Basically this refers to the use of modern industrial concepts of production reutilization, procurement through strategic alliances, coordination, and contracting in the food marketing system.

Marketing Functions

One way to analyze markets is to study how the various functional activities are performed. There are mainly two major classes of market functions.

(i) Primary Function

There are four major primary functions such as creating time, place, form, and possession utility. These four utilities are created by the transportation system, the storage system, the processing system, and the exchange system. But these are not the only four functions in a marketing system. The other functions are called the facilitating functions.

(ii) Facilitating Functions

Markets operate more efficiently if buyers and sellers can agree on a price without a physical examination of the product. To facilitate this there must be a system of grades and standards that both buyers and sellers agree on. In some cases it is the government that creates grades and standards, and in other cases the industry will impose grades and standards upon itself. A second facilitating function is financing. The creation of the time utility implies storage costs, but it also implies a financial cost for the time value of money for whoever has ownership of the commodity while it is in storage. So financing the ownership of a commodity during the marketing period of that commodity becomes a part of the marketing cost that the consumer must eventually pay.

A third facilitating function is risk bearing. During the marketing process there are two significant risks that the owner of the commodity faces. There is a physical risk that the commodity may be destroyed in a fire or accident. And there is the price risk that between the time the good is bought and sold, its price may have changed. A final facilitating function is market information. For markets to work efficiently and effectively, both buyers and sellers need full information about prevailing prices and quantities of goods that are moving at those prices.

Conclusion

Between 1950 and 1984, World grain production expanded 2.6 fold, outstripping population growth by a wide margin and raising the grain harvested per person by 40 per cent. However, recently these trends in food output per person have been reversed with unanticipated abruptness especially in developing countries with a quest on the food security front. The present chapter discussed the international linkages of hunger and food security challenges along with food marketing. Food marketing refers to all the activities that occur between the farmer and the consumer of food, which creates utility. The food bill as a percentage of disposable income will decline when economies develop. The marketing bill varies substantially among food products depending on how much utility has been added in the marketing process. Increasing marketing efficiency—that is, lowering marketing costs—is a win-win situation in which both producers and consumers are made better off.

REFERENCES

Chambers, J.D. and Mingay, G.E. (1966), *The Agricultural Revolution, 1750-1880*, Schocken Books, New York.

Cohen, M.M. (1977), *The Food Crisis in Prehistory*, Yale University Press, New Haven.

Hollist, W. Ladd and Lamonmd Tullis (eds.) (1987), *Pursuing Food Security: Strategies and Obstacles in Africa, Asia, Latin America and the Middle East*, Lynne Rienner Publishers, London.

Lipton, M. and Lonhurst, R. (1989), *New Seeds and Poor People*, Unwin Hyman, London.

Pinstrup-Anderson, P. and Rosegrant, M.W. (1999), *World Food Prospects: Critical issues for the Early Twenty-First Century*, International Food Policy Research Institute, Washington D.C.

14

World Trade and Agriculture

Introduction

In the modern era countries world-wide are more vigilant with regard to the international trade and liberalization of trade regimes have started with great pace. Trade occurs because individuals, firms, governments, or nations anticipate economic gains from the exchange of goods or services. People make money in international commerce by purchasing goods or services in the country, where they can be produced the cheapest and selling those goods or services in the country where they are worth the most. Each country is endowed with a unique set of human, institutional, and natural resources that give rise to different prices and trade relationships among countries.

The basis for trade is differing opportunity costs among nations. To receive gains from trade, nations must specialize in the production of goods for which they are most efficient and exchange those goods with other nations. Through increased specialization and exchange, all nations can benefit from trade, and world economic welfare will be increased.

Exports and Imports of Farm Commodities: Demand for Exports and Imports

The influence of exogenous factors on Indian agriculture can be illustrated as follows:

The supply and demand for food for the rest of the world (ROW) are given by Sw and Dw in Panel-A of Fig. 14.1. With no international trade, equilibrium price and output in the ROW equal Pw1 and Qw1. However, we assume that the ROW does not have a comparative advantage in food production, that the price Pw1 is higher than the price of Indian food available in the international market. The ROW thus imports food. To obtain the Indian demand for exports (for imports from the ROW view point) we subtract laterally Sw from Dw in Panel-A, plotting the result in Panel-B. The Dx curve is the demand for Indian exports. In general for any Qw > Qw1, the Dw curve will be more inelastic than will be the Dx curve for the corresponding import quantity.

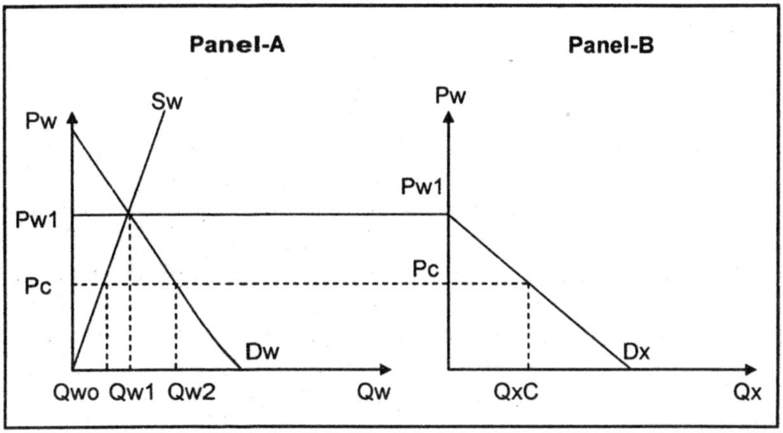

Fig. 14.1: ROW Domestic Demand and Supply for Food and Export Demand

If time is allowed for ROW output to respond to price changes, the demand for exports likely tends to be more elastic than the domestic demand. Under free trade conditions, the demand for exports would likely add elasticity to the farm-level demand for Indian farm output.

Indian supply and demand for food are given by Se and De in Panel-B of Fig. 14.2. For any Pe > Peo India produces more than it consumes. To derive the supply for Indian supply for Indian exports, we subtracts laterally Indian demand from supply, plotting the result for all prices not less than Peo in

Panel-A. The demand for Indian exports Dx from Fig. 14.1 is reproduced in Fig. 14.2.

The competitive equilibrium is given by the intersection of the demand and supply for Indian exports, by the intersection of Dx and Sx in Panel-A of Fig. 14.2. Equilibrium price and quantity are given by Pc and Qxc. By construction Qxc = Qe1 – Qeo. Going back to Fig. 14.1, we see that Qxc equals, also by construction (Qw2 – Qwo).

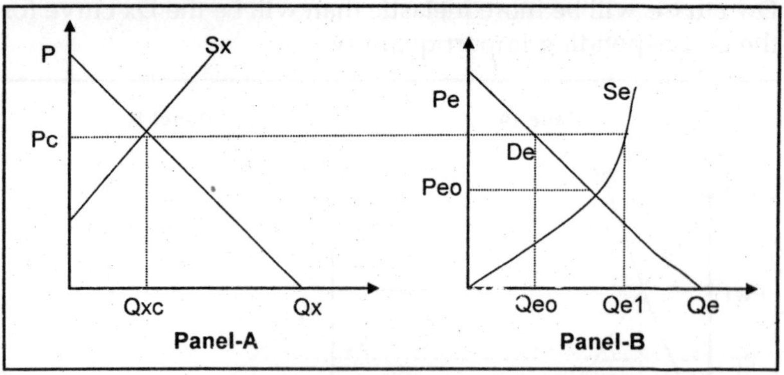

Fig. 14.2: Indian Domestic Demand and Supply for Food and Export Demand and Supply

Elasticity

The elasticity of export demand is closely linked to the elasticities of the ROW demand and supply. The elasticity of total demand is a weighted average of the elasticities for the demand for domestic consumption and the demand for exports.

The elasticity of total demand equals the elasticity of the demand for domestic consumption, weighted by the ratio of domestic consumption to domestic production, plus the elasticity of the demand for exports, weighted by the ratio of exports to domestic production. At present, there is widespread disagreement as to the magnitude of export demand elasticity, particularly in the long run. As a consequence, there is also much uncertainty as to the elasticity of total demand.

The existence of production lags and uncertainty does, however, call attention to a dynamic issue that is important in understanding the pricing of farm outputs. Time is required for the response of Indian and ROW outputs to changes in prices. If we hold constant planned production both inside and abroad and ignore the demand for stocks, the stage is set for unstable markets and for wide price swings depending on the weather. Favourable weather both here and abroad increases Indian output at the same time export demand contracts. Also, in the very short run, with fixed farm output abroad, the demand for Indian farm exports is likely high inelastic. The price in India, and in the ROW, too, could collapse because of high yield.

Move Towards Trade Liberalization

Increased world market instability, declining commodity prices, and lower farm incomes led to record levels of government support to the farm sector during the mid-1980s world-wide. When distortions to agricultural trade continued to drive up farm programme costs, world leaders called for major reform of the agricultural trading system. The result was the initiation of the multilateral trade negotiations under the General Agreement on Tariffs and Trade (GATT) and finally, the birth of the World Trade Organization. The Uruguay Round of Agreements, which involved 125 nations, was completed on December 15, 1994 and was implemented on January 1, 1995, and concluded in 2001.

The major objectives of these trade liberalization movements included the following:

1. Provide market access by converting quotas to tariff equivalents, then phase in a reduction of tariffs by an average of 36 per cent over six years, with a minimum of 15 per cent reduction for each tariff and minimum market access growing from 3 per cent to 5 per cent of domestic consumption.
2. Reduce export subsidies by 36 per cent in expenditure and 21 per cent in tonnage over six years.

3. Lower trade distorting domestic agricultural support by 20 per cent over 6 years.
4. Use accepted international standards for food safety and animal and plant health regulations, harmonize those standards in order to prevent their use as non-tariff barriers to trade, and establish disease/pathogen free zones within geographic boundaries of countries affected by certain diseases and pests. Countries may maintain standards more stringent than the international standards if they are based upon sound scientific evidence.

Basis of Trade

Trade occurs because of inter-regional or international differences in production efficiencies and therefore in the costs of production. These differences may be due to natural resource endowments, technological advantages, or differences in resources productivities. A country will import those goods that it produces (or could produce) at relatively high opportunity cost and exports those goods it produces at relatively low opportunity cost.

Goods that are differentiated are called products. Most products are sold under a brand name to identify one producer's product as being different from another's. While the trade in products is also driven by relative costs of production, there are additional forces that determine the flow of trade. Products are differentiated to cater to the unique tastes and preferences of individual consumers. When consumers buy a product, the purchase decision is usually made on the basis of value—a balance between the perceived satisfaction of using the product and the price of the product. And since different people have different perceptions, they behave differently.

While the trade in commodities is usually unidirectional, flowing from the country with lower relative costs to the country with higher relative costs, the flow of products in multidirectional, driven by the variety of tastes and preferences. In the case of products it is value (a perception of the individual consumer) rather than costs that dictate the flow of trade.

Trade Model

The concepts of import demand and export supply can be used to illustrate how cost differentials between two countries explain the flow of trade.

The model is based on the following assumptions:

1. Two countries, both of which produce and consume a single good—call it stuff.
2. There are no transportation costs and no barriers to trade such as tariffs or taxes.

Because of different resource endowments and resource productivities, one country is a lower cost producer of stuff while the other is a higher cost producer.

The domestic supply and demand diagrams for both countries are shown in the right and left panel of Fig. 14.3. Country A is a relatively high cost producer of stuff, while country B is a relatively low cost producer. Without trade between the two, a price of Pa would prevail in country A and a price Pb would prevail in country B. The price differential between the two countries suggests that there is an incentive to trade. The center panel of the figure shows the import demand of country A (the high cost producer wants imports) and the export supply of country B (which seeks markets for what it can produce at a low opportunity cost).

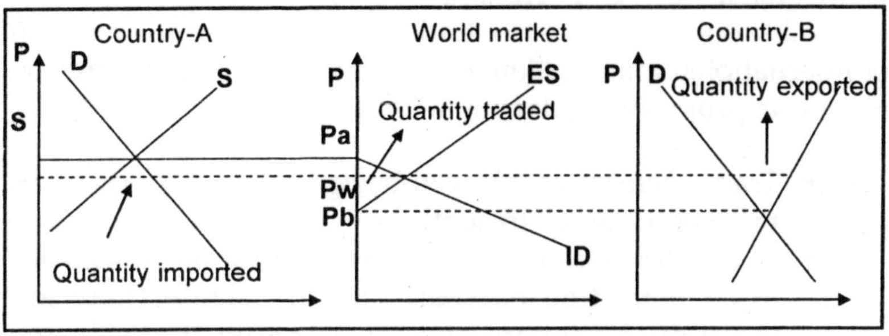

Fig. 14.3: Two Country One Commodity Model

The import demand and export supply on the world market operate like any other supply-demand situation. The interaction of potential buyers and sellers determines an equilibrium price at which the market is cleared. This is shown as Pw. At this price the quantity that country B is willing to export is equal to the quantity that country A is willing to import and the world market clears. At this one unique price, the three line segments (quantity imported, quantity exported, and quantity traded) are of equal length showing that the international market clears with quantity demanded equals quantity supplied.

Producers in country B are happy because they are selling more stuff at higher prices than prevailed without trade. Likewise, consumers in country A are delighted because they can now consume more stuff at a lower price. So, the impulse to trade internationally comes from differences in domestic prices that would prevail in the absence of trade. These differences arise because of different resource endowments and different resource productivities.

Gains from Trade

Trade, whether among regions or among nations, encourages resources to seek those employments where they are relatively efficient. From a global point of view, this reallocation of resources has the effect of increasing global production and hence global well-being. This improvement in global well-being is possible only so long as free trade is unobstructed by national or international intervention. Economists universally agree on two basic propositions dealing with trade.

- Trade increase global well-being by causing resources to be used more efficiently.
- Trade increases the overall well-being of the citizens of each trading partner. That is, while there are individual winners and losers from trade, in the aggregate gains of the winners will outweigh losses of the losers.

To illustrate the first point let's use a simple two-country, two-good model. Assume that the US and India both produce wheat and cloth. The productivity of labour in both countries for both goods is shown in Table 14.1. Clearly the US is able to produce wheat more efficiently that India, while the latter is more efficient in the production of cloth. Therefore, if trade were allowed between the two countries, we would expect the US to export wheat and India to export cloth.

Table 7.1: Output per Unit of Labour

Country	*Wheat*	*Cloth*
United States	10 units	6 units
India	5 units	10 units

To illustrate that trade and the resulting reallocation of resources would improve the global well-being, let's conduct the following exercise.

Assume that each country has a fixed number of labourers involved in the production of each commodity. Now assume that each country reallocates just one unit of that labour into the production of the product that is produced more efficiently. The result is given in Table 14.2. In the US when one unit of labour is withdrawn from the relatively inefficient cloth industry and reallocated to wheat production, we find that cloth production fall by 6 units while wheat production increases by 10 units. In India, a similar reallocation in the other direction causes wheat production to fall by 5 units while cloth production increases by 10 units.

Table 7.2: Impact of Reallocating One Unit of Labour in each Country

Country	Wheat	Cloth
US	+10 units	-6 units
India	–5 units	+10 units
World	+5 units	+4 units

Restraints to Trade

In the real world, we often find that trade among nations is restricted by tariffs, quotas, or other barriers. A tariff is a tax imposed by the importing country that is levied at the point of entry. A quota is a quantitative limitation of the quantity of a good that may be imported per unit of time. Such restraints to trade are usually imposed by the importing country in order to protect entrenched domestic factors of production from foreign competition.

(i) *Tariffs*: A tariff is a tax or surcharge levied on an imported good. Tariffs may be either *ad valorem,* which means the tariff is computed at a fixed rate per Rupees of imported value, or 'specific', which means the tariff amount is quoted as so many Rupees per unit imported. The main justification for imposing tariffs today is to reduce foreign competition in order to protect domestic producers. Tariffs are also a revenue source for the government imposing the tariff. Today tariffs are important tax sources in many developing countries.

(ii) *Quotas*: A quota is a restriction on the quantity of a goods that is allowed to be imported during a given period of time. Like other trade restrictions, the purpose of a quota is to protect domestic resources from foreign competition.

(iii) *Restrict Domestic Demand*: A third trade restraint policy is to introduce programmes to restrict domestic demand for the imported product. Presumably, if domestic demand for the imported goods can be restrained, then imports of the goods will fall.

Trade Agreements

The trade history of the past century can be divided into two broad epochs, with the Second World War as dividing line. The first half of the century saw increasing isolationism in the form of higher and higher trade barriers, and the second half saw trade liberalization with lower and lower trade barriers. The primary instrument of trade liberalization has been the General Agreement on Tariffs and Trade (GATT).

In 1947 representatives from many of the leading nations of the world completed a multilateral trade agreement known as the GATT. This Agreement established rules for fair trade among the signatories and called for mutual reductions in tariffs. Since then additional 'rounds' of discussions have resulted in additional treaties liberalizing trade incrementally.

The latest round, which was completed in 1994, was known as the Uruguay Round. This round was very important for several reasons. First, trade in agriculture, services, and intellectual property was included in the agreement for the first time. Agricultural trade was, and continues to be, very contentious issue. Second, the name of the organization was changed from GATT to WTO (World Trade Organization). Third, domestic trade dispute resolution was turned over to a panel of independent judges, who have final say in trade disputes.

Balance of Payments

The movement of goods across national borders usually requires the movement of money in the opposite direction and hence each country keeps an accounting record of its international transactions. The accounting record of the international transaction of a country is known as balance of payments. The balance of payments of a country, therefore, is a summary statement of all economic transactions between the residents of the reporting country and residents of all other countries during some specific period of time.

The balance of payments is a system of accounts in which all transactions of producers and consumers in one country with the producers and consumers of other countries are summarized. This system of accounts is called a balance, because the bottom line is always zero. The BOP has three payments: the current account, the capital account, and official reserves. The current account shows trade in goods and services and transfers. In BOP accounting, exports are always treated as a positive entry and imports as a negative entry. The BOP on the current account shows the net trade position of the country.

The balance of payments is divided into those transactions which involve receipts and those which involve payments.

Receipts are those financial payments made for whatever reason to residents of the reporting country by residents of other countries. Payments are those financial payments made to residents of other countries by residents of the reporting country. When a country's receipts are equal to its payments it is said that the balance of payments is in equilibrium. When a country's receipts exceed its payments the country is said to have a balance of payments surplus.

Conclusion

This chapter reviewed trends in global agriculture trade, focusing on the importance of trade to the over all economy and the gains from and restraints on trade. The increase in the gains from international trade in developing countries is based on the terms of trade, which will be reflected in the balance of payments. The basis of trade is differing opportunity costs among nations. To receive gains from agriculture trade nations must specialize in the production of farm products for which they are most efficient and exchange those with other nations. Through increased specialization and exchange, all nations can benefit from trade, and world economic welfare wili be increased.

REFERENCES

Drummond, Evan H. and John W. Goodwin (2001), *Agricultural Economics*, Prentice Hall, New Jersey.

Helmberger, Peter G. and Jean Paul Chavas (1996), *The Economics of Agricultural Prices*, Prentice Hall, New Jersey.

John, M. Antle and Daniel A. Sumner (1996), *The Economics of Agriculture: Selected Papers of D. Gale Johnson*, University of Chicago Press, Chicago.

Laurens van der Laan H. *et al.* (eds) (1999), *Agricultural Marketing in Tropical Africa*, African Studis Centre, Leiden.

Yotòpoulos, P.A. (1968), 'On the Efficiency of Resource Utilization in Subsistence Agriculture,' *Food Research*, Institute in Agricultural Economics, Trade and Development, Vol. 8, No. 2.

PART III
RURAL DEVELOPMENT

15

Introduction to Rural Development

Introduction

The term rural development is a subset of the broader term development. Development is a universally cherished goal of individuals, families, communities and nations all over the world. It is also natural in the sense that all forms of life on Planet Earth have an inherent urge to survive and develop.

Development is a subjective and value-added concept, and hence there cannot be a consensus as to its meaning. The term is used differently in diverse contexts. It basically means 'unfolding,' 'revealing,' or 'opening up' something which is latent. When applied to human beings, it therefore means 'unfolding' or 'opening up' their potential powers. Generally speaking, the term development implies a change that is desirable. Since what is desirable at a particular time, place and in particular culture may not be desirable at other places, or at other times at the same place and in the same cultural milieu, it is impossible to think of a universally acceptable definition of development. At best, development in the context of rural society could be conceptualized as a set of desirable societal objectives which society seeks to achieve. Thus development means it is cherished by all individuals, communities and nations, irrespective of their culture, religion and spatial location.

In the present world sustainable development has become a buzzword. According to the World Commission on Environment and Development (WCED), 'Sustainable development is one that meets the needs of the present generation without compromising the ability of future generations to meet their own needs.' In other words, sustainable development is a process in which the set of desirable societal objectives, or the development index, does not decrease over time. Constancy of natural capital stock, including natural resources and the environment, is a necessary condition for sustainable development. The set of 'sufficient conditions' includes an appropriate institutional framework and governance system for implementation of sustainable development policy.

The term rural development connotes overall development of rural areas with a view to improve the quality of life of rural people. In this sense, it is a comprehensive and multi-dimensional concept, and encompasses the development of agriculture and allied activities, village and cottage industries and crafts, socio-economic infrastructure, community services and facilities, and above all, the human resources in rural areas.

- As a phenomenon, rural development is the end-result of interactions between various physical, technological, economic, socio-cultural and institutional factors.
- As a strategy, it is designed to improve the economic and social well-being of a specific group of people—the rural poor.
- As a discipline, it is multi-disciplinary in nature, representing intersection of agricultural, social, behavioural, engineering and management sciences.

In the words of Robert Chambers, 'Rural development is a strategy to enable a specific group of people, poor rural women and men, to gain for themselves and their children more of what they want and need. It involves helping the poorest among those who seek a livelihood in the rural areas to demand and control more of the benefits of rural development.' The group includes small scale farmers, tenants, and the landless. Thus the term rural development may be used to imply anyone of the above mentioned connotations. That is, rural development is defined as a process leading to sustainable improvement in the quality of life of rural people, especially the poor.

In addition to economic growth, this process typically involves changes in popular attitudes, and in many cases even in customs and beliefs. In a nutshell, the process of rural development must represent the entire gamut of change by which a social system moves away from a state of life perceived as 'unsatisfactory' towards a materially and spiritually better condition of life.

Basic Elements of Rural Development

Whatever be the geographic location, culture and historical stage of development of a society, there are at least three basic elements which are considered to constitute the true meaning of rural development. They are:

(i) Basic Necessities of Life

People have certain basic needs, without which it would be impossible for them to survive. The basic necessities include food, clothes, shelter, basic literacy, primary health care and security of life and property. When anyone or all of them are absent or in critically short supply, we may state that a condition of absolute underdevelopment exists. Provision of the basic necessities of life to everybody is the primary responsibility of all economies, whether they are capitalists, socialists, or mixed. In this sense, we may claim that economic growth is a necessary condition for improvement of the quality of life of rural people, which is rural development.

(ii) Self-respect

Every person and every nation seeks some sort of self-respect, dignity or honour. Absence or denial of self-respect indicates lack of development.

(iii) Freedom

In this context, freedom refers to ideological freedom, economic freedom and freedom from social servitude. As long as a society is bound by the servitude of men to nature, ignorance, other men, institutions, and dogmatic beliefs, it cannot claim to have achieved the goal of development. Servitude in any form reflects a state of underdevelopment.

The new economic view of rural development considers reduction or elimination of poverty, inequality and unemployment as an important index of development. The questions to ask about a country's rural development are, therefore:

- What has been happening to poverty?
- What has been happening to unemployment?
- What has been happening to inequality?

If all the three of these have declined from high levels, then, beyond doubt, this has been a period of rural development in the country concerned. If one or two of these central problems have been growing worse, especially if all the three have, it would be strange to call the result development even if per capita income doubled.

Growth *versus* Development

While economic growth is an essential component of development, it is not the only one, as development is not a purely economic phenomenon. In the ultimate sense, it must encompass more than the material and financial sides of people's lives. Development should, therefore, be perceived as a multi-dimensional process, involving the reorganization and reorientation of both economic and social systems. In addition to improvements in the level and distribution of incomes and output, it involves radical changes in institutional, social and administrative structures. Finally, although development is usually defined in a context, its widespread realization may necessitate fundamental modifications of the international economic, social and political systems as well.

Expectations of Rural Societies and the Concept of Development

The common rural man in developing countries expects a higher standard of living for himself, his family, his community and his nation. Particular expectations, of course, differ from person to person and from region to region, but the expectation of marked improvement in material conditions of life is general throughout the world. People want and expect to have better diet, clothes, houses, education, a secure life and freedom from servitude. This is the revolution of expectation that has swept over rural societies in developing countries.

There are many explanations for this phenomenon.

(i) The demonstration effect of the rural elite; urban rich and foreign tourists engaging in ostentatious consumption of exotic and luxurious goods has distorted the consumption and utility functions of the rural poor.
(ii) Films, radio, television and advertising have exposed the masses to modern gadgets and lifestyles, and have thus aroused their expectations.
(iii) Local and national politicians in all countries world-wide have assured the rural poor of the modern amenities of life, if they would vote for them.
(iv) The central governments world over have declared time and again that the eradication of poverty is their major policy goal.

Through these media, the common man has first learned about the new products, gadgets and services, then come to want them, and now to demand them. The economies of most of developing countries cannot possibly fulfil these expectations in the immediate future, and there is bound to be a collision between rising expectations and economic reality.

The outcome will vary from country to country, but it will certainly involve disillusionment, demoralization, agitation and political upheaval. It is this that makes rapid agricultural and economic development a national imperative.

Rural Development and Rural Change

Development in rural areas is both a cause and a consequence of change. There is a two-way relationship between them; that is development influences, and is influenced by, a change. The change implies a physical, technological, economic, social, cultural, attitudinal, organizational, or political change. Whereas all manifestations of development can be traced to some change somewhere, sometimes not all changes lead to development; a change may be either for the better or the worse.

In the context of rural development, a change may be considered to be an instrument which can be used to promote rural development. The introduction of technological changes such as high-yielding varieties of crops, fertilizers, improved farm machinery, modern milk processing and feed processing plants, artificial insemination of dairy animals, etc. triggered local economic development. In Taiwan and China, agricultural development was largely a result of institutional reforms, especially land reforms and technological advances. Karl Marx was one of the great advocates of revolutionary change as an instrument of development.

A change may occur naturally or autonomously, or may be induced. A development manager may accelerate the pace of development by both inducing a desirable change in a given system, and by properly directing the autonomous change. It is important that the likely impacts of a contemplated change on various segments of society be carefully evaluated before the change is introduced.

Important Dilemmas in Rural Development

Literature on development abounds in a variety of dilemmas and dogmas, such as rural *versus* urban development, agricultural *versus* industrial development, primacy of capital *versus* labour, and natural *versus* induced development; which are discussed in detail as follows:

Rural versus *Urban*

Economic development has been associated with growing urbanization, as reflected in the increasing proportion of the urban population. Hence, urbanization was treated as an index of development. Growing urbanization is obviously the consequence of the growing concentration of infrastructural networks and capital intensive industrial enterprises in urban centres. This type of concentration has resulted in the existence of what is known in the literature on the economic development as 'dualism', or co-existence of two separate economic subsystems in an economy, especially in many developing countries. On one hand, there exists a small but highly modern and developed urban sector, which absorbs most of the material, financial and educated and talented manpower resources; on the other hand, a very large but traditional and underdeveloped rural sub-sector, characterized by widespread poverty, unemployment and low productivity, which forms the majority of the population. In many developing countries, both the sub-sectors coexist, but without those linkages between them that were once the main factors which contributed to the development of today's developed countries.

At the other extreme, there is another dogma rapidly emerging in many developing countries, that rural development is a prerequisite for overall development, and hence it deserves the highest priority in terms of allocation of resources. In their enthusiasm to promote the cause of rural development, the proponents of this school thought usually tend to either disregard or underplay the linkages between the rural and the urban sub-sectors of the economy. What is needed is a new approach to development, which explicitly recognizes the inter-linkages and complementarity between the rural and the urban sub-sectors, and provides for integrating them completely.

Agricultural versus *Industrial*

Closely analogous to the rural *versus* urban development dilemmas is the dogma that industrialization alone can modernize agriculture and thereby raise agricultural productivity, wage rates and provide employment to labour displaced by mechanization of agriculture. This has led many development economists to associate development with industrialization. Following this dogma, many developing countries have established highly capital-intensive and sophisticated industrial enterprises, similar to those in developed countries. Such efforts. however, have often led to bitter disappointment when the desired results failed to materialize. Such projects are mere showcases, whose contribution to development is negligible, and sometimes even negative, because they are built at the expense of enterprise that meet the basic needs of people. Nations with high agricultural potential spend enormous resources on agricultural imports and depend heavily on imported technology, capital and management. At the same time, local agriculture stagnates and nutritional standards remain far lower than in the advanced countries. Distribution of incomes is titled in favour of industrialists against farmers, workers and consumers.

At the other extreme is agricultural fundamentalism, which holds that in the initial stages of development when per capita incomes are low, agriculture alone can serve as an instrument of development, and that increased agricultural productivity is a prerequisite to increased income and industrialization. The proponents of this dogma argue for allocation of more resources and attention to agriculture, rather than to industry. They do not, however, realize that agriculture cannot develop alone, and that concomitant development of industry and supporting infrastructure is essential not only for the growth of the national economy, but for the advancement of agriculture itself. The non-agricultural sector must be developed to the extent that it is able to provide the agricultural sector with new farm inputs and services vital to its development, as also to absorb the manpower rendered surplus as a result of increased labour productivity in agriculture.

The establishment of small and less capital intensive industrial enterprises in rural areas, along with introduction of new technology in agriculture, is likely to establish linkages between agriculture and industry.

Capital versus *Labour*

This is a legacy inherited by today's development economists from their predecessors in the developed countries, who considered capital to be the key instrument of development. The Harrod-Domar model represents a typical example of this dogma. In this model, the rate of growth is expressed as the product of the savings rate and the output-capital ratio. Under the assumption that capital and labour cannot be substituted for each other, and that labour is in surplus supply, capital becomes the overriding constraint on economic growth. This dogma received a further fillip from those techno-economists who held that all new technology is embodied in capital.

Capital fundamentalism has been accepted by development economists and planners in the developing countries. This has led to the promulgation of a number of policies in these countries, all aimed at increasing savings, redistributing income from the workers to the capitalists, granting monopoly rights to national and multinational corporations, transferring resources from the private to the public sector, increasing dependence on foreign aid and loans, and under pricing capital, particularly foreign exchange for capital goods. This has resulted in a number of adverse effects on the economies of these nations. For example, under pricing exchange for capital goods has killed the incentive to develop labour-intensive technologies adapted to domestic needs and circumstances, and has led to premature and excessive mechanization in a number of sectors, resulting in unemployment of labour and underutilization of other domestic resources.

Capital fundamentalism has extended to cover human capital formation as well. Higher education is highly subsidized in most developing countries, with the result that millions of college and university graduates are added annually to the pool of the unemployed white-collar proletariat.

Autonomous versus *Induced*

In every country, some development takes place naturally or autonomously overtime, but its level and pace may not be adequate to maintain a reasonably satisfactory standard of living. In such situations, some sort of intervention is needed to speed up the pace of natural development. Development planning is one of the forms of intervention that becomes a fad in many developing countries of the world, and is considered a magic door to development. In fact, even the advanced countries have come to realize the need for some sort of planning or government intervention in the economic processes. It seems that there is a growing consensus around the statement that any planning is better than no planning at all, and decentralized planning is better than centralized planning.

However, we need to realize that planning can be positive contribution only if it realizes the achievement of development objectives more rapidly and more efficiently than is development followed natural forces. It is now becoming increasingly apparent that the development effort cannot be left to the government alone; it must be shared by private, cooperative, corporate and other non-governmental organizations and agencies, and above all by the people themselves. Planning by the government should complement and supplement the efforts of individuals and non-governmental organizations.

REFERENCES

Griffin, Keith (1973), 'Policy Options for Rural Development', *Oxford Bulletin of Economics and Statistics*, Vol. 35, No. 4, November.

Johnston, B.F. and Clark, W.C. (1982), *Redesigning Rural Development: A Strategic Perspective*, John Hopkins University Press.

Sandbrook (1982), *The Politics of Basic Needs*, Heinemann.

Singh, Katar (1999), *Rural Development Principles: Policies and Management*, Sage Publication Inc.

Todaro, M. (1992), *Economics from a Developing World*, Third Edition, London and New York: Longman.

16

Basic Theories Underlying Rural Development

Introduction

A theory is expected to perform two major functions, namely, explanation and prediction of a phenomenon. There is no universally acceptable theory of rural development which can explain the existing phenomenon of rural development and predict its future course. What we have is a set of hypothesis and propositions that constitute higher level generalizations in the field of development. To the extent that rural development is a subset of development, hypotheses of development apply to rural development as well. Many such hypotheses emphasize both economic and non-economic determinants of development, that is, they are quite comprehensive. Another characteristic of some of the hypotheses propounded by development theorists is that they are not fully operational, in the sense that it is very difficult to test them, that is, they are refractory.

The economists of the late eighteenth and early nineteenth centuries were primarily concerned with the conditions of economic growth. This was the period of the 'Industrial revolution' in Europe. The classical economists—including Adam Smith, David Ricardo, Thomas Robert Malthus, John Stuart Mill and Karl Marx—lived through the period of take-off into sustained growth. The observations of these economists regarding the nature and causes of economic growth are, therefore, of considerable interest. An interesting element of the arguments of the classical economists was the concept of circularity that characterized the interrelationship between technology, investment and profit. The circularity was inherent in their assertion that the level of technology depends on the level of investment, investment depends on profits, and profits depend partly on the level of technology.

The classical economists did not focus their attention on development or rural development *per se;* they perhaps assumed that economic growth would naturally lead to development. It was towards the end of Second World War around 1945, that development became an important field of study and attracted several scholars. Most of the initial writings on the subject dwelt on explaining the meaning of development, identifying factors affecting development, and exploring inter-relationships among the factors. Two distinct schools of thought emerged in the fifties, namely Capitalist and Marxist, and two distinct theories corresponding to them, namely modernization theory of the capitalist school and the dependency theory of the Marxist school.

The Modernization Theory

The dominant arguments of the capitalist school are embodied in what is known as the modernization theory, or the 'free world' model of development. The modernization theory was the justification for US hegemony in the context of the cold war. The essence of the theory was the transfer of western technology and rationality, without changing class structure as means of development and removal of all social and ideological obstacles to such a process.

The modernization theory was based on the following assumptions:

(i) Application of western science and technology in order to increase production is essential for achieving development.

(ii) The process of development can be delineated into a series of stages, and all societies pass through those stages.

(iii) In the process of development, traditional social and political institutions are replaced by modern ones.
(iv) Traditional feudal forms of political power will be replaced by democratic forms of governance.

In a nutshell, the modernization theory presented the 'American way of life' as the epitome of modernity. It envisages that development can be achieved only through industrialization and urbanization, along with technological transformation of agriculture—an insight validated by the experience of newly industrialized countries of East Asia and South East Asia.

In the context of rural development, the modernization theory offers quite a few useful insights, such as the inevitability of the use of modern technology for increasing agricultural production, and need for replacing traditional feudal institutions by new democratic ones, for a shift towards greater scientific temper, and secular values and norms. However, the theory has lost much of its appeal due to its failure to predict and explain many economic phenomena, such as the faltering of the post-Second World War boom in the 1960s, world-wide depression in the 1970s, and the shift in the terms of international trade in favour of developed countries. The theory also did not foresee the adverse environmental impacts of the capitalist/free market model of development, and its unsustainability.

The recent financial turmoil in East Asian countries has proved that the free market economy model, or the capitalist path, cannot guarantee stable and sustainable economic development characterized by fast-improving living standards. From Japan and South Korea to Malaysia and Indonesia, mounting bankruptcies, growing unemployment and rising inflation have engendered not only the loss of economic self-confidence, but also threatened the region's political and military stability.

There is yet another reason for the failure of the Modernization Theory to be relevant in the context of developing countries and that is the non-existence or ineffective implementation of rules and controls aimed at preventing private companies or groups from dominating their domestic markets.

The Dependency Theory of the Marxist School

The growing disenchantment with the Modernization theory, owing to its failure to explain growing inequalities, poverty, violence and military coups in the newly independent nations in Africa and Asia, forced development scholars to ask new questions and seek new answers, using an alternative paradigm. The intellectual foundation of the new paradigm was rooted in the ideas of Karl Marx, Friedrich Engels and other Marxist thinkers. Marx and Engels believed that the process of social change was not gradual and evolutionary, as assumed by the Modernization theory. Instead, it was characterized by conflict of interests between classes in society, or class struggle. The Marxists saw class struggle as the engine of social change and development.

The Marxist argued that imperialism, rather than being a benign political outgrowth of European civilization (as argued by the Modernization theorists), was an exploitative system of economic, social and political relations. The system changed the colonized nations into sources of cheap inputs to production in the capitalist nations, as well as markets for their products. This arrangement always worked to the advantage of the imperial power. Such a view of the dynamics at work in the capitalist system meant a complete reversal of the logic of modernization from the promise of development to impoverishment. This was the fundamental argument of Marxist school of thought, which came to be known as the Dependency theory.

The following are the main arguments of the Dependency theory:

(i) The developed countries could not have achieved the level of development that they have, without the systematic exploitation of the developing countries.

(ii) The process of development passes through a series of stages is an illusion. Developing countries cannot attain development following the path adopted by developed countries, so long as the exploitative world system exists.

(iii) Countries that are now poor were not so to begin with; rather they have been forced into the stage of underdevelopment by a global system of capitalist exploitation.

(iv) Developing countries. can develop only by snapping their links with the developed countries.

The dependency theory was very popular in the 1970s, as it provided a plausible explanation to the perpetuation of the problem of poverty and stagnation in developing countries, despite concerted efforts at solving them. However, in the 1980s, the theory lost much of its initial popularity, and was criticized as being too deterministic and too simplistic. The basic argument of the theory that underdevelopment in developing countries is the result of development in developed countries, was falsified by the experience of the East Asian countries.

In the context of rural development it could be seen that the theory provides a useful caveat that, while identifying the determinants of rural development, we should critically examine various inter-sectoral linkages (backward and forward) and interactions, and determine whether they are beneficial to rural people or not. If not, necessary policy measures should be suggested to make the linkages and interactions beneficial to rural people. A similar exercise needs to be done at the national level, to find out which international economic and political relationships are beneficial, and which are harmful to economic development in general, and rural development in particular.

Rosenstein-Rodan's Theory of the 'Big Push'

According to this theory, there is a minimum level of resources that must be devoted to development programme, if it is to have any chance of success. Launching a country into self-sustaining growth is a little like getting an airplane off the ground. There is a critical ground speed which must be passed before the craft can become airborne. The essence of this theory is that proceeding bit by bit will not add up in its effects to the sum total of the single bits. A minimum quantum of investment is necessary, though not sufficient, condition of success.

Rosenstein-Rodan identifies three different kinds of indivisibilities, which may be considered the main obstacles to the development of developing countries. They are:

- Indivisibility in the supply of social overhead capital (lumpiness of capital);
- Indivisibility of demand (complementarity of demand); and
- Indivisibility (kink) in the supply of savings.

He argues that a big push in terms of a high quantum of investment is required to scale the economic obstacles to development created by these three kinds of indivisibilities, and the external economies to which they give rise. This implies that the development process is a series of discontinuous jumps, and each jump requires a big push. Besides, there may finally be a phenomenon of indivisibility in the vigour and drive required for successful development policy. Isolated and small efforts may not add up to a sufficient impact on growth. An atmosphere of development may arise only after a critical minimum level of investment has been reached.

Rosenstein-Rodan does not offer any specific and practicable suggestions to overcome the adverse effects of the indivisibilities, but he suggest that international trade may reduce the size of the minimum push required to obviate the effect of indivisibility of demand. Mobilization of sufficient resources to provide the required big push continues to be the biggest hurdle, which developing countries cannot overcome on their own. Rosenstein-Rodan recommends that a trust, with capital from outside, be established to plan and finance investment for the entire area simultaneously. A major criticism of this theory is that the resources required to give the big push are of such a high order, that a developing country cannot afford them. In fact, a country capable of mobilizing the requisite quantum of resources would not be a poor country. However, conceptually, this paradigm continues to be appealing to planners and scholars.

Leibenstein's 'Critical Minimum Effort Thesis'

The central idea of Harvey Leibenstein's thesis is that in order to attain sustained secular growth, it is essential that the initial stimulant to development be of a certain critical minimum size. According to Leibenstein, economic backwardness is characterized by a set of interrelated factors, which have a certain degree of stability at their small equilibrium values. The actual values are different from the equilibrium values, because the economy is always being subjected to stimulants or shocks. The stimulants have a tendency to raise per capita incomes above the equilibrium level. But in backward economies, long-term economic development does not take place because the magnitude of stimulants is too small. In other words, efforts to escape from economic backwardness, be they spontaneous or forced, are below the critical minimum needed for sustained growth.

For small values of the stimulant, the general income-depressing factors are, in the long run, more significant than the induced income-raising forces, but the reverse is the case with high values of the stimulant. Population growth may be cited as an example of this phenomenon. A small increase in capital through raising incomes will stimulate more than an equivalent increase in population, and a proportional decline in per capita incomes. The need for a minimum effort arises to overcome internal and external diseconomies of scale, to overcome income-depressing obstacles which may be generated by the stimulants to growth, and to generate sufficient momentum in the system, so that the factors that stimulate growth continue to play their part.

Leibenstein's critical minimum effort thesis is explained in Fig. 16.1; where the 45° line measures induced increases and decreases in per capita income. The curve X_1X_1 represents all per capita income raising forces and the curve Z_1Z_1 the per capita income depressing forces. If the stimulants raise per capita income from the equilibrium level O_e to O_m, the income raising forces, thus, generated will raise the per capita income by na. But at this level, the income-depressing forces fb are greater than the income-raising forces af, which will, therefore, generate the downward path abcd, until it reaches the equilibrium position E. It is only when the investment programme raises the per capita income to Ok level that the path of sustained growth starts. Thus, if the per capita income level in a period is raised to Ok, the income-raising forces generated will raise the income level to sG, which will in turn generate the path of endless expansion of per capita income as shown by arrows rising above G. Raising the per capita income to Ok level and beyond point G is the critical minimum effort case.

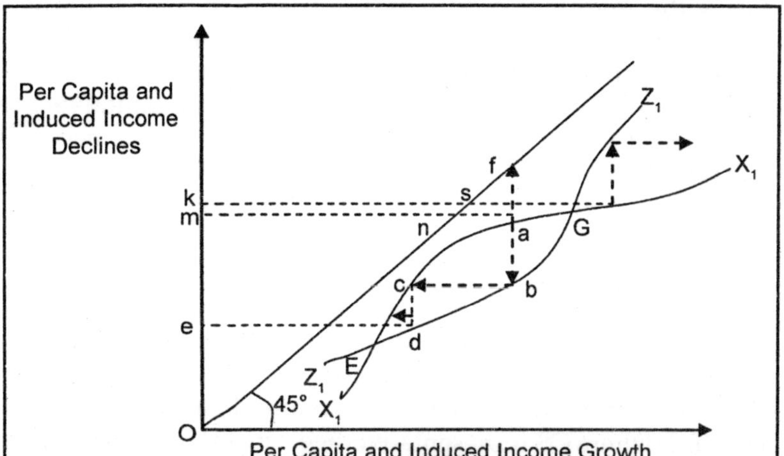

Fig. 16.1: Leibenstein's Critical Minimum Effort Thesis

Lewis' Model of Economic Development with Unlimited Supplies of Labour

W. Arthur Lewis' model is based on the fact that in many developing countries, there exist large reservoirs of labour whose marginal productivity is negligible, zero, or even negative. This labour is available in unlimited quantities, at a wage equal to the subsistence level of living, plus a marginal sufficient to overcome the friction of moving from the subsistence sector to the capitalist sector, which may be called subsistence-plus wage. As the supply of labour is unlimited, new industries can be set up and the existing ones can be expanded without limit, at the ruling wage rate. The capitalist sector also needs skilled workers. But Lewis maintains that skilled labour is only a temporary bottleneck and can be removed by providing training facilities to unskilled workers.

Since the marginal productivity of labour in the capitalist sector is higher than the ruling wage rate, there results a capitalist surplus. This surplus is used for capital formation, which makes possible employment of more people from the subsistence sector. The increase in investment by the capitalists raises the marginal productivity of labour, which induces capitalist employers to increase their labour force till the marginal productivity of labour falls to a level equivalent to the ruling wage rate. This process goes on till the capital-labour ratio rises to the point where the supply of labour becomes inelastic. Some critics have pointed out that Lewis' optimism concerning development by absorption of disguised unemployment from agriculture is unfounded, because it is not possible to transfer a large number of workers permanently and on a full-time basis from agriculture to industry, without a drop in agriculture output, that is, the marginal productivity of labour in Agriculture is not zero.

The Lewis' theory can be explained with the help of Fig. 16.2; where OS represents average subsistence wage in the subsistence sector, and OW the capitalist wage. At OW wage in the capitalist sector, the supply of labour is unlimited, as shown by the horizontal supply curve of labour WW. In the beginning, when ON_1 labour is employed in the capitalist sector, its marginal productivity curve is P_1L_1 and the total output of this sector is $OP_1Q_1N_1$. Out of this, workers are paid wages equal to the area OWQ_1N_1. The remaining area WP_1Q_1 shows surplus output. This is the capitalist surplus or total profit earned by the capitalist sector. When this surplus is reinvested, the curve of marginal productivity shifts upward to P_2L_2. The capitalist surplus and employment are now larger than before being WP_2Q_2 and ON_2 respectively. Further reinvestment raise the marginal productivity curve and the level of employment to P_3L_3 and ON_3 and so on, till the entire surplus labour is absorbed in the capitalist sector. After this, the supply curve WW will slope from left to right upward like an ordinary supply curve, and wages and employment will continue to rise with development.

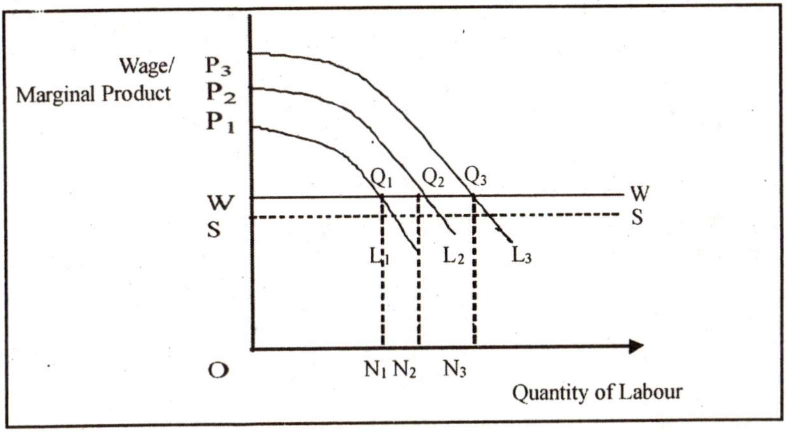

Fig. 16.2: Lewis Model

Lewis model seems to provide a good framework to understand the process of economic development in labour-surplus developing countries. Its basic premise is that labour productivity in agriculture must increase substantially in order to generate surplus in the form of food to be used for development of the non-farm sector, and to release the surplus labour from agriculture for meeting the growing needs of the non-farm sector. However, the relevance of the model is constrained by a number of factors.

(i) Labour unions may push the wage rate up as labour productivity increases, and keep the rate of profit and rate of capital formation lower than expected.

(ii) The capitalist employers may use the surplus for speculative or non-productive purposes. This is, in fact, what has been happening these days in developing countries.

(iii) To meet their rising expectations, rural people may consume more and save less than predicted by the model, and thereby dampen the pace of development.

Gunnar Myrdal's Thesis of 'Spread and Backwash' Effects

Gunnar Myrdal highlighted low level of income world-wide and international disparities in income, wealth and investment. Myrdal finds the theoretical approach (automatic self-stabilization) inadequate to grapple with the problems of inequality. In his opinion, in the normal case, a change does not call forth countervailing changes, but, instead, supporting changes which move the system in the same direction as the first change, but much faster—the principle of circular and cumulative causation. As a result of such circular causation, a social process tends to move faster. A social process can be stopped by introducing new exogenous changes in the system.

He also emphasized the role of non-economic factors in development, and the backwash effects of growth brought out by the free play of market forces. The clustering of labour, capital, goods and services in certain localities and regions leave the remaining areas, mostly rural, more or less in the backwaters and accentuate regional inequality. Concentration of firms, capital, and talented individuals in certain localities (growth points) at the expense of surrounding areas (in backwash) lowers the level of economic development below what it would have been, if growth points had never emerged.

Against the backwash effects there are, however, certain centrifugal 'spread effects' of expansionary momentum from the centres of economic expansion to other regions. Empirical evidence shows that 'backwash effects' are neutralized by 'spread effects' only at a high level of development. This is one of the reasons why rapid sustained progress becomes an almost autonomous process, once a country has reached a high level of development. At low levels of development, the 'spread effects' are either very weak, or are just strong enough to cancel the 'backwash effects', and the result in both cases is poverty and stagnation.

Similarly, at the international level, trade, capital movement and migration have strong backwash effects on the developing countries. Examples can easily be cited of developing countries whose cultures have been impoverished as a result of the establishment of trading contacts with the outside world.

The Human Capital Model of Development

This model emphasizes the importance of human capital investment in the process of economic and social development. By human capital, we mean acquired mental and physical ability through education, training, health care, and pursuit of some spiritual methods. The acquisition of human capital is largely through the investment of human effort and money. The simplest and most important of this type of model is a schooling model, which relates economic development to schooling. It was Theodore Schultz, who elaborated the concept of human capital, and explicitly considered the investment in human capital as an important determinant of economic development. Subsequently, quite a few other scholars got interested in the economics of human capital, especially the economics of education, and a large number of studies were conducted on the subject. The model considers the totality of human potential, and emphasizes the need to harness it for the good of the people. It respects people's culture and religion, and social values and structures.

The human capital approach to rural development is based on the following two assumptions:

(i) Human physical and mental capabilities are partly inherited and partly acquired, and they vary from individual to individual.

(ii) Human capital directly contributes to development through its positive effect on productivity, and through reduction in resistance to the diffusion of new technologies in the economy, especially in the rural sector.

Thus this model shifts the emphasis from physical capital formation to human capital formation and from industrial development to rural development, as a basis for overall development. This model seems most appropriate for labour-surplus developing countries; where a lot of underdeveloped human capital resources having high potential for development exist. Besides, human resources are renewable, and hence inexhaustible. Therefore, human capital can be substituted for exhaustible non-renewable physical capital in the process of development, and thus relax the constraint on development imposed by inadequacy of physical capital to a large extent. As a matter of fact, strategies for development of the tertiary sector, which is the fastest growing sector all over the world, requires skilled, experienced, and innovative human resources for their success. Human resource development through nutrition, health care, appropriate education, training and empowerment deserves the highest priority now.

Gandhian Model of Rural Development

Influenced by Tolstoy and Ruskin, Gandhiji placed more emphasis on moral and spiritual values than economic motives as a means of overall development. It is based on the following values and premises:

(i) A nation is found not in its cities, but in its villages;
(ii) The revival of villages is possible only when the villages are exploited no more;
(iii) Simple living and high thinking, implying voluntary reduction of materialistic wants, and pursuit of moral and spiritual principles of life;

(iv) Dignity of labour, everyone must earn his bread by physical labour, and one who labours must necessarily get his subsistence;
(v) Preference to the use of indigenous products, services and institutions; and
(vi) Balance between the end and the means.

The principal components of the Gandhian model are the following:

- Self-sufficient village economy
- Decentralization
- Development of village and cottage industries

He prescribed some important institutional structure and instruments for implementing the above strategies such as decentralized local governments, cooperatives and trusteeship for the ownership of resources and a new educational system by giving emphasis to the development of full potential of children and adults.

Rural Development Theories from Other Social Sciences

Rural development is a complex process which is affected by both economic and non-economic factors. The importance of non-economic factors in development was duly recognized by the Classical school. J.S Mill thought that non-economic factors like belief, habits of thought, customs and institutions play an important role in economic development, and he attributed the backwardness of underdeveloped countries to the despotic and anti-progressive character of their customs, institutions, and beliefs.

Boeke attempts to explain underdevelopment in terms of sociological dualism, which he defines as 'the clashing of an imported social system with an indigenous social system of another style.' On the basis of his analysis, largely based on the Indonesian experience, he concludes that the kindest thing the Western world can do for developing countries is to leave them alone; any effort to develop them along Western lines can only hasten their retrogression and decay. The acceptance of the dualism leads to two policy conclusions:

(i) As a rule, one policy for the whole country is not possible, and
(ii) What is beneficial for one section of society may be harmful for another.

An appraisal of Boek's theory would reveal that whereas there can be no question about the existence of dualism, its explanation lies not in the nature of society as Boeke perceives it, but in economic and technological terms. This is proved by the fact that not all efforts to promote development in the developing countries through technical and capital assistance from the West have been in vain.

McClelland's "Need for Achievement Motivation" (N-Ach) theory seeks to establish a relationship between N-Ach and economic development. His theory rests on the following two propositions:

(i) Group differences in the average level of certain motives, such as N-Ach, predict differences in the rate of economic growth; and
(ii) Certain motive combinations predispose individuals to act like successful business entrepreneurs, who have played key roles in all previous economic development.

On the basis of studies and analyses, he concludes if we are to promote economic growth, it is necessary to first change the values and motives of individuals; which can be done by:

- Persuasion or education;
- Introducing changes in social system; and
- Early character training.

Of these three, the third is by all odds the one most likely to succeed; that is, values can be in-built from the very beginning. Early character training can be imparted by a corps of specially qualified nursery and primary school teachers carefully selected for the purpose.

Conclusion

Although there is no universally valid theory of rural development available so far, the various paradigms and hypotheses of development reviewed in this chapter furnish many valuable insights into the processes and determinants of rural development. There is a set of elements/factors that is common to most of the paradigms of development. The common set comprise natural resources, new technology, enterprising and motivated human resources with values and ethos congenial to rural development, and an appropriate institutional and organizational framework.

REFERENCES

Booth, D. (1994), *Rethinking Social Development: Theory, Research and Practice*, Longman Scientific and Technical, Harlow.

Daniel Thorner, *et al.* (eds.) (1966), *The Theory of Peasant Economy*, Irwin Inc, Illinois.

Fassil G., Kiros (eds.) (1977), *Rural Development*, IDR, AAU.

Johnston, B.F. and Clark, W.C. (1982), *Redesigning Rural Development: A Strategic Perspective*, John Hopkins University Press.

Singh, Katar (1999), *Rural Development Principles: Policies and Management*, Sage Publications, New Delhi.

17

Measures of Rural Development

Introduction

Quantitative measurement of the level and pace of rural development is needed to indicate the extent of economic and social well-being of rural people, to serve as a benchmark for future planning, to serve as instruments of monitoring, evaluation and control of ongoing programmes; to facilitate spatial and temporal comparisons of development and to serve as criteria for advancing loans. Needless to emphasize, if the measures are to be meaningful, they must be consistent with the objectives of rural development.

The main objectives of rural development in all societies, irrespective of their economic, political and socio-cultural system are:

(i) To increase the availability and improve the distribution of life-sustaining goods, such as food, clothes, shelter, health and security;

(ii) To raise per capita purchasing power and improve its distribution by providing better education, productive and remunerative jobs and cultural amenities; and

(iii) To expand them from servitude and dependence.

Therefore, a measure of rural development should provide an indication of per capita availability of life-sustaining goods or per capita income in rural areas, as well as some idea of the distribution of income, assets and other means of socio-economic welfare. There is at present no single indicator of rural development which adequately captures its multifaceted nature. A variety of indicators have been used by economists to reflect the multiplicity of goals which characterize rural development. For the sake of simplicity, the indicators of rural development can be categorized into two classes:

- Measures of the level of rural development, and
- Measures of distribution of income.

Measures of the Level of Rural Development

The following measures are commonly used to measure the level of rural development at a particular time in a particular place, as well as over time and across space.

Per Capita Gross National Product in Rural Areas

Gross National Product (GNP) is the market value of all final goods and services produced in a year, and attributable to the factors of production supplied by the normal residents of the country concerned. Real GNP is the GNP adjusted for changes in prices, and is computed by dividing GNP by the general price index. Per capita real GNP is the most widely used measure of the economic well-being of people. If computed for rural people separately, it could be used as a measure of the economic component of rural development. More real GNP per capita means that, on the average, we are economically better off.

However, the GNP does not include everything that contributes to human happiness, and does not exclude everything that diminishes it. Despite all its weakness, per capita GNP is the only quantitative indicator of the economic component of rural development available for comparisons over time and over space.

Per Capita Consumption Expenditure of Rural People

This measure of rural development is considered a better measure of rural development. Per capita consumption expenditure is a reasonably good proxy variable for per capita income. Like nominal income, nominal consumption expenditure also should be adjusted for changes in the general price index over time and across space, to make it useful for comparison purposes.

Per Capita Public Expenditure on Community Facilities and Services in Rural Areas

The level of rural development in a country is a function of the per capita quantity of various goods and services consumed by its rural population, in a particular reference period of time. It does not matter whether the goods and services consumed are purchased by a person with his personal income, or whether he receives them without specific expenditure on his part. Certain services, facilities and civic amenities, such as schools, hospitals, roads, parks, police protection and street lights, are provided by the government free or at a nominal cost to its people. The availability of these facilities and services represents 'real income', and therefore, constitutes part of the level of living. Per capita public expenditure on such services and amenities is a good measure of socio-economic welfare. For comparisons over time and space, this measure should also be adjusted for changes in the general price index.

Physical Quality of Life Index (PQLI)

This measure was developed by Morris and McAlpin to determine the impact of development projects on their target groups. It supplements per capita real GNP, which is the most widely used measure of economic growth. PQLI has three components:

- Infant mortality,
- Life expectancy at age one, and
- Basic literacy.

These three component indicators are simple to compute and follow, are sensitive to changes in distribution of benefits of development; which do not reflect the values of any specific cultures, and reflect results, not inputs.

In calculations of GNP, various goods and services can be combined *via* a common element; market price. But the three component indicators of PQLI do not have any common element that values them all. Instead, a simple indexing system is used to combine them into a single-index PQLI. For each indicator, the performance of individual states/countries is evaluated on a scale of zero to 100, where zero represents an absolutely defined worst performance, and 100 represents the best performance. Once the performance for each indicator is called to this common measure, a composite index is calculated by averaging the three indicators, giving equal weight to each of them. The resulting PQLI is also scaled zero to 100.

Morris and McAlpin computed the PQLI for 150 countries. The range for each component index was based on the examination of the historical experience of the countries concerned. The literacy index ranged from zero to 100 per cent literacy for the population aged 15 years and over, the infant mortality rate from 229 to 7 per thousand births, and life expectancy at age one from 38 to 77 years. The corresponding index numbers are calculated according to the following formula (All variables have equal weights):

(a) Years of life expectancy are converted to an index;

$$\frac{\text{Life expectancy at age 1} - 38}{0.39}$$

(b) Infant mortality rate is converted to an index;

$$\frac{229 - \text{Infant mortality rate per 1000}}{2.22}$$

(c) Literacy index numbers correspond to the actual data.

The PQLI estimated for Nigeria and USA are given in Box 17.1. They argue that PQLI measures the combined effects of nutritional status, public health facilities, family income and social relations. The PQLI is used to measure the quality of life of the rural communities using the primary level or factual data.

Box 17.1: Estimation of Physical Quality of Life Index

Country	Life Expectancy at age 1		Infant Mortality		Literacy		PQLI
	years	Index No.	Per 1000 live births	Index No.	Per cent	Index No.	
Nigeria	49	28	180	22	25	25	25
USA	72	87	16	96	99	99	94

Source: Morris and McAlpin, 1982.

Human Development Index (HDI)

Rediscovering the truth that people must be at the centre of all development, the UNDP decided to bring out every year, beginning in 1990, a report on the human dimensions of development. The Human Development Report 1990 was the first such report; which addresses the question of how economic growth will promote human development. It discusses the meaning and measurement of human development, proposes a new composite index of human development, summarizes the record of human development over the past three decades, and sets forth strategies for human development in the 1990s.

The Human Development Report (HDR) 1990 defined human development as the process of increasing people's options. It stressed that the most critical choices that people should have include the options to lead a long and healthy life, to be knowledgeable, and to find access to the assets, employment and income needed for a decent standard of living.

The HDI composed of three indicators:

- Life expectancy,
- Adult literacy, and
- Income expressed in logs.

The subsequent HDRs have made some refinements in the procedure of defining the component indicators and computed the HDI. The refinements include the following:

(i) Adjustment of income for differences in purchasing power and disparities in income distribution,
(ii) Combining adult literacy and mean years of schooling into an index of educational attainment, and
(iii) Computing disaggregated HDI for males and females and for different population group.

In addition, HDI has also been supplemented by Human Freedom Index, and indicators of human security for selected countries for which data are available.

The HDI is calculated (from 1994 onwards) as follows.

Maximum and minimum values are fixed for the four basic variables (HDR, 1994 figures are shown) as follows on the basis of historical data and rational envisions.

- Life expectancy – 85 and 25 years,
- Adult literacy – 100 per cent and zero per cent,
- Mean years of schooling – 15 and zero years (100 per cent and zero per cent), and
- Income adjusted for differences in purchasing power and expressed in terms of PPP – \$40000 and \$100.

For income, threshold value was taken to be the global average real GDP per capita of PPP \$5120. Multiples of incomes beyond the threshold were discounted using a progressively higher rate. The formula used for adjusting the income is as follows.

Adjusted income = Global Average per capita GDP + 2 (Per capita GDP of the country concerned – Global Average per capita GDP)$^{1/2}$. The adjusted income estimation of Greece is given in Box 17.2.

Box 17.2: Illustration of Adjusted Income Estimation

Greece's per capita GDP is \$7680, and the threshold (Global Average per capita GDP) is \$5120.

The adjusted income of Greece = 5120 + 2 (7680 – 5120)$^{1/2}$
= 5120 + 101 = 5221

The formula used for the preparation of index for each of the component variables of HDI is

$$\text{Component Index} = \frac{\text{Actual value} - \text{Minimum value}}{\text{Maximum value} - \text{Minimum value}}$$

An illustration of calculating the HDI is given in Box 17.3.

Box 17.3: Calculation of Human Development Index of Costa Rica

(i) *Calculating the Life Expectancy Index*: The life index measures the relative achievement of a country in life expectancy at birth. For Costa Rica, with a life expectancy of 78 years in 2002, the life expectancy index is 0.884.

$$\text{Life expectancy index} = \frac{78-25}{85-25} = 0.884$$

(ii) *Calculating the Education Index*: The education index measures a country's relative achievement in both adult literacy and combined primary, secondary and tertiary gross enrolment. First, indices for adult literacy and for combined gross enrolment are calculated. Then these two indices are combined to create the education index, with two-thirds weight given to adult literacy and one-third weight to combined gross enrolment. For Costa Rica, with a, adult literacy rate of 95.8 per cent in 2002 and a combined gross enrolment ratio of 69 per cent 2001-02, education index is 0.870.

$$\text{Adult Literacy Index} = \frac{95.8-0}{100-0} = 0.958$$

$$\text{Gross Enrolment Index} = \frac{69-0}{100-0} = 0.690$$

Education Index = 2/3 (Adult literacy index) + 1/3 (Gross enrolment index)

= 2/3 (0.958) + 1/3 (0.690) = 0.870

(iii) *Calculating the GDP Index*: The GDP index is calculated using adjusted per capita income (PPP US$). In the HDI income serves as a surrogate for all the dimensions of human development not reflected in a long and healthy life and in knowledge. Income is adjusted because achieving a respectable level of human development does not require unlimited income. Accordingly the logarithm of income is used. For Costa Rica, with a GDP per capita of $8840 (PPP US$) in 2002, the GDP index is 0.748.

$$\text{GDP Index} = \frac{\log(8840) - \log(100)}{\log(40000) - \log(100)} = 0.748$$

(iv) Calculating the HDI: Once the dimension indices have been calculated, determining the HDI is straightforward. It is a simple average of the three dimension indices.

$$\text{HDI} = \frac{0.884 + 0.870 + 0.748}{3} = 0.834$$

Source: UNDP, Human Development Report, 2004.

The human development indicators of Ethiopia are given in Table 17.1. The HDI can be used for analyzing the rural development; for that village level HDI are to be framed.

Table 17.1: Human Development Indicators of Ethiopia, 2004

Indicators	*Value*
1. Life Expectancy at birth (years)	45.5
2. Adult literacy rate (percentages 15 and above)	41.5
3. Combined gross enrolment ratio for primary, secondary, and tertiary schools (%)	34
4. GDP per capita (PPP US$)	780
5. Life expectancy index	0.34
6. Education index	0.39
7. GDP index	0.34
8. HDI	0.359
9. HDI Rank	170/177

Source: UNDP, Human Development Report, 2004.

Measures of Distribution of Income

There are wide variety of measures which are used by economists to measure income distribution; including Pareto index, the shares of the bottom 20 per cent and top 20 per cent of households in the aggregate income, standard deviation of logarithms of incomes, the Lorenz curve and the Gini Concentration Ratio. A good measure of income distribution should possess the following two characteristics.

- It should be unaffected by equal proportional increase in all incomes, so that if the distribution of income for the year X is simply a scaled-up version of that for the year Y, then we should regard them as characterized by the same degree of inequality.
- It should be sensitive to disproportionate changes at all levels of income, so that if from year X to year Y, the incomes of lower income households increase proportionately more than the incomes of the higher income households, this ought to lead to a strictly positive reduction in the index of inequality, and not merely leave it unchanged.

Some of the commonly used measures of income distribution are mentioned below.

The Lorenz Curve

This is a graphical measure of income distribution and income inequality. The information required to draw a Lorenz Curve consists of a frequency table showing the distribution of income by deciles group of households. That is, the table should show for each of the deciles groups, its share in the aggregate income, as is shown in Table 17.2. To draw a Lorenz Curve, the cumulative percentage of income-receiving households is represented on the horizontal axis, the cumulative percentage of aggregate income on the vertical axis, and the curve represents the locus of all the combinations of the two cumulative percentages. The Lorenz Curves shown in Fig. 17.1 are drawn on the basis of the figures presented in Table 17.2. The diagonal line represents a perfectly equal distribution of income and hence is known as the line of equality. That is, the farther the Lorenz Curve is from the equality, the higher the degree of income inequality.

Table 17.2: Relative Shares of Aggregate Income Received by Various Decile Groups of Households in Village-X and Village-Y

Deciles Group	*Percentages of Aggregate Income*			
	Village-X		*Village-Y*	
(Percentages)	*Simple*	*Cumulative*	*Simple*	*Cumulative*
< 10	0.42	0.42	0.77	0.77
10-20	0.20	0.62	2.37	3.14
20-30	2.29	2.91	3.57	6.71
30-40	4.06	6.97	5.12	11.83
40-50	6.10	13.07	6.71	18.54
50-60	8.00	21.07	8.89	27.43
60-70	10.31	31.38	11.55	38.98
70-80	13.94	45.32	13.86	52.84
80-90	18.39	63.71	17.56	70.40
90-100	36.29	100.00	29.60	100.00

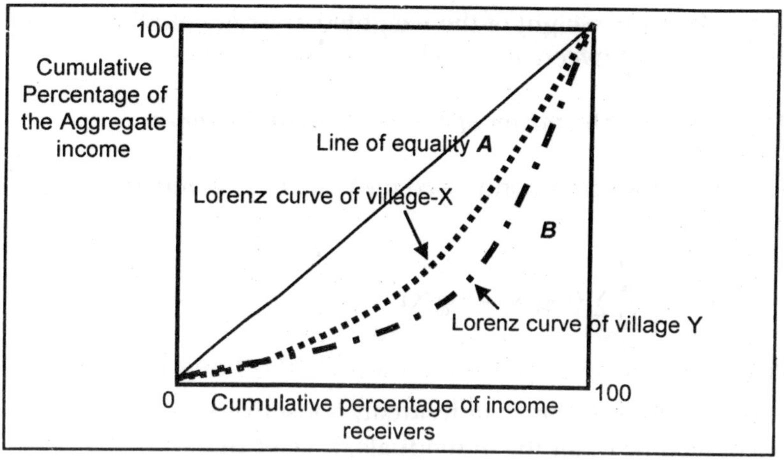

Fig. 17.1: Model Lorenz Curves of Villages X & Y

The Gini Concentration Ratio (GCR)

This ratio was invented by Corrado Gini in 1913, and is the most commonly used measure of income inequality these days. This ratio can be approximated either from the Lorenz Curve, or the mean difference. When approximated from the Lorenz Curve, it represents the proportion of the area lying between the diagonal and the Lorenz Curve, to the total area under diagonal. If we denote the area inside the Lorenz Curve as 'A' and outside the Lorenz Curve as 'B', the ratio would be A/(A+B). Hence the range of this ratio is from zero to one; zero being perfect equality, and one perfect inequality.

When computed from the mean difference; the Gini concentration ratio may be defined as:

$$GCR = \sum_{i=1}^{n} \sum_{j=1}^{n} \frac{f_i f_j / X_i - X_j /}{2\overline{X}N}$$

Where n is the number of income classes, f_i and f_j are the frequencies in the ith and j^{th} classes, x_i and x_j the mean incomes of the ith and j^{th} classes, N is the total number of income receivers, and $\overline{X}$ the overall mean income. Hence, the ratio is one-half of the weight of the weighted average of all absolute differences, between all possible pairs of incomes.

The Standard Deviation of Logarithms of Incomes

This is another commonly used measure of income inequality. It is defined as:

$$SD = \left[\frac{1}{N}\sum_{i=1}^{n}(\log X_i - \log \overline{X})^2\right]^{1/2}$$

Where n is the total number of individuals/households and x_i is the income of the ith individual/household, and $\overline{X}$ is the mean income of all the individuals/households.

Measures of Rural Poverty

The term rural poverty is the opposite of the term rural development. Poverty implies a condition of life characterized by deprivation of some sort or the other, and perceived as undesirable by the persons concerned or others. It is a multidimensional concept and phenomenon. Generally, there is a consensus among scholars about poverty being conceived and defined as absolute or relative. Absolute poverty implies a person's lack of access to objectively determined, reasonably adequate quantity of goods and services, to satisfy his/her material and non-material basic needs.

Relative poverty, on the other hand, means that a person's access to the basic access of life is relatively lower, as compared to some reference group of people. Between two households or two persons, one may be considered as poor, while the other in comparison may not be so, even though both may be in a position to fulfil their basic material needs. The magnitude of poverty at any point in time depends on the criteria or norms used to define poverty and determine the poverty line. There are two criteria or norms usually employed to define the poverty line:

- The norm based on the concept of a nutritionally adequate diet; and
- The norm based on the concept of a minimum level of living.

Some of the most important commonly used measures/ indicators of poverty are the following.

Poverty Ratio or Head Count

This measure estimates the percentage of population below a special poverty line. To compute this measure, it is necessary to define and determine a poverty line. Given the diversity of the basic necessities of life and intra-regional and inter-regional variations in the mix a 'basket of basic necessities,' the poverty line must of necessity be expressed in monetary terms, as it is not possible to have any meaningful physical common denominator to aggregate different elements of the basic necessities of life.

Besides per capita income/consumption expenditure, there are quite a few other commonly used single variate measure of poverty or human development. They include:

(i) Life expectancy,
(ii) Literacy rate,
(iii) Birth rate,
(iv) Death rate, and
(v) Infant mortality rate.

Housing Index

Gibbons (1997) proposed this index as a cost-effective measure/ tool for identifying the poor. The Housing Index has three components, namely

(i) The size of the house,
(ii) The physical condition of the house, as reflected in the materials used in its construction, and

(iii) The type of materials used for making the roof of the house.

Participatory Rural Appraisal (PRA)

PRA method of wealth ranking has been found to be useful. In the PRA method, all the villagers are brought together to find out who are the very poor, poor, not-so-poor and not poor at all. This method is found to be suitable in terms cost-effectiveness and the time taken. It is used by governmental and non-governmental organizations engaged in rural development, for identifying the poor for targeting their projects.

Human Poverty Index (HPI)

HPI measures deprivations in the three basic dimensions of human development in the HDI.

- *A long and healthy life*: Vulnerability to death at a relatively early age, as measured by the probability at birth of not surviving to age 40.
- *Knowledge*: Exclusion from the world of reading and communications, as measured by the adult illiteracy rate.
- *A decent standard of living*: Lack of access to overall economic provisioning, as measured by the unweighted average of two indicators, the percentage of the population without sustainable access to an improved water sources and the percentage of children under-weight for age.

Calculating the HPI is more straightforward than calculating HDI. The indicators used to measure the deprivations are already normalized between 0 and 100 (because they are expressed as percentages), so there is no need to create dimension indices as for the HDI.

Measuring the deprivation in a decent standard of living is an unweighted average of the two indicators, as follows:

Unweighted average = ½ (% of population without sustainable access to an improved source) + ½ (% of children underweight for age)

Calculation of HPI is based on the following formula:

$$HPI = [1/3 (P^{\alpha}_1 + P^{\alpha}_2 + P^{\alpha}_3)]^{1/\alpha}$$

Where, P_1 probability at birth of not surviving to age 40 (times 100)

P_2 adult illiteracy rate

P_3 unweighted average of population without sustainable access to an improved water source and children underweight for age.

α is 3

The illustration of calculating the HPI is given in Box 17.4.

Box 17.4: Calculating Human Poverty Index of Cambodia

Population without sustainable access to an improved water source = 70%
Children underweight for age = 45%
Unweighted average of deprivation of standard of living (P_3)
= ½ (70) + ½ (45) = 57.5%
Probability at birth of not surviving to age 40 (P_1) = 24%
Adult illiteracy rate (P_2) = 30.6%
Unweighted average of population without sustainable access to an improved water source and children underweight for age (P_3) = 57.5%

$$HPI = [1/3 (24^3 + 30.6^3 + 57.5^3)]^{1/3} = 42.6$$

Conclusion

There is no universally acceptable measure of rural development that captures its multifaceted nature. The choice of measure depends upon the purpose of measurement, and the availability of required data/information. Commonly used measures of rural development can be categorized into two classes, namely, measures of the level of rural development, and measures of the distribution of rural development. Of all the measures of level, the Human Development Index, when computed separately for the rural population, could be the most appropriate indicator of rural development.

REFERENCES

Griffin, Keith (1973), Policy Options for Rural Development, *Oxford Bulletin of Economics and Statistics*, Vol. 35, No. 4.

Harriss, J. (1992), *Rural Development: Theories of Peasant Economy and Agrarian Change*, Huttchinson, London.

Johnston, B.F. and Clark, W.C. (1982), *Redesigning Rural Development: A Strategic Perspective*, The John Hopkins Press, London.

Sen, A. (1981), *Poverty and Famines: An Essay on Entitlement and Development*, Oxford University Press.

Singh, Katar (1999), *Rural Development: Principles, Policies and Management*, Sage Publications, New Delhi.

Todaro, M. (1992), *Economics for a Developing World*, Longman, London.

UNDP, *Human Development Reports*, Various years.

18

Dynamics of Demography and Rural Development

Introduction

The consequences of population growth on economic development have attracted the attention of economists ever since Adam Smith wrote his *Wealth of Nations.* To Adam Smith, 'The annual labour of every nation is the fund which originally supplies it with all the necessaries and convenience of life.' It was only Malthus and Ricardo who created an alarm about the effects of population growth on the economy. But their fears have proved unfounded because the growth of population in Western Europe has led to its rapid industrialization. Population growth has helped the growth of such economies because they are wealthy, have abundant capital and scarcity of labour. In such countries, the supply curve of labour is elastic to the industrial sector so that even a high growth rate of population has led to a rapid increase in productivity. However, the impacts of population growth on developing countries and in particular with regard to rural development are not that much encouraging.

Population and Rural Development

The consequences of population growth on the development of rural economies are not the same that we mentioned above because the conditions prevailing in the developing countries are quite different from those that in the urbanized developed world. The rural economies are poor, capital-scarce and labour abundant. The population growth adversely affects their economic development in the following ways:

(i) Faster population growth makes the choice scarcer between higher consumption now and the investment needed to bring higher consumption in the future.
(ii) Rapid population growth tends to over use the rural economies' natural resources. This is particularly the case where the majority of people are dependent on agriculture for their livelihood. With rapidly rising population, agricultural holdings become smaller and unremunerative to cultivate. There is no possibility of increasing farm production through extensive cultivation, in particular in overpopulated developing countries. Consequently it will affect the poverty-stricken rural economies. In fact, rapid population growth leads to the overuse of the land thereby jeopardizing the welfare of future generations.
(iii) With rapidly growing population, it becomes difficult to manage the adjustments that accompany economic and social changes. Besides, growing population threatens permanent environmental damage through urbanization in rural areas.

In LDCs people mostly live in rural areas and agriculture is their main occupation. With population growth, the land-man ratio is disturbed; pressure of population on land increases because the supply of land is inelastic. It adds to disguised unemployment and reduces per capita productivity further. As the number of landless workers increases, their wages fall. Thus low per capita productivity reduces the propensity to save and invest. As a result, the use of improved techniques and other improvements on land are not possible. Capital formation in agriculture suffers and the economy is bogged down to the subsistence level. The problem of feeding the additional population becomes serious due to acute shortage of food products.

Rapid population growth leads to environmental damage in rural areas. Scarcity of land due to rapidly increasing population pushes large number of people to ecologically sensitive areas such as hillsides and tropical forests. It leads to overgrazing and cutting of forests for cultivation leading to severe environmental damage. Moreover, the pressures of rapid population growth force people to obtain more food for themselves and their livestock. As a result, they over cultivate the semi-arid areas. This leads to desertification over the long-run when land stops yielding anything. Besides, rapid population growth leads to the migration of large numbers to urban areas with industrialization.

The Theory of Demographic Transition

According to this theory, every country passes through five different stages of population development. According to C.P. Blacker, they are:

- The high stationary phase marked by high fertility and mortality rates;
- The early expanding phase marked by high fertility and high but declining mortality;
- The late expanding phase with declining fertility but with mortality declining more rapidly;
- The low stationary phase with low fertility balanced by equally low mortality; and
- The declining phase with low mortality, lower fertility and an excess of deaths over births. These stages are explained in Fig. 18.1.

First Stage

In the first stage the country is backward and is characterized by high birth and death rates with the result that the growth rate of population is low. People mostly live in rural areas and their main occupation is agriculture which is in a state of backwardness. There are a few simple, light and small consumer goods industries. The tertiary sector consisting of transport, commerce, banking and insurance is underdeveloped. All these factors are responsible for low incomes and poverty of the masses. Large family is regarded as a necessity to augment the low family income. Children are an asset to the society and parents. The existence of the joint family system provides employment to all children. People being illiterate, ignorant, superstitious and fatalists are averse to any methods of birth control. Children are regarded as God-given and preordained. All these economic and social factors are responsible for a high birth rate in the country. Along with high birth rate, the death rate is also high due to non-nutritional food with a low caloric value, lack of medical facilities and the lack of any sense of cleanliness. People live in dirty and unhealthy surroundings in ill ventilated small houses.

The high birth and death rates remain approximately equal overtime so that a static equilibrium with zero population growth prevails. This is illustrated in Fig. 18.1—A by the time period HS (High stationary) stage and by the horizontal portion of the P (Population) curve in the lower portion.

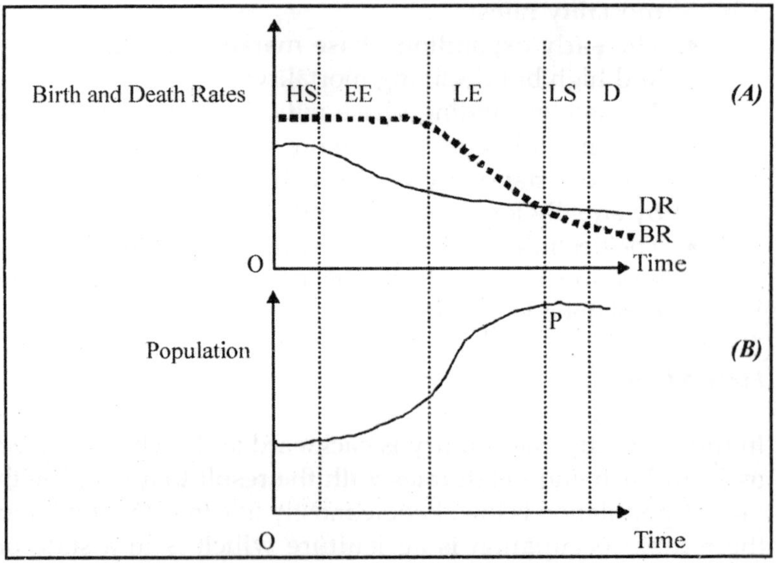

Fig. 18.1: Demographic Transitions

Second Stage

In this stage the economy enters the phase of economic growth. Agricultural and industrial productivity increases, means of transport develop and there is a greater mobility of labour, along with expansion in education and income. People get more and better quality food products and medical and health facilities. All these factors bring down the death rate. However, the birth rate is almost stable. People do not have any inclination to reduce the birth of children because with economic growth employment opportunities increase and children are able to add more to the family income. With improvements in the standard of living and the dietary habits of the people, the life expectancy also increases. People do not make any effort to control the size of family because of the presence of religious dogmas and social taboos towards family planning. Of all the factors in economic growth it is difficult to break with the past social institutions, customs and beliefs. As a result of these factors, the birth rate remains at the previous high level. With the decline in the death rate and no change in the birth rate, population increases at a rapid rate. This leads to population explosion. This is an 'Early Expanding' (EE) stage in population development when population grows at an increasing rate, as shown in Fig. 18.1-B, with the decline in death rate and no change in birth rate, as shown in the upper portion.

Third Stage

This is the 'Late Expanding' (LE) stage of population growth. In this stage, declining birth rates accompanied by death rates and declining more rapidly. As a result, population grows a diminishing rate, as shown in the figure.

Fourth Stage

In this stage, the fertility rate declines and tends to equal the death rate so that the growth rate of population declines. As growth gains momentum and people cross the subsistence level of income, their standard of living rises. The leading growth sectors expand and lead to an expansion in output in other sectors through technical transformations. Education expands and permeates the entire society. People discard old customs, dogmas and beliefs, develop individualistic spirit and break with the joint family. Men and women prefer to marry late; the desire to have more children to supplement parental income declines. People readily adopt family planning devices. All these trends to reduce the birth rate which along with an already low death rate brings a decline in the growth rate of population. The advanced countries are passing through this 'Lower Stationary' (LS) stage of population growth as shown in the figure; with zero population growth.

Fifth Stage

A continuing decline in birth rates when it is not possible to lower death rates further, in the advanced countries leads to a 'declining' (D) stage of population. The existence of this stage in any developed country is a matter of speculation.

The demographic transition theory is superior to all the theories of population because it is based on the actual population growth trends of the developed countries. Some of the very backward countries in Africa and Asia are still in the first stage where as the others are either in the second or in the third stage.

Rural-Urban Migration

The classic theory of rural-urban migration is based on Harris-and Todaro. The main idea of the Harris-Todaro model is that the formal urban sector pays a high wage to workers and it is this high wage that creates urban unemployment. The high wages in the urban formal sector may be because of unionization in the sector; and is often treated as the showcase of government policy, so that minimum wage laws, pension schemes, unemployment benefits, day care, and other facilities may be required by law; which raise the worker's utility. The firms in the urban formal sector pay higher wages to attract the best working force.

In contrast to the high wages paid in the formal urban sector, the informal urban sector and the rural sector have low wages that fluctuate according to supply and demand considerations. There is no unionization and the government policy is difficult to implement. Moreover, if the bulk of labour is family labour or if the bulk of labour effort is readily monitorable, then there will be little incentive for employers in these sectors to pay higher wages as a potential threat. Migration in the Harris-Todaro model is then viewed as a response to the significant wage gap that prevails between the two sectors.

The Basic Model

In this model it is assumed that there are only two sectors in the economy; a rural sector and a formal urban sector. Fig. 18.2 captures the basic theory. The width of the horizontal axis is the entire labour force in the economy, which is divided between the agricultural sector (Denoted by A) and the formal urban sector (denoted by F). The left axis of the figure records various formal wages in the urban sector, whereas the right axis records agricultural wages. The curve AB is the demand curve for labour in the urban formal sector, and that of the agricultural sector is CD. Just as in the urban sector, more agricultural labour can be absorbed only at a lower wage.

To alleviate persistent migration between one sector and the other, the wages in the two sectors must be equalized. This occurs at the intersection of the curves AB and CD, and will determine the equilibrium wage and labour supply. In Fig. 18.2, the equilibrium wage is w^*, with L_A^* individuals in the agrarian sector and L^*_F individuals in the urban sector.

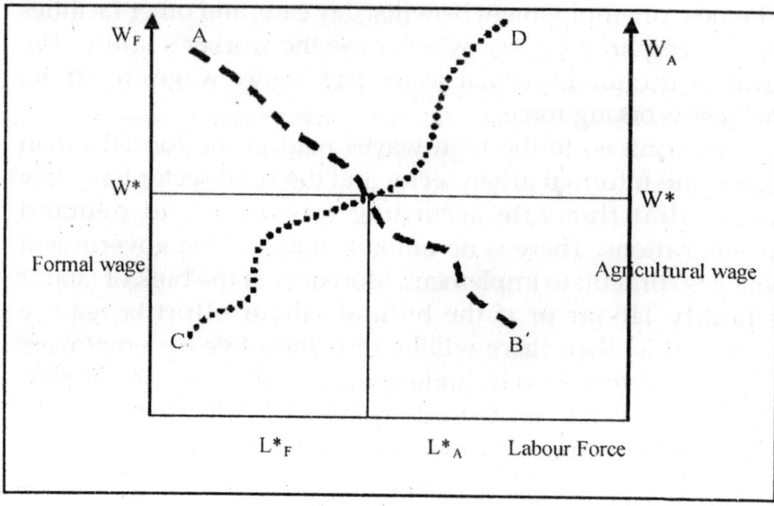

Fig. 18.2: Market Equilibrium with Flexible Wages

Floors on Formal Wages

Imagine that the wage rate in the formal sector is fixed at too high a level of market equilibrium w* to occur. Fig. 18.3 capture this situation by drawing the minimum formal wage rate $\overline{W}$, at a level that lies above the intersection of the two absorption curves. It follows that private sector formal firms will hire no more than the amount L_F of labour at this wage. All the remaining individuals are employed in the agricultural sector. In that case, Fig. 18.3 tells that the wage in the agricultural sector must drop to $\overline{W}$. Now in both the sectors we have full employment, so that no individual job seekers needs to fear unemployment if he/she looks for a job in either sector. Nonetheless, the wages, $\overline{W}$ and $\underline{W}$ are different. This cannot be an equilibrium state for the economy, because with full employment in both sectors, workers will wish to migrate to the sector with the higher wage.

Figure 18.3 reveals that only an amount L_A can be soaked up in the agricultural sector. If the formal and the agricultural sectors are the only two sectors in the economy, we must have a pool of unemployed people. In Fig. 18.3, U denotes the size of the resulting unemployed pool. Given that agriculture has flexible wages, the unemployed workers cannot be physically located in agriculture. If they were, they would simply pour into that labour market and consequently drive the wages down. Therefore, they must be located in the urban sector. Now we have a situation in which these workers rationally migrate to the urban formal sector, even though the wages there are the same as those in agriculture and there is significant risk of unemployment.

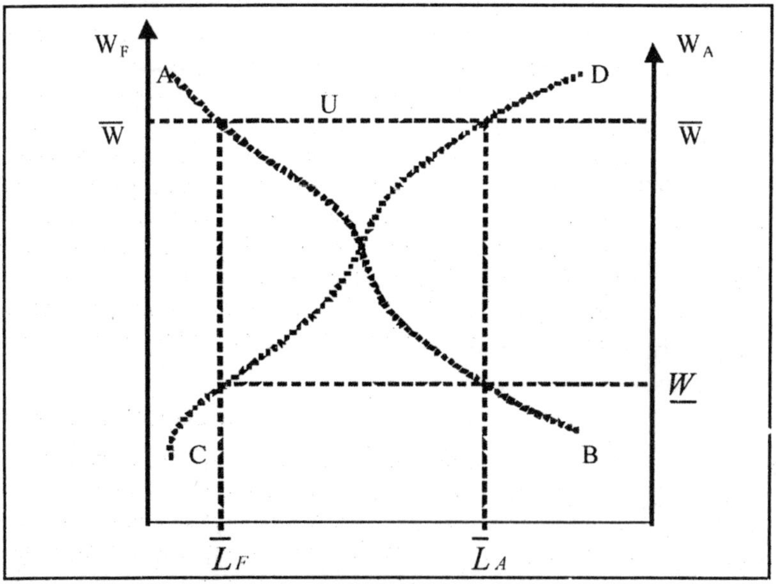

Fig. 18.3: Floor on the Formal Wage

The main idea is that potential migrants choose between a relatively safe option, which is to stay in the agricultural sector, and the gamble of moving to the urban sector, where a high-paying formal job is determined by the ratio of formal job seekers to available formal jobs. Those who do not get a job might be referred to as the unemployed, and where the informal sector comes in. Frustrated formal job seekers may enter the informal sector, where jobs or businesses are easy enough to find but pay a pittance. Fig. 18.4 schematically capture the gamble that is involved.

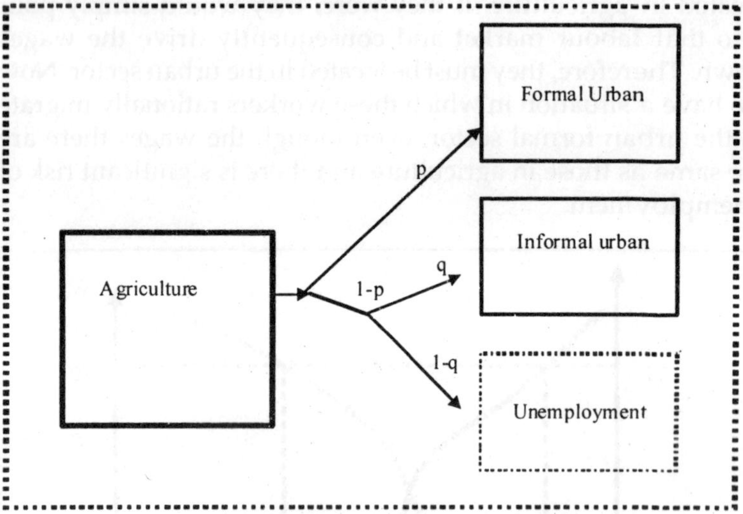

Fig. 18.4: Options Open to a Potential Migrant

In Fig. 18.4, there are two sets of boxes; the left set is a single box, agriculture, with its wage w_A and the right set describes the various options open in the urban sector, together with the probabilities of access. First, there is the formal sector at some high wage $\overline{W}$. The probability of obtaining such a job depends on the ratio of vacancies to job seekers. Denote this by *p*. There is the informal urban sector, in which migrant can get absorbed in the event that no formal jobs is forthcoming. Denote the wage rate in the informal sector by w_1 and assume that it is fixed regardless the number of people in that sector.

The expected value, that is required, is calculated in the usual way: weigh each outcome by its probability of occurrence and add up over all outcomes. Thus the expected wage in the urban sector is neither $\overline{W}$ nor w_1, but the combination as shown below:

$$P\overline{W} + (1 - P)w_1$$

It is this expected wage that is compared to the wage in the agricultural sector. It is reasonable to assume that not every, one is guaranteed to receive even the lower income w_1 in the informal sector. It may be that some individuals do not get any employment at all, so that they are openly unemployed. The additional option is displayed by the dotted box in Fig. 18.4, with associated wages equal to zero.

We need to know the probability of getting an informal sector job, conditional on having been turned away from the formal sector; denote this by q. Thus after being turned away from the formal sector, the migrant manages to join the informal sector with probability q and remains openly unemployed with probability $1-q$. The expected value of this latter set of possibilities is $qw_1 + (1 - q)\,0 = qw_1$. Thus the overall expected wage is now $P\overline{W} + (1-P)qw_1$.

In the urban sector, suppose that we use L_1 to denote informal employment, then we can see that the ratio:

$\frac{L_F}{L_F + L_I}$ captures the probability of getting a job in the formal sector. The number of employed people L_F explains how many jobs are there, whereas the number $L_F + L_1$ is the measure of the total number of potential job seekers. The ratio of the two thus gives us the chances that an urban dweller will get a job in the formal or informal sector.

Migration from the rural sector may be thought of as an irreversible decision, at least for the proximate future. Because the fate of a potential migrant is not known, we must consider the expected income from migration and compare it with the actual income received in agriculture. That is:

$$\frac{\overline{L}_F}{\overline{L}_F + L_1}\overline{W} + \frac{L_1}{\overline{L}_F + L_1}w_1 = w_A .$$

This is the equilibrium where no person wishes to migrate from one sector to the other. This is the Harris-Todaro equilibrium condition.

Conclusion

A rapidly increasing population leads to an increased demand for food products, clothes, houses, etc. But their supplies cannot be increased in the short run due to the lack of co-operant factors like raw materials, skilled labour, capital, etc. Consequently, their costs and price rise which raise the cost of living of masses, especially in the rural economies. This brings down further already low standard of living; poverty breeds large number of children which increases poverty further and the vicious circle of poverty, more children and low standard of living continues. The consequences of rapidly increasing population are to retard all development effort in rural economies unless accompanied by high rates of capital accumulation, and technological progress. But these counteracting factors are not available and the result is that population explosion leads to declining agricultural productivity, low per capita income, low living standards, mass unemployment, and low rate of capital formation, other than rural urban migration.

REFERENCES

Booth, D. (1994), *Rethinking Social Development: Theory, Research and Practice*, Longman Scientific and Technical, Harlow.

Eicher, Carl K. and John M. Stazz (1984), *Agricultural Development in the Third World*, The John Hopkins Press, London.

Johnston, B.F. and Clark, W.C. (1982), *Redesigning Rural Development: A Strategic Perspective*, The John Hopkins Press, London.

Ray, Debraj, *Development Economics*, Princeton University Press, New Jersey.

Sen, A. (1981), *Poverty and Famines: An Essay on Entitlement and Development*, Oxford University Press.

Todaro, M. (1992), *Economics for a Developing World*, Longman, London.

19

Agricultural Transformation and Rural Development

Introduction

It is the fact that over two-thirds of the world's poorest people are located in rural areas and engaged primarily in subsistence agriculture. Their basic concern is survival. Many hundreds of millions of people have been bypassed by whatever economic progress has been attained. It is estimated that more than 800 million of these people do not have enough food to meet their basic nutritional needs. In their daily struggle to subsist, their behaviour may have often seemed irrational to many observers who, until recently, had little comprehension of the precarious nature of subsistence living and the importance of avoiding risks. If development is to take place and become self-sustaining, it will have to include the rural areas in general and the agricultural sector in particular. The core problems of widespread poverty, growing inequality, rapid population growth, and rising unemployment all find their origins in the stagnation and too often retrogression of economic life in rural areas.

Traditionally, the role of agriculture in economic development has been viewed as passive and supportive. Based on the historical experience of western countries, economic development was seen as requiring a rapid structural transformation of the economy from one predominantly focused on agricultural activities to a more complex modern industrial and service society. As a result, agriculture's primary role was to provide sufficient low-priced food and manpower to the expanding industrial economy, which was thought to be dynamic 'leading sector' in any overall strategy of economic development.

However, today development economists are less sanguine about the desirability of placing such heavy emphasis on rapid industrialization. They have come to realize that far from playing a passive, supporting role in the process of economic development, the agricultural sector in particular and the rural economy in general must play an indispensable part in any overall strategy of economic progress, especially for the low income developing countries.

An agricultural and employment based strategy of economic development requires at minimum the following three basic complementary elements:

- Accelerated output growth through technological, institutional, and price incentive changes designed to raise the productivity of small farmers;
- Rising domestic demand for agricultural output derived from an employment-oriented urban development strategy; and
- Diversified, non-agricultural, labour-intensive rural development activities that directly and indirectly support and are supported by the farming community.

To a large extent agricultural and rural development has come to be seen by many as the *sine qua non* of national development. Without such integrated rural development, industrial growth either would be stultified or, if it succeeded, would create such severe internal imbalances in the economy that the problems of widespread poverty, inequality, and unemployment would become even more pronounced. In this chapter we will try to find out solutions to the following questions:

- How can total agricultural output and productivity per capita be substantially increased in a manner that will

directly benefit the average small farmer and the landless rural dweller while providing a sufficient food surplus to support a growing urban, industrial sector?
- What is the process by which traditional low-productivity peasant farms are transferred into high-productivity commercial enterprises?
- When traditional family farmers and peasant cultivators resist change, is their behaviour stubborn and irrational, or are they acting rationally within the context of their particular economic environment?
- Are economic and price incentives sufficient to elicit output increase among peasant agriculturists, or are institutional and structural changes in rural farming systems also required?
- Is raising agricultural productivity sufficient to improve rural life, or must there be concomitant off-farm employment creation along with improvements in educational, medical, and other socials services? In other words, what do we mean by rural development, and how can it be achieved?

Structure of Agrarian Systems

When we look at the state of contemporary agriculture in most poor countries, we realize the enormity of the task that lies ahead. A brief comparison between agricultural productivity in the developed nations and the underdeveloped nations makes this clear (*see*, Table 19.1). World agriculture, in fact, comprises two distinct types of farming:

- The highly efficient agriculture of the developed countries, where substantial productive capacity and high output per worker permit a very small number of farmers to feed entire nation, and
- The inefficient and low-productivity agriculture of developing countries, where in many instances the agricultural sector can barely sustain the farm population, let alone the burgeoning urban population, even at a minimum level of subsistence.

The gap between the two kinds of agriculture is immense. This is illustrated by the disparities in labour productivity. In 1960, the agricultural population of the developed nations came to about 115 million people. They produced a total output amounting to $78 billion, or about $680 per capita. In contrast, the per capita product of the agricultural population in the underdeveloped countries in 1960 was only $52. In other words, agricultural labour productivity in developed countries was more than 13 times that in the less developed countries. By 2000, this productivity gap had widened to more than 50 to 1.

Table 19.1: Land Productivity in Developed *vs* Developing Countries, 2000

Country	*Average Grain Yield (kg/Ha.)*
1. United Kingdom	6975
2. Japan	5971
3. United States	5794
4. Indonesia	3915
5. Bangladesh	2786
6. Mexico	2660
7. Brazil	2660
8. India	2293
9. Pakistan	2255
10. Nigeria	1208
11. Congo	781

Source: World Bank, 2001.

In the developed countries, there has been a steady growth of agricultural output since the mid-eighteenth century. This growth has been spurred by technological and biological improvements, which have resulted in ever higher levels of labour and land productivity. The growth rate accelerated after the First World War and particularly after the Second World War. The end result is that fewer farmers are able to produce more food. This is especially the case in the US, where in 2000 only 3 per cent of the total workforce was in agriculture, compared with more than 70 per cent in the early Nineteenth century.

The picture is entirely different when we turn to the agricultural production experience of developing countries. In many poor countries, agricultural production methods have changed relatively low over time. Rapid rural population growth has compounded the problem by causing great pressure to be exerted on existing resources. Where fertile land is scarce, especially throughout South and Southeast Asia but also in many parts of Latin America and Africa, rapid population growth has led to an increase in the number of people living on each unit of land. Given the same farming technology and the use of traditional non-labour inputs (*e.g.*, simple tools, animal power, traditional seeds), we know from the principle of diminishing returns that as more and more people are forced to work on a given piece of land, their marginal productivity will decline. The net result is a continuous deterioration in real living standards of rural peasants in some areas.

Peasant Agriculture in Latin America, Asia and Africa

In many developing countries, various historical circumstances have led to a concentration of large areas of land in the hands of a small class of powerful landowners. This is especially true in Latin America and parts of the Asian subcontinent. In Africa, both historical circumstances and the availability of relatively more unused land have resulted in a different pattern and structure of agricultural activity; however, in terms of levels of farm productivity, there is little to distinguish among the three regions.

A common characteristic of agriculture in all three regions, and for that matter in developed countries, is the position of the family as the basic unit of production. For the vast number of farm families, whose members constitute the main agricultural workforce, agriculture is not merely an occupation or a source of income; it is a way of life. This is particularly evident in traditional societies, where farmers are closely attached to their land and devote long, arduous days to its cultivation. Any change in farming methods brings with it changes in the farmer's way of life. The introduction of biological and technical innovations must, therefore, be adapted to the natural and economic conditions, but perhaps even more to the attitudes, values, and abilities of the mass of producers, who must understand the suggested changes, must be willing to accept them, and must be capable of carrying them out.

Thus in spite of the obvious differences between agricultural systems in Asia, Latin America, and Africa and among individual nations within each region, certain broad similarities enables us to make some generalizations and comparisons. In particular, agrarian systems in many parts of Asia and Latin America show more structural and institutional similarities and differences, and subsistence farmers in all three regions exhibit many of the same economic behaviour patterns.

Box 19.1: Latin American *vs.* Asian Peasants

Both the Latin American and Asian peasants are rural cultivators whose prime concern is survival. Subsistence defines his concept of life. He may strive to obtain his and his family's minimal needs by tilling an inadequate piece of land which is his own, or more often, which is rented from or pawned to a landlord or moneylender, or by selling his labour for substandard wages to a commercial agricultural enterprise. Profits which might come to him through the fortunes of weather of market are windfalls, not preconceived goals. Debt rather than profit is his normal fate, and therefore, his farming techniques are rationally scaled to his level of disposable capital: human and animal power rather than mechanized equipment; excrement rather than chemical fertilizers; traditional crops and seeds rather than experimental cultivation.

No effective social security, unemployment insurance, or minimum wage laws ease his plight. His every decision and act impinges directly upon his struggle for physical survival. In countries with a high proportion of peasantry, traditional food crops which a rural family can itself covert readily into the daily fare for its grain—or tuber based diet dominate the agriculture; corn in Mexico, rice in Indonesia, Mandioca in Brazil and Soybeans in China.

The Latifundio-Minifundio Pattern and Resource Utilization in Latin America

In Latin America, as indeed in Asia and Africa, agrarian structures are not only part of the production system but also a basic feature of the entire economic, social, and political organization of rural life. The agrarian structure that has prevailed in Latin America since colonial times and has provided much of the region with its social organization is the pattern of agricultural dualism known as Latifundio-Minifundio. Latifundios are very large landholdings. They are defined in Latin America as farms large enough to provide employment for more than 12 people, though some employ thousands. In contrast, Minifundios are the smallest farms. They are defined as farms too small to provide employment for a single family (two workers) with the typical incomes, markets, and levels of technology and capital prevailing in each country or region.

According to FAO, 1.3 per cent of landowners in Latin America hold 71.6 per cent of the land under cultivation. If we exclude countries that have carried out drastic land reforms during the last Century (Mexico, Bolivia, and Cuba), Latin America's agrarian structures seems to follow a uniform pattern. This pattern is basically one in which a small number of Latifundios control a large proportion of the agricultural land while a vast number of Minifundios must scratch out a survival existence on a meagre fraction of the occupied land. Table 19.2 provides a clear picture of the unequal distribution of landholdings in seven Latin American countries during the latter half of the 20th century. In no case did Minifundios, which comprised up to 90 per cent of the farms, occupy more than 17 per cent of the total agricultural land.

Table 19.2: Latifundios and Minifundios in the Agrarian Structure of Selected Latin American Countries

(per cent)

Country	*Minifundios*		*Latifundios*	
	Farms	*Occupied Land*	*Farms*	*Occupied Land*
1. Argentina	43.2	3.4	0.8	36.9
2. Brazil	22.5	0.5	4.7	59.5
3. Chile	36.9	0.2	6.9	81.3
4. Colombia	64.0	4.9	1.3	49.5
5. Ecuador	89.9	16.6	0.4	45.1
6. Guatemala	88.4	14.3	0.1	40.8
7. Peru	88.0	7.4	1.1	82.4

Source: Celso Furtado (1970).

But, Latifundios and Minifundios do not constitute the entire gamut of Latin American agricultural holdings. A considerable amount of production is also earned on family farms and medium-sized farms. The former provides work for two to four people (recall that the Minifundio could provide work for fewer than two people), and the latter, also sometimes known as multifamily farms, employ 12 workers (just below Latifundios). In Venezuela, Brazil, and Uruguay, these intermediate farm organizations account for almost 50 per cent of total agricultural output and employ similar proportions of agricultural labour. These farms use a more efficient balance between labour and land, and studies show that they have much higher total factor productivity than either Latifundios or Minifundios, as the law of diminishing returns suggests.

The economic and social ramifications of heavy land concentration in the hands of a few large landowners are compounded by the relative inefficiency of Latifundios in comparison with other Latin American farm organizations. Some economists have assumed that large farms use productive resources more efficiently than small ones on the ground that large enterprises can take advantage of economies of large-scale production and thereby lower costs. In terms of agriculture, the efficient utilization of large tractors and combine harvesters requires large tracts of land—otherwise this capital equipment will be grossly underutilized.

Evidence from a wide range of developing countries, however, clearly demonstrates that small farms are more efficient (lower-cost) producers of most agricultural commodities. For example, Minifundios in Argentina, Brazil, and Chile yield more than twice the value of output per hectare under cultivation than the Latifundios and more than 10 times the value per hectare of total farm land. Moreover, a 1990s land survey in Brazil showed that small farms of under 10 hectares had production of $85 per hectare, while the largest farms, in excess of 500 hectares, had a gross output of only $2 per hectare.

A major explanation for the relative economic inefficiency of farming the fertile land on the Latifundios in comparison with Minifundios is simply that the wealthy landowners often value these holdings not for their potential contributions to national agricultural output but rather for the considerable power and prestige that they bring. Much of the land is left idle or farmed less intensively than Minifundios. Also, Latifundio transaction costs, especially the cost of supervising hired labour, are much higher than the low effective cost of using family labour on peasant farms. It follows that raising agricultural production and improving the efficiency of Latin American agrarian systems in particular will require much more than direct economic policies that lead to the provision of better seeds, more fertilizers, less distorted factor prices, higher output prices, and improved marketing facilities. It will also require reorganization of rural social and institutional structures to provide Latin American peasants, who now constitute almost 70 per cent of the rural population, a real opportunity to lift themselves out of their present state of economic subsistence and social subservience.

Fragmentation and Subdivision of Peasant Land in Asia

If the major agrarian problem of Latin America can be identified as too much land under the control of too few people, the basic problem in Asia is one of too many people crowded onto too little land. For example, the per capita availability of arable land in India, China, and Bangladesh in the middle of 1990s was 0.19, 0.08, and 0.07 hectares, respectively. Central Java in Indonesia is an extreme example of the pressure of population on limited land that characterizes the Asian agrarian scene. It has the dubious distinction of possessing the world's record population density—over 1500 persons per square kilometre.

The present land owners in Asia are an absentee owner who lives in the town and turns over the working of the land to sharecroppers and tenant farmers. In many respects, therefore, his position of power in the economic, political, and social structure of the rural community is analogous to that of the Latin American 'patron'. There is a difference in that the former is an absentee owner, whereas the latter often lives on his Latifundio. But the efficiency and productivity implications are the same.

Sharecropping is widespread in both Asia and Latin America but more pervasive in Asia. It has been estimated that of all tenanted land, some 84.5 per cent is sharecropped in Asia while only 16.1 per cent is sharecropped in Latin America. Moreover, this institution is almost unknown in Africa, where farms operated under tribal or communal tenure forms continue to be dominant.

The creation of individual titles to land made possible the rise to power of another dubious agent of change in Asian rural socio-economic structures, the moneylender. Once private property came into effect, land became a negotiable asset that could be offered by peasants as security for loans and, in the case of default, could be forfeited and transferred to the often unscrupulous moneylender.

The final major force altering the traditional agrarian structure in Asia has been the rapid rate of population growth, especially over the past 30 or 40 years. Myrdal notes in reference to the population phenomenon that, "When and where expansion in the cultivated area was a feasible alternative—whether for physical, technical, social, economic, or institutional reasons—population growth was reflected, in the first instance, in the cumulative subdivision and fragmentation of the acreages already under cultivation. Later this process, in combination with the emergence of private property and the rise of commercial agriculture and money lending, often contributed to the rise of large land owners, the demise of small peasant proprietors, and the increase of the landless." The ultimate impoverishment of the peasantry was the inevitable consequence of this process of fragmentation, economic vulnerability, and loss of land to rich and powerful landlords. As these holdings shrink even further, production falls below the subsistence level, and chronic poverty becomes a way of life.

Subsistence Agriculture and Extensive Cultivation in Africa

As in Asia and Latin America, subsistence farming on small plots of land is the way of life for the vast majority of African people. However, the organization and structure of African agriculture systems differ markedly from those found in contemporary Asia or Latin America. Except in former colonial settlement areas like White Highlands of Kenya and some of the large sugar, cocoa, and coffee plantations of East and West Africa, the great majority of farm families in tropical Africa still plant their output primarily for their own subsistence. Since the basic variable input in African agriculture is farm family and village labour, African agriculture systems are dominated by the following three major characteristics:

- The importance of subsistence farming in the village community;
- The existence of some (though rapidly diminishing) land in excess of immediate requirements, which permits a general practice of shifting cultivation and reduces the value of land ownership as an instrument of economic and political power; and
- The rights of each family (both nuclear and extended) in a village to have access to land and water in the immediate territorial vicinity, excluding from such access use by families that do not belong to the community even though they may be of the same tribe.

The low productivity subsistence farming characteristic of most traditional African agriculture results from a combination of three historical forces restricting the growth of output:

(i) In spite of the existence of some unused and potentially cultivable land, only small area can be planted and weeded by the farm family at a time when it uses only traditional tools such as the short-handled hoe, the axe, and the long-handled knife. In some countries, use of animals is impossible because of the notorious tsetse fly or lack of fodder in the long dry seasons, and traditional farming practices must rely primarily on the application of human labour to small parcels of land.

(ii) Given the limited amount of land that a farm family can cultivate in the context of a traditional technology and the use of primitive tools, these small areas tend to be intensively cultivated. As a result, they are subject to rapidly diminishing returns to increased labour inputs. In such conditions, shifting cultivation is the most economic method of using limited supplies of labour on extensive tracts of land. Under shifting cultivation, once the minerals are drawn out of the soil as a result of numerous cropping, new land is cleared, and the process of planting and weeding is repeated. In the meantime, formerly cropped land is allowed to recover fertility until it can be used again. Under such a process, manure and chemical fertilizers are unnecessary, although in most African villages some form of manure (mostly animal waste) is applied to nearby plots that are intensively cultivated in order to extent their period of fertility.

(iii) Labour is scarce during the busiest part of the growing season, planting and weeding times. At other times, much of the labour is underemployed. Because the time of planting is determined by the onset of the rains and because much of Africa experiences only one extended rainy season, the demand for workers during the early weeks of this rainy season usually exceeds all available rural labour supplies.

The net result of these forces had been a relatively constant level of agricultural total output and labour productivity throughout much of Africa. As long as population size remained relatively stable, this historical pattern of low productivity and shifting cultivation enabled most African tribes to meet their subsistence food requirements. But the feasibility of shifting cultivation has now broken down as population densities increased. It has largely been replaced by sedentary cultivation on small owner-occupied plots. As a result, the need for other non-human productive inputs and new technologies grows, especially in the more densely populated agricultural regions of Kenya, Nigeria, Ghana, and

Uganda. Moreover, with the growth of towns, the penetration of the monetary economy, soil erosion and deforestation of marginal lands, and the introduction of land taxes, pure subsistence-agricultural practices are no longer viable. Mixed and modern commercial farming must appear, as indeed they have in parts of Sub-Saharan Africa.

Role of Women in Agrarian Development

A major and often overlooked feature of LDC agrarian systems, particularly in Africa and Asia, is the crucial role played by women in agricultural production. In Africa, where subsistence farming is predominant and shifting cultivation remains important, nearly all tasks associated with subsistence food production are performed by women. Although men who remain home generally perform the initial task of cutting trees and bushes on a potentially cultivable plot of land, women are responsible for all subsequent operations, including removing and burning felled trees, sowing or planting the plot, weeding, harvesting, and preparing the crop for storage or immediate consumption.

Women provide an important source of labour for cash crop production, cultivate food for household consumption, raise and market livestock, generate additional income through cottage industries, collect firewood and water, and perform household chores, including the processing and cooking of foods. Due to the time-consuming nature of their diverse responsibilities, women tend to work longer hours than their male counterparts. Studies concerning the allocation of women's time among different activities have greatly increased recognition of the importance of rural women's economic contribution. It has become clear that since women produce a large share of agricultural output, successful agricultural reform will require raising women's productivity.

When the structure of agriculture is becoming more commercialized, women's roles and thus their economic status are changing. In many developing regions, women are still unremunerative for the long hours they contribute to the tending of commercial crops. As revenue-generating cash cropping rises in importance, the proportion of resources controlled by women tends to diminish. This is largely due to the fact that household resources, such as land and inputs, are transferred away from women's crops in order to promote the production of cash crops.

Though efforts to increase the income of women by providing direct access to credit and inputs have experienced considerable success, programmes that work indirectly with women have frequently fallen short of their stated goals. Studies have found that projects are most likely to elicit the cooperation of women when resources are placed directly under their control. Clearly, projects that depend on the unremunerated labour of women are likely to obtain only minimal support. Adoption of new crops and technologies will be more effective where patterns of production are consistent with the interests of female household members. Because the active participation of women is critical to agricultural prosperity, policy design should ensure that women benefit equally from development efforts.

Towards a Strategy of Agricultural and Rural Development: Main Requirements

If the major objective of agricultural and rural development in developing nations is the progressive improvement in rural levels of living achieved primarily through increase in small-farm incomes, output and productivity, it is important to identify the principal sources of agricultural progress and the basic conditions essential to its achievement. These are necessarily interrelated, but for purposes of description we may separate them into two and further divide each into three components.

Sources of Small-scale Agricultural Progress

Agricultural and rural development that benefits the masses of people can succeed only through a joint effort by the government and all farming community, not just the large farmers.

(i) Technological Change

In most developing countries, new agricultural technologies and innovations in farm practices are preconditions for sustained improvements in levels of output and productivity. In many parts of Africa and Latin America, however, increased output in earlier years was achieved without the need for new technology simply by extending cultivation into unused but potentially productive lands. Almost all of these opportunities have by now been exploited, however, and there is not much scope for further significant improvement. The following two major sources of technological innovation can increase farm yields:

- Introduction of mechanized agriculture to replace human labour.
- Biological (hybrid seeds), water control (irrigation), and chemical (fertilizers, pesticides, insecticides, etc.) innovations.

These are land augmenting by improving the quality of existing land through raising yield per hectare.

(ii) Appropriate Government Economic Policies

A development innovation with great potential for alleviating rural poverty and raising agricultural output can turnout to be anti-developmental if public policies and social institutions militate against the active participation of the small farmers in evolving agrarian structure. Another area calling for major improvements in government policies relates to the pricing of agricultural commodities, especially food grains and other staples produced for local markets; so as to ensure fair incomes to the rural farmers.

(iii) Supportive Social Institutions

Although the new hybrid 'miracle seed' varieties together with needed irrigation and chemicals are scale-neutral and thus offer the potential for small-farm progress, the social institutions that accompany their introduction into the rural economy often are note scale-neutral.

Conditions for General Rural Development

It is for the humane reason as well as for reasons of higher agricultural output and the simultaneous achievement of both greater efficiency and more equality that land reform is often proposed as a necessary first condition for agricultural development in LDCs. Even where land reform is not necessary but where productivity and incomes are low, the broad network of external support services, along with appropriate governmental pricing policies related to both farm inputs and outputs, is an essential condition for sustained agricultural progress.

(i) Modernizing Farm Structures to Meet Rising Food Demands

Farm structures and land tenure patterns must be adapted to the dual objectives of increasing food production and promoting a wider distribution of the benefits of agrarian progress.

(ii) Creating an Effective Supporting System

The full benefits of small-scale agricultural development cannot be realized unless government support systems are created that provide the necessary incentives, economic opportunities, and access to needed credit and inputs to enable small cultivators to expand their output and raise their productivity.

(iii) Changing the Rural Environment to Improve Levels of Living

Rural development, though dependent primarily on small farmer agricultural progress, implies much more. It encompasses:

- Efforts to raise both farm and non-farm rural real incomes through job creation, rural industrialization, and the increased provision of education, health and nutrition, housing and variety of related social and welfare services;
- A decreasing inequality in the distribution of rural welfare services; and
- The capacity of the rural sector to sustain and accelerate the pace of these improvements over time.

Conclusion

The above mentioned experiences point out that the future of most developing countries will depend to a large extent on what happens to their agriculture, there has been a marked shift in rural development thinking and policy making. This shift, which began in the late 1970s and has continued in the 1990s, has been away from the almost exclusive emphasis on rapid industrialization towards a more realistic appreciation of the overwhelming importance of agricultural and rural development for national development. The first step towards understanding what is needed for agricultural and rural development, however, must be a comprehensive of the nature of agricultural systems in diverse developing regions and, in particular, of the economic aspects of the transition from subsistence to commercial agriculture.

REFERENCES

Bardhan, Pranab (1984), *Land, Labour and Rural Poverty: Essays in Development Economics*, Columbia University Press, New York.

Berry, R. Albert (1979), *Agrarian Structure and Productivity in Developing Countries*, John Hopkins University Press, Baltimore.

Furtado, Celso (1970), *Economic Development in Latin America*, Cambridge University Press, New York.

Robson, Peter and Dennis A. Lury (1969), *The Economies of Africa*, Allen and Unwin, London.

Yudelman, Montague, *et al.* (1971), *Technological Change in Agriculture and Employment in Developing Countries*, OECD, Paris.

20

Factor Markets and Rural Development

Introduction

Some countries have adopted successful agricultural and rural development strategies as if by accident, and have stayed with them. Other countries experienced dramatic failures and some painful learning experiences before they abandoned poor policies. Some continue to cling to misguided prescription of the past, support by political equilibria that do not provide adequate voice to large segments of their rural populations. Severe external shocks and adverse policies of developed countries have often contributed to their poor performance. Poor agricultural and rural development performance has retarded economic growth and increased poverty.

During the early days of development economics—in the 1950s—rural poverty was often explained by the backwardness of traditional smallholder agriculture. The sector was considered to have almost no potential for development. It is, therefore, not surprising that the solution to the reduction in rural poverty was almost universally seen as being associated with urban growth and rural-to-urban migration. It was assumed that rural population and employment would decline, if not in absolute terms, at least as a proportion of the labour force.

The promised elimination of rural poverty *via* migration to the cities has not materialized. Today many developing countries have two to three times as many poor rural people as in 1950. Much of the massive population transfer to the cities has been into the informal sector and into slum areas. Most of these countries are characterized by high rates of rural violence and urban crime, and many of these countries have undergone decades of land-related uprisings and land invasions. Finally, many smallholders who cannot gain access to land *via* purchase, rental, or land reform eventually turn to environmentally destructive cultivation of marginal land, petty trading activities, or to crime.

Land Markets and Rural Development

Proper functioning of the land market is very important for the overall development of the rural economy. If land is held unequally and many individuals fail to obtain access to it, they are likely to leave agriculture in search of a less precarious source of living. This can lead to a situation in which large numbers of rural migrants crowd the cities—a situation that can be politically, environmentally, and economically unpalatable. Quite apart from political acceptability, there is the narrower question of economic efficiency in agriculture. Input markets such as the land market exist to bring the ratios of various inputs into line for efficient production.

Ownership and Tenancy

Although there is substantial inequality in Asia, land inequalities in Latin America are higher by an order of magnitude. The low per capita holdings of land in Asia and the high inequality of landholdings in Latin America have a similar effect: a significant fraction of the farms are owner operated and cultivated. The African countries are somewhat of an outlier in this respect. Much of the land is held under forms of group or communal tenure, and individual claims on such plots are weak. Several countries provide for ownership or use rights to tenants who have worked the land for some pre-specified number of years. This legal stipulation often lowers the amount of tenancy, and in the case of Asia there may be substantial amount of informal tenancy that goes unrecorded. Several countries in Latin America also uphold as a basic principle that the land belongs to those who farm it and have legalized this principle by regarding tenancy as a basis for granting use rights or ownership. See Table 20.1 for the distribution tenure status of land in different parts of world.

Table 20.1: Distribution of Farms and Farmland Tenure Systems

Countries	Asia	Africa	Latin America	Europe	North America	World
1. Farms (Million)	93.3	3.5	8.6	11.9	3.1	120.4
2. Farm size (Hectares)	2.3	0.5	46.5	7.6	161.2	10.0
3. Distribution of Farm (%)						
(i) Owner cultivation	85.8	5.2	60.3	67.6	63.2	79.2
(ii) Pure Tenancy	5.9	1.6	17.1	9.3	12.0	7.1
(iii) Owner-*cum*-Tenancy	8.2	6.9	6.6	23.0	24.8	10.0
(iv) Others	0.0	86.3	16.0	0.1	0.0	3.7
4. Distribution of Farmland (%)						
(i) Owner cultivation	84.0	9.2	80.4	58.9	36.6	61.1
(ii) Pure tenancy	5.9	3.0	6.2	12.5	11.9	9.0
(iii) Owner-*cum*-tenancy	10.1	29.1	5.6	28.5	51.5	27.2
(iv) Others	0.0	58.7	7.8	0.1	0.0	2.7
5. Percentage of share tenancy in tenanted land	84.5	0.0	16.1	12.5	31.5	36.1

Source: Otsuka, Chuma, and Hayami, 1992.

In a country with large landholdings, agriculture may take on a highly mechanized and capitalistic form, using wage labour where labour is required. In such a regime, it may be better for smaller landowners to give up their land to large owners in exchange for a rent.

Suppose that a landowner wishes to rent out his land to a potential tenant. Several contractual forms are available. The simplest form of tenancy contract is what is called a 'fixed-rent contract,' one in which the landlord charges a sum of money for the rental of the land and, in turn, allows the tenant to carry out production. This sort of contract is found wherever land rentals are observed. A second type of contract is commonly referred to as 'sharecropping'. Sharecropping comes in many flavours, but all of them involve the sharing of the tenant's output in some pre-assigned proportion between the landlord and the tenant. The proportions vary from country to country and across regions within a country, although a 50-50 division is commonly observed. Variations on the sharecropping contract include different proportions of division of the output depending on whether input costs are also shared between the landlord and the tenant, and tied credit arrangements.

There is a simple but useful way to write down a class of rental contracts that contains fixed rent and sharecropping contracts as special cases. If 'Y' denotes agricultural output on the rented land, then write the total rent as:

$$R = \alpha Y + F$$

If $\alpha = 0$ and $F > 0$, this is a fixed-rent contract with rent F. If $F = 0$ and α lies between 0 and 1, then this is a sharecropping contract, where the share to the landlord is α and the share to the tenants is $1 - \alpha$. Finally, if $\alpha = 0$ and $F < 0$, this can be interpreted as a 'pure wage contract,' where the wage is simply $w = -F$; the tenant is not a tenant at all, but a labourer on the landlord's land.

Land Reforms

To realize the gains, we left with the option of land transfers from rich to poor, either without adequate compensation or with full compensation paid by the government or by foreign donors, but not entirely by the beneficiaries. Unless the government wishes to spend its budget on compensating beneficiaries, or unless some enlightened foreign donors earmark funds especially for this purpose, it is hard to see how a successful land reform can come about. It takes tremendous political will to push a land reform programme through. There is some possibility that large landowners will agree to some reform if they are faced with the credible threat of violence or forced expropriation. Otherwise, major land reforms have been the product of political upheavals in society, as in Cuba, Japan, Korea, and Taiwan. Political upheaval has the advantage that large landowners are viewed as enemies, or collaborators with the previous regime, and so there is immense popular support for land reform.

There are intermediate steps that lie between government inaction and large-scale redistribution. Providing tenants with unlimited use rights to land is one of them. Although such reforms undoubtedly go in the right direction and can have significant effects on productivity, they fall short of reaping the full gains in an environment of imperfect credit markets. Without ownership rights, land cannot be pledged as collateral for productivity enhancing investments. Seized land also may be redistributed as collectives, as in Mexico or Peru. Finally, land ceilings may be used to curtail ownership of large plots. Even though such ceilings are in force in many developing countries, they are easily sidestepped by holding land in several parcels under the names of friends and relatives.

Labour Markets and Rural Development

Land and labour markets emerge because there is an imbalance between the ownership of various inputs of production in rural areas. One such imbalance might occur in the inputs of land and labour themselves. Specifically, landholdings may be more unequally distributed than endowments of labour. In such a situation a land market, or labour market, or both will have to emerge to create a balance between the operational holdings of land and labour. Land and labour markets may be complementaries instead of substitutes. This is especially so with agricultural activities that are mechanized and must take place on a large scale. In this situation both land and labour are employed by those individuals with access to capital.

Even in a geographically contiguous region, there is no single, homogenous labour market. Hired labour is broadly classified into two.

(i) Labourers that are hired on a casual basis, perhaps on some daily arrangement or for some pre-specified short duration (such as the harvesting period), and

(ii) Labourers that are under some long-term contract with their employer.

The distinction between these two categories is important, because their markets work quite differently.

Casual labour is normally hired to carry markets that are easily amenable to observation. Harvesting and weeding fall into this category. The tasks of long-term labour are somewhat more mixed. On large plots of land, a long-term employee may serve in a supervisory capacity, along with the owners of the farm. They might be responsible for tasks that require special care and are relatively difficult to monitor, such as the application of fertilizer and pesticides or the application of water. In addition, long-term employees might work at 'standard' tasks along with their casual counterparts, participating in the harvesting process, for instance.

Poverty, Nutrition and Labour Markets

Labour supply depends on the work capacity of the rural population. Relationship between nutrition and work capacity, which is known as the 'capacity curve' is shown in Fig. 20.1. The horizontal axis is labelled 'income'; the implicit assumption is that all income is converted to nutrition. Nothing if substance is lost by amending this to a more realistic situation where, say 70 per cent of income is spent on nutrition. The vertical axis is labelled work capacity; a measure of the total number of tasks an individual can perform during a given period, say the quantity of wheat that he can harvest during a day. The capacity curve is found by linking different nutrition (Income) points to the corresponding levels of work capacity that are generated by the individual.

The shape of the capacity curve is because, most nutrition initially goes into maintaining the body's resting metabolism. In this stretch very little extra energy is left over for work, so work capacity in this region is close to zero and does not increase too quickly as nutrition levels change. Once resting metabolism is taken care of, however, there is marked increase in work capacity with nutrition. Finally there is a phase of diminishing returns, as natural bodily limits restrict the conversion of increasing nutrition into ever-increasing work capacity.

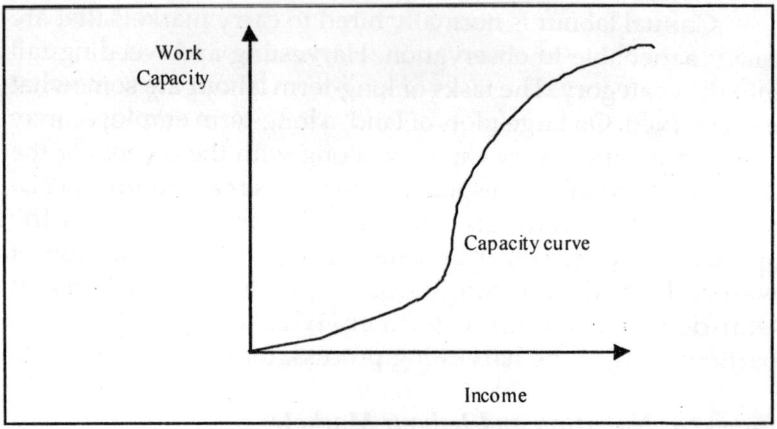

Fig. 20.1: The Capacity Curve

The shape of the capacity curve is because, most nutrition initially goes into maintaining the body's resting metabolism. In this stretch very little extra energy is left over for work, so work capacity in this region is close to zero and dose not increase too quickly as nutrition levels change. Once resting metabolism is taken care of, however, there is marked increase in work capacity with nutrition. Finally, there is a phase of diminishing returns, as natural bodily limits restrict the conversion of increasing nutrition into ever-increasing work capacity.

Piece Rates

Income determines work capacity, but work capacity determines income as well. Let's try to capture this in the simplest possible way. Imagine that incomes are generated by working in a labour market where piece rates are paid. This is payment on the basis of tasks completed. Piece rates have an easy pictorial representation along the same axes used for Fig. 20.1. If income is paid per unit of task, then we can see that there is a relationship between the number of tasks that are performed and total income. Fig. 20.2 draws the obvious graph that portrays this relationship. A piece rate, then, appears as a relationship between the number of tasks performed and the total income of a person.

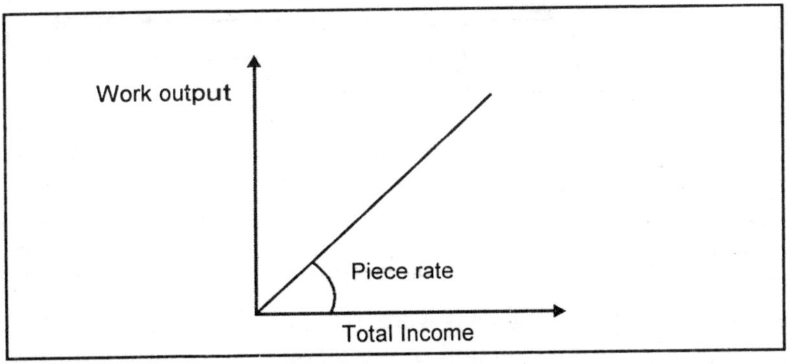

Fig. 20.2: Piece Rate

Now super impose Fig. 20.1 on Fig. 20.2. The result is shown in Fig. 20.3. Four piece rates are shown, V_1, V_2, V_3 and V_4. Thus v_1 means something like the labour get paid V_1 for every quantity of wheat harvested. And also, V_1 is larger than V_2, which in turn exceeds V_3, which is larger than V_4.

Labour Supply

Assume that a laborer tries to obtain the highest possible level of income that he can possibly earn, given the constraints imposed by his capacity curve. Suppose, first, that the going piece rate is V_1. The labourer clearly chooses the point A, which yields the largest possible feasible income for him. As the piece rate drops to V_2, this maximum income falls. On Fig. 20.3, the labourer now slides down to point B, which involves less total work and lower income.

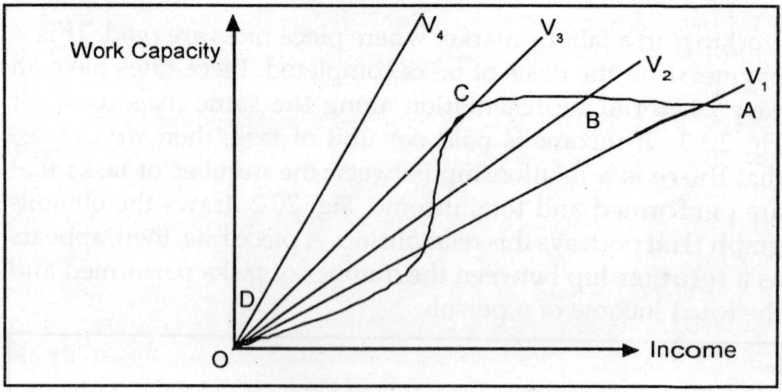

Fig. 20.3: Piece Rates and Work Effort

At V_3, something interesting happens, this is a piece rate that has the property that it is just tangent to the capacity curve along its hump. At this piece rate the labourer can just about choose the point C. If the piece rate drops a little more, then the amount of work that the labourer can supply drops dramatically, jumping, as it were, from a point like C to point D (which is the intersection of the lowest piece rate with the capacity curve). This jump occurs precisely because the capacity curve is shaped the way it is shaped, with low levels of nutrition permitting only very low levels of work, and moderate to high levels of creating a rapid increase in work capacity.

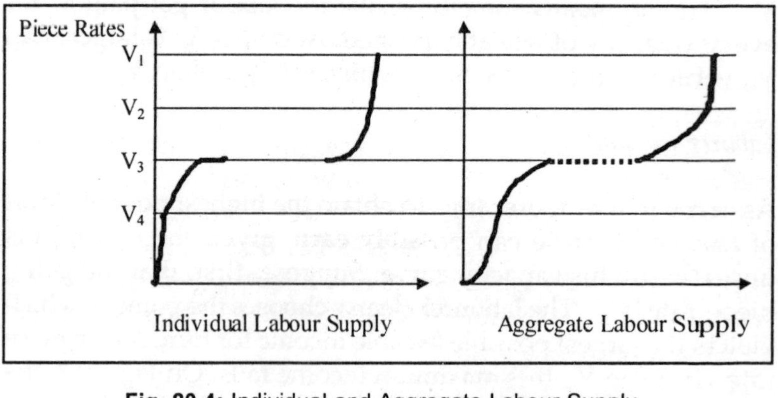

Fig. 20.4: Individual and Aggregate Labour Supply

By using this information it is possible to generate a supply curve of labour, which tells the different levels of labour power supplied at different piece rates. Fig. 20.4 shows the transition from individual labour supply to aggregate labour supply. The left-hand panel shows individual labour supply, by simply transplanting the information from Fig. 20.3. The gap in labour supply at the piece rate V_3 captures that after a certain threshold wage, individual labour supply must jump discontinuously. The right-hand panel effectively multiplies this individual supply curve by the number of labourers. Two things happen; first, the horizontal axis gets blown up by the number of labourers for each piece rate, and secondly, the 'dotted' gap.

Equilibrium

The demand for labour is a perfectly standard one, which is downward slopping to capture the fact that if labour is cheaper, employers will demand a larger quantity of it. Fig. 20.5 shows the demand and supply curves on the same Figure. Here two cases are of interest; in the first case, represented by the left-hand panel, the demand curve for labour cuts the supply curve at a point that is beyond the gap in the supply curve. This case is perfectly normal: the market determines an equilibrium piece rate V* and everybody gets to supply a high level of work effort, that is, a level of work effort that is somewhere on the hump of the capacity curve for each labourer. The market clears in a standard fashion; this case obtains if demand is large relative to supply.

The interesting case is represented by the right-hand panel; here supply is large relative to demand, so that the demand curve passes through the dotted gap in the aggregate supply curve. If the piece rate is larger than v*, there is excess supply, which brings the piece rate down. On the other hand, for piece rates below this critical level, there is excess demand, so that wages are bid up.

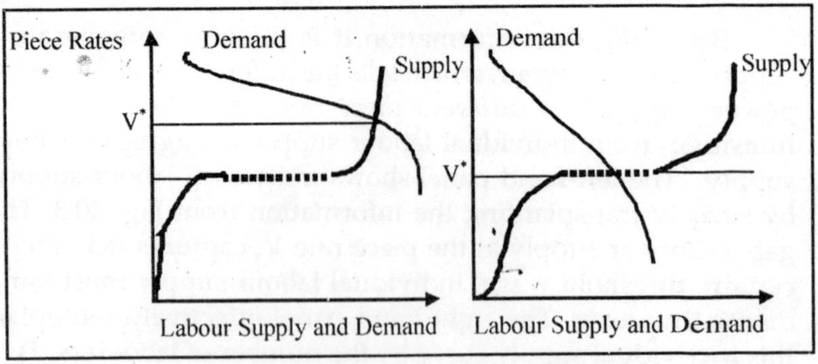

Fig. 20.5: Equilibrium in the Labour Market

Rural Credit Markets

Many economic activities are spread out over time. The adoption of a new technology or a new crop requires investment today, with the payoffs coming on later. Even on-going productive activity requires inputs in advance, with revenue realized at a later point in time. This is especially true for casual labour or the self-employed; income streams may fluctuate, and such fluctuations will be transmitted to consumption unless they are smoothed through some form of credit. The following two important features of rural credit markets make it problematic.

- It is often very difficult to monitor exactly what is being done with a loan. A loan may be taken for an ostensibly productive reason, but may be used for other needs (such as consumption) that cannot be easily transformed into monetary repayment. Alternatively, a loan may be put into a risky productive activity that may fail to pay off. This creates the problem of 'inability to repay' or involuntary default, at which point there is little that a lender can do get his money back.
- The second problem is voluntary or strategic default, a situation in which the borrower can repay the loan, in principle, but simply does not find it in his interest to do so. Such a state of affairs is especially pertinent

in contexts where the legal system of loan enforcement is weak.

Rural credit markets are usually been served by either institutional or informal lenders.

Institutional Lenders

There are the institutional lenders or formal lenders such as government banks, commercial banks, credit bureaus, and so on. Often special banks are set up, as in Thailand, Philippines and India, and in many developing countries, to cater to the needs of rural population. The main problem with the formal lenders is that they often do not have personal knowledge regarding the characteristics and activities of their clientele. Often, these agencies cannot precisely monitor just how the loans are used. The problem is not just production *versus* consumption; for example, the fear that a loan taken ostensibly for some productive purposes may be squandered to meet the expenses of a wedding. There are other, more subtle reasons for a systematic divergence between what lenders want and done with the money and what borrowers want.

Informal Lenders

The right sort of informal money-lender may be willing to accept collateral in any form. A large land-owner who has land adjacent to that of a poor farmer may be interested in the tiny plot as collateral (indeed, perhaps more interested in the plot than in getting the loan back). An employer of rural labour will accept labour as collateral, in case the labourer-borrower fails to repay.

It is no surprise, therefore, to find that formal banks cannot effectively reach out to poor borrowers, whereas informal money-lenders (the landlord, the shopkeeper, the trader, etc.) do a much better job. Quite apart from the ability to accept collateral in exotic forms, the informal money-lender often has much better information regarding the activities and characteristics of his clientele.

Characteristics of Rural Credit Markets

Following are the important characteristics of rural credit markets.

(i) Informational Constraints

The fundamental feature that creates imperfections in credit markets is informational constraints; which occur at two basic levels:

- There is the lack of information regarding the use to which a loan will be put.
- There is the lack of information regarding the repayment decision.

This deficiency includes limited knowledge of innate characteristics of the borrower that may be relevant in such a decision, as well as limited knowledge of the defaulter's subsequent needs and activities, which place limits on his incentive to default. All the important features of credit markets can be understood as responses to one or the other of these informational problems.

(ii) Segmentation

Another characteristic of the rural credit market is its tendency towards segmentation. Many credit relationships are personalized and take time to build up. Typically, a rural money-lender serves a fixed clientele, whose members he lends to on a repeated basis; he is extremely reluctant to lend outside this circle. Most often, money-lender's clients are from within his villages or from close by, so that the money-lender has close contact with them and is well informed about their activities and whereabouts. Repeat lending—a phenomenon in which a money-lender lends funds to individuals to whom he has lent before (or has close interactions with) is very common.

(iii) Inter-linkage

A majority of village moneylenders do not pursue usury as their sole occupation; most of them are wealthy landlords, shopkeepers, or traders dealing in the marketing of crops. Given a segmented market, it probably won't come as a surprise to learn that landlords tend to give credit mostly to their tenants or farm workers, whereas traders favour lending to clients from whom they also purchase grains. Thus segmentation often takes place along occupational lines, and the complementarity of some production relationship (tenant and landlord or farmer and trader) facilitates the credit relationship. This interlocking of market—people who conduct their business in different markets (land, labour, credit) with the same trading partners, and indeed make the terms of transaction in one market depend on the terms and conditions in the other—is a far cry from the impersonal and independent functioning of markets.

(iv) Interest Rate Variation

Segmentation has a natural corollary; informal interest rates on loans exhibit great variation, and the rates vary by geographical location, the source of funds, and the characteristics of the borrower. Sometimes the rate of interest is extraordinarily high.

(v) Rationing

Informal credit markets are characterized by widespread rationing; that is, upper limits on how much a borrower receive from a lender. Rationing meant that at the going rate of interest, the borrower would like to borrow more but cannot. In this sense credit rationing is a puzzle; if the borrower would like to borrow strictly more than what he gets, there is some surplus here that the money-lender can grab by simply raising the rate of interest a wee bit more. This process should continue until the price (interest rate) is such that the borrower is borrowing just what he wants at that rate of interest. As a special case, rationing also include the complete exclusion of some potential borrowers from credit transactions with some lenders. That is, at the going terms offered by the lenders, some borrowers would like to borrow, but the lender does not lend to them. In this sense rationing is intimately connected to the notion of segmentation.

(vi) Exclusively

Many informal credit transactions are characterized by exclusive dealings. Money lenders dislike situations in which their borrowers are borrowing from more than a single source. They insist that the borrower deal with them exclusively; that is, approach no other lender for supplementary loans.

Microfinance

The Grameen Banks (Village Banks)

It is also possible for institutional lending to closely mimic and exploit some of the features of informal lending. For instance, it may be possible to design an innovative rural credit scheme in a rice-growing area in which a formal-sector institution acts both as lender and a miller. The combined activity will permit the formal institution to accept rice output as repayment for loans. By mimicking the activities of a trader-moneylender, the formal institution may actually be able to carry out lending activities that reach small borrowers and are profitable at the same time.

Even if such mixed institutions are difficult to put into practice, there are ways in which the information base of a community can be put to use by a cleverly constructed lending institution. An example of this is the Grameen Bank of Bangladesh. In Bangladesh, as in many other developing countries, subsidized rural credit offered by government banks laid the basis for its rural credit policy. However, repayment rates were low, and loans (or the forgiveness of the past loans) were often used for political reasons, undercutting the effects of the policy.

The Grameen Bank, started in mid-1980s in Bangladesh lends to very poor households, and lends to groups of borrowers rather than individuals. A typical group consists of five borrowers, and lending to individuals within the group occurs in sequence. The average loan size was around $100; no collateral is required and the nominal rate of interest was around 20 per cent (roughly 12 per cent real). Over 90 per cent of the borrowers are women and average repayment rates were over 97 per cent.

Some of the most important features of Grameen Banks are the following:

(i) Group Lending and the Use of Information: The central feature of Grameen Bank's lending policy is that in the event of a default, no group member is allowed to borrow again. This means that a group has to be formed carefully by the individuals to weed out bad borrowers who could jeopardize the creditworthiness of the group as a whole. The borrowers themselves have the incentive to use this information to form groups, and this induces a form of self-sufficient that no individual-based banking scheme can mimic.

(ii) Positive Assortative Matching: Self-selection typically takes the form of positive assortative matching, where good credit risks come together. To be sure, both bad and good risks equally want to team up with the good risks, but if the good risks can identify other good risks, they will form a group together. Thus group formation has the property that it can drive risky types out of the market, because some of the costs of their riskiness are borne by other borrowers instead of the bank alone.

(iii) Peer Monitoring: The arguments so far assume that borrowers are intrinsically safe or risky. This is a valid assumption in many situations; group members may not be able to control a fellow member does with her money, although they might still be able to predict what she is going to do (for instance, because they know her personality). In other situations, group members might be able to monitor and

influence the choice of individual projects. In that case, the group will want these projects to be safe, relative to the safety levels they would choose as individual borrowers.

The Grameen Bank type rural credit institutions are also not free from limitations. The following are the most important limitations:

(i) The most serious of this occurs when one member of the group runs into genuine financial difficulties and must default. In that case it is a dominant strategy for other group members to default on their outstanding loan as well, because one member's genuine difficulties have destroyed the group's credit rating anyway. The Grameen Bank avoids this problem by lending sequentially to group members, thus minimizing the contagion effect of an individual default.

(ii) The peer monitoring effects might backfire as well; that is, there may be excessive pressures to choose overly safe outcomes that are not socially optimal in terms of average profitability. For instance, a group sees as its potential loss the costs of a project failure (which is a social loss as well) as well as the cost future exclusion from borrowing. The latter cost necessarily exists because the no-lending threat must be used to avoid voluntary or strategic default, but this drives a wedge between the group's calculation of private cost and the true social loss of project failure (which is thereby smaller). Therefore, a group will have some tendency to be over-conservative in its choice of projects.

(iii) Finally, group-based schemes may lack flexibility; which can happen in rapidly changing environments in which some group members fare much better than others. In that case, the worst-performing member slows down the group as a whole.

As far as viability of Grameen Banks are concerned, they are lending to the poor; there are limits on the interest rate that it can charge without seriously affecting repayment capacity and loan sizes are very small. This means that each loan comes with a high administrative overhead. There are costs of providing, tracking, and ensuring repayment of the loan, and these are fixed costs per borrower, so that small loan sizes raise these costs.

Other Microfinance Institutions

The Grameen Bank spawned, by example, many other microfinance programmes. Several countries in Latin America, Africa and Asia, and US have adopted finance programmes based on the Grameen Bank. Some of these programmes have been more successful than Grameen if one goes by the narrow criteria of economic viability. For instance, the BancoSol in Bolivia lends to groups rather than individuals, just as the Grameen Banks does, but the groups are significantly richer than the clientele of Grameen. Thus average loan sizes are larger, and so are interest rates, allowing BancoSol to turn a profit. The Bank Rakyat Indonesia (BRI) lends to individuals and asks for collateral. Here also the economic characteristics vary from those of their Bangladeshi counterparts. Thus Grameen Banks remain a role model on two counts: because of the pioneering and innovative inroads it has made into small-scale lending and because it has reached out to very poor individuals.

Conclusion

The important factors underlying rural development include land, labour and credit markets and the efficiency with which they are functioning. A proper functioning of the land market including ownership and utilization is very important for the overall development of the rural economies, as the rural livelihood is based on agricultural operations. Like land markets, labour markets are devices of adjustment between the ownership pattern of factors and the way they are put to operational use. Typically credit is taken to finance ongoing production (working capital) or to finance shortfalls in consumption (consumption credit). Credit may be sought for new venture, such as the overhead expenditures needed to switch to a new crop (fixed capital). In this chapter, we have seen that with land and labour as inputs for rural development must be greatly qualified by the functioning of the credit markets as well.

REFERENCES

Bardhan, P.K. (1984), *Land, Labour and Rural Poverty: Essays in Development Economics*, Oxford University Press, New York.

Berry, R.A. and W.R. Cline (1979), *Agrarian Structure and Productivity in Developing Countries*, ILO, Geneva.

Bose, P. (1997), 'Formal-Informal Sector Interaction in Rural Credit Markets', *Mimeograph*, Department of Economics, University of Memphis.

Caselli, F. (1997), 'Rural Labour and Credit Markets,' *Mimeograph*, Department of Economics, Harvard University.

Huppi, M. and G. Feder (1990), 'The Role of Groups and Credit Cooperatives in Rural Lending.' *World Bank Research Observer-5.*

Powelson, J.P. and R. Stock (1987), *The Peasant Betrayed: Agriculture and Land Reform in the Third World*, Gunn and Hain, MA: Oelgeschlager, Boston.

Ray, Debraj (1998), *Development Economics*, Princeton University Press, New Jersey.

Otuska, H., H. Chuma and Y. Hayami (1992), 'Land and Labour Contracts in Agrarian Economies', *Journal of Economics Literature*, Vol. 30.

21

Rural Development

Policies, Strategies and Instruments

Introduction

The most common social and political usage of the term policy refers to a course of action or intended course of action conceived of as deliberately adopted after a review of possible alternatives and pursued, or oriented to be pursued. The policy process is the formulation, promulgation and application of these courses of action. In this chapter we will concern ourselves with public rural development policy, strategies and different instruments, by which we mean actions taken by the government in pursuit of certain objectives of rural development.

Policy is a comprehensive term and connotes a set of intended actions. It subsumes programmes which are narrower in scope than policy, but more specific with regard to what is to be done, how, by whom and where. A policy has to be translated into a number of programmes before it can be implemented. Programmes and projects are interrelated. A project is highly specific and detailed in terms of its objectives, location, duration, funds and executing agency, and lends itself to planning, financing and implementation as a unit. A programme may consist of several projects. A rural development project may be defined as an investment activity, where resources are expended to create a producing asset from which we can expect to realize benefits over an extended period of time.

Need for a Rural Development Policy

When we move from simple, small scale handicraft industry and self-contained and subsistence agriculture, a greater need develops for public policy in the economic field. The individual, as a producer and as a consumer, depends more and more upon the general conditions of the market, of employment, output and production efficiency of the nation as a whole, and upon the way income is distributed among the people; in short, upon the economic welfare of the country. Some of the specific reasons favouring government intervention in the rural sector are as follows:

(i) Achieving Socialist Pattern of Society

It means that the basic criterion for determining the lines of development must not be private profit, but social gain, and that the pattern of development and the structure of socio-economic relations should be so planned that they result not only in appreciable increase in national income and employment, but also in greater equality in incomes and wealth. However, the experience of developing countries so far has been that the benefits of development have not been equally shared by all. This has aggravated the problem of poverty, which has manifested itself in various forms, including rising unemployment, malnutrition, growth of slums, fall in real wages, and impoverishment of marginal and small farmers. The growing poverty in rural and urban areas undermines the principal objective of planned development, which is improvement in the standard of living of the masses. It has been acknowledged that a high rate of growth is not a substitute for deliberate policies to ensure equitable distribution of the gains of development. Therefore, there is need for a public policy to ensure growth with social equity or social justice.

(ii) To Stabilize Agricultural Production, Prices and Incomes

Agricultural production, being biological in nature, is more vulnerable to the vagaries of nature than non-farm production, and hence fluctuates more violently than does industrial production in response to erratic rainfall or other natural phenomena. Fluctuations in agricultural output lead to still higher fluctuations in agricultural prices and hence agricultural incomes. This is because the demand for most agricultural produce is inelastic, or because of higher price flexibility of agricultural produce with respect to changes in the supply. Most farmers, being small-scale operators and poor, cannot bear the consequences of fluctuations in farm outputs, prices and incomes. They need some protection from the adverse effects of the free market and niggardly nature. Such protection can be provided only by the government in the form of price support, insurance and credit policies.

(iii) Eradication of Rural Poverty and Equitable Income Distribution

The average per capita income in rural areas is not only lower than in urban areas, but is also more unevenly distributed. The injustice of the plight of rural people is reason enough for government intervention to support rural income and improve its distribution through anti-poverty programmes.

(iv) Strengthening Rural Enterprises

Most rural enterprises are small, scattered and unorganized. Due to these characteristics, their owners have very low or practically no bargaining power *vis-à-vis* those to whom they sell their produce, and from whom they buy their supplies. This results in exploitation on both fronts—selling as well as supplies. This heightens the need for government policies aimed at equalizing opportunities, at strengthening the bargaining power of individuals and groups in rural areas, and restraining the powerful from exploiting the weak.

(v) Development of Basic Infrastructure in Rural Areas

Rural areas are at a great disadvantage in relation to urban areas, as far as provision of basic infrastructural facilities and services such as roads, drinking water, electricity, schools, hospitals, police protection, transport and communication, etc. are concerned. Not only are these public facilities and amenities in rural areas inadequate, but they are also very poorly organized and undependable. As a result, poor villagers are damned, generation after generation, to poor education, poor health, unemployment and poverty. Improvement of their plight requires intensive government intervention.

Goals of Rural Development Policy

Rural development policies are designed to improve the conditions under which rural people work and live. The goals of policies are governed by what people desire, and the measures of policies by what people think the government can and ought to do to bring about the desired change. This is the theory of public policy. Changes are desired only when people do not like the way things are going. Pressure for public action arises when people feel that they, individually, cannot bring about the desired adjustments. They have in mind some 'norm', some image of an ideal situation towards which they strive. These norms become the goals of policy towards which objectives of specific programmes are directed.

There are two dominant goals of economic policy; first, increasing the national income, and second, improving the distribution of national income among the members of society. To achieve these, following goals are to be attained:

(i) Priority to agriculture and rural development, with a view to generating adequate productive employment and eradication of poverty.
(ii) Accelerating the growth rate of the economy with stable prices.
(iii) Ensuring food and nutritional security for all, particularly the vulnerable sections of society.
(iv) Providing the basic minimum services of safe drinking water, primary health care facilities, universal primary education, shelter, and connectivity to all in a time bound manner.

(v) Containing the growth rate of population.
(vi) Ensuring environmental sustainability of the development process through social mobilization and participation of people at all levels.
(vii) Empowerment of women and socially disadvantaged groups.
(viii) Promoting and developing people's participatory institutions like Local Governments, cooperatives and self-help groups.
(ix) Strengthening efforts to build self-reliance.

The above objectives, which seek to achieve 'growth with equity', need to be seen in the context of the following four important dimensions:

- Quality of life of the rural population
- Generation of productive employment
- Regional balance
- Self-reliance

All these objectives seem to be worthwhile, and therefore, deserve serious pursuit by policy makers. However, to be of any use to society, these objectives should be translated into specific programmes and projects that are manageable under the existing conditions. Many rural development policies are complex combinations of various goals, different sets of means or instruments, and are limited by various conditions. To understand such policies, we should divide them into several programmes or projects. For each programme, a clearly defined objective may be designated, which a particular government agency should pursue. The programme measures can then identified and appraised as to whether they are appropriate and efficient in serving the objective, and adapted to the conditions outside the influence of that particular programme. These conditions are often the decisive factor determining whether or not a certain programme is administratively feasible.

Hierarchy of Policy Goals

Given the multiplicity of policy goals, it is necessary to study the relationships among them and to see that how they converge towards public interest. This can be done if various policy goals and programme objectives are arranged in the form of a pyramid, as shown in Fig. 21.1. Descending the steps of the pyramid of policy goals from the lofty top of generality to the practical base of concrete issues would reveal the following hierarchy.

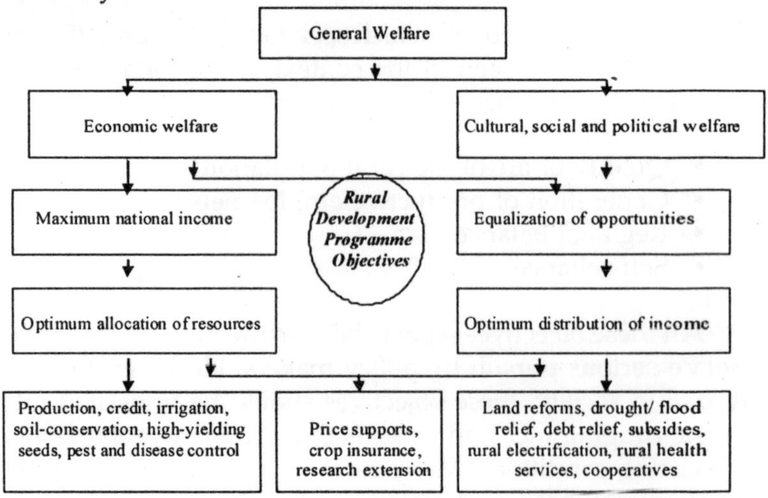

Fig. 21.1: Hierarchy of Rural Development Policy Goals

(i) The master goal of economic policy is to promote general welfare, which comprises economic welfare and cultural, social, and political welfare. The master goal is served by two superior goals, namely, maximum national income, and equalization of opportunities. The master goal and the superior goals together constitute the top level of the hierarchy.

(ii) Descending from the top level of the hierarchy, a series of goals is developed at a lower plane of generality. These goals deal with specific maladjustments in the various sectors of the economy, and may be called the central goals of major national policies. Each of these central goals is still quite general in scope and complex in nature; for practical application, these goals have to be divided further into more specific programme objectives directed at a great variety of situations, and concerning various groups of people, regions, and commodities.

(iii) At the next level, we find the objectives of specific government programmes designed to correct maladjustments, or to remove the source of dissatisfaction suffered by certain groups of people. The central goal of agricultural policy, for instance, is divided in various programme objectives assigned to irrigation, soil conservation and agricultural credit, marketing, research, education and extension.

(iv) We descend then to the lowest, most specific level of programme units, the objectives of which are relatively simple and clear-cut. These are supporting specific farm commodities at specific prices, making loans to farmers for specific purposes, inducing farmers to follow certain soil conservation practices, and developing dams and irrigation systems.

The method of formulating programmes in which the objective and its means are clearly defined is indispensable for the study of policies. But the method is not simple to apply. Objectives become means and means become objectives, depending upon how one looks at them. An objective in the context of a more specific programme appears as a means in a more general action system. In evaluating the appropriateness of means, we take the objective for granted; in order to evaluate the appropriateness of an objective, we must place it in the position of a means serving a superior end.

Strategies of Rural Development

There are basically four important strategies of rural development, which are most important for the developing countries. The strategies are the following:

(i) Growth Oriented Strategy

This is based on the philosophy that rural people, like any other people, are rational decision makers, who, when given adequate opportunity and a proper environment, will try to maximize their incomes. The role of the state in this strategy is to build infrastructure, and maintain a favourable climate to stimulate the growth of rural enterprises. The critical assumption of this strategy is that the benefits of increased production will gradually 'trickle down' to the poor. The regulation and coordination of the activities of private and public agencies is primarily through market mechanisms. This paradigm formed the basis of the predominant agricultural development strategies in developing countries.

(ii) Welfare Oriented Strategy

This seeks to promote the well-being of the rural population in general, and the rural poor in particular, through large-scale social programmes like the minimum needs programme, nutrition programme, etc. The primary means used in this strategy are free provision/distribution of goods, services and civic amenities in rural areas. The critical assumptions of this strategy are that people are not competent to identify and resolve their problems, and that government specialists can identify their needs and meet them with the financial and administrative resources available with the government. The role of villagers is that of passive receptors of services. This strategy has a paternalistic orientation. The performance of the programme is judged by the quantity of goods, services, and civic amenities delivered.

(iii) Responsive Strategy

This is aimed at helping rural people help themselves through their own organizations and other support systems. Its concern is with responding to the felt needs of the rural people, as defined by them. The role of the government is to facilitate the self-help efforts of villagers by providing technologies and resources that are not locally available. The critical assumption of this strategy is that the rural poor will identify and resolve their own problems if provided with minimal support, and otherwise left to their own devices and initiatives. Community participation in, and control of, project activities is the primary performance indicator of this strategy.

(iv) Integrated or Holistic Strategy

This combines all the positive features of the earlier three strategies, and is designed to simultaneously achieve the goals of growth, welfare, equity and community participation. This paradigm takes a very comprehensive but integrated view of the basic problem of poverty, unemployment and inequality, and seeks to address the physical, economic, technological, social, motivational, organizational and political bases of these problems. The multiple goals of this strategy are sought to be achieved by building the capacity of the community to involve itself in development in partnership with the government.

Rural Development Policy Instruments: Conceptual Framework

An instrument is the means by which an objective is pursued. A measure is the use of a particular instrument at a particular time in order to promote one or more objectives; for instance, the decision to raise the bank rate on a certain day, or to reduce income tax in a particular budget year. The removal of a measure, for instance, the removal of price control, is also a measure. Knowledge about what instruments can be used to achieve the objectives of various rural development programmes is essential for rural development policy makers and managers in order for these programmes to be effective and successful.

Perhaps the most useful framework to illustrate the relationship among policy instruments, target variables and social welfare, and for policy analysis, has been provided by

Nobel Laureate Jan Timbergen, which is illustrated in Fig. 21.2. The important elements of the framework for policy analysis are W, the Y_i, the Z_j and the structural relationships that link the Z_j to the Y_i.

(i) Social Welfare Function (W)

Economists call W the social welfare function. It reflects the level of well-being achieved by the society. As such, it represents the aggregate of the satisfaction reached by the individuals comprising society. Utility is consumed ultimately only by individuals, and no social or community welfare function exists independent of the well-being achieved by individuals. Because no method has been found to measure utility or well-being W is entirely psychological and subjective. Social, political, and cultural factors as well as economic ones must be included in any conceptualization of welfare; and must be evaluated in any policy analysis.

(ii) Policy Goals (Y_i)

The Y_i are the articulated goals of policy. They are deduced from the values of W. An element of W may be an improvement in the range of opportunities for members of the society—the target goal may be a rise of per capita incomes of 5 per cent per annum, a rise in the literacy level of 70 per cent, or the complete eradication of poliomyelitis. It should be obvious that W and the Y_i are related, and the precise nature of the relationship between the two should be as clear as possible.

The policy maker may well decide the Y_i. A great deal of thought and care should be given to the matter of selecting appropriate target variables. It is especially important that the Y_i be framed in such a way that they are capable of being evaluated. Vaguely stated goals often cannot be easily appraised. The second is specific and quantitative, and can be readily evaluated.

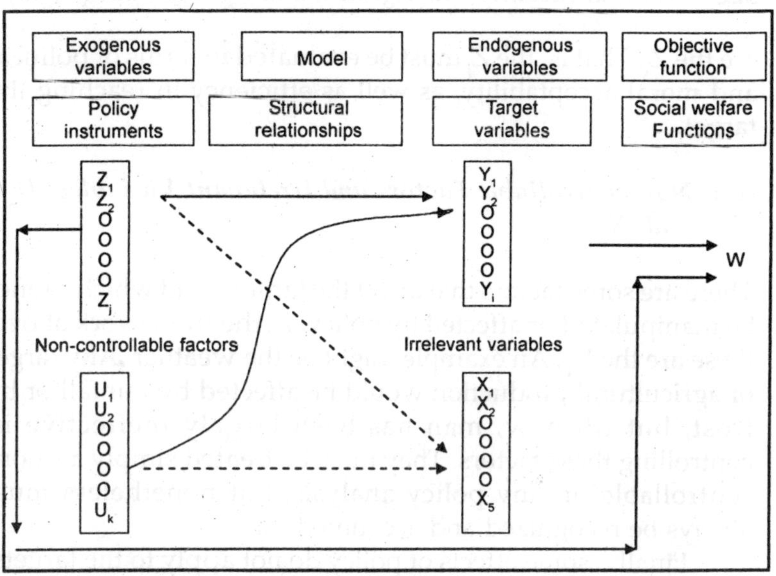

Fig. 21.2: A Conceptual Framework for Policy Analysis

(iii) Policy Instruments (Z_j)

The policy instruments available to achieve the target goals are the Z_j. For example, to reduce unemployment to 5 per cent of the workforce (a target to be sought), various policies (Z_j) may be utilized. The government may increase the quantity of money in the economic system, believing that more demand for goods will ultimately reduce unemployment. Or, a tax reduction may be given to businesses which invest in new capital equipment, under the theory that capital growth will produce more jobs. A great number of policies may be alleged to contribute to the accomplishment of the target. Policy analysis is largely composed of looking for and evaluating alternative ways to achieve the target goals. The great bulk of science, and most of economics, is concerned with these tasks.

A set of statistical relationships must be established that reveal the process of getting from the Z_j to the Y_i, and how efficient the processes are. It should be remembered that just as the Y_i are prescribed by the ultimate values of society, so are the Z_j. That is, the Z_j must be evaluated in terms of political and moral acceptability, as well as efficiency in reaching the target.

(iv) Non-controllable Factors and Irrelevant Variables (U_k) and (X_s)

There are some factors that affect the targets, and which cannot be manipulated or affected by policy. In the framework above, these are the U_k. An example might be the weather. Any target of agricultural production would be affected by rainfall or by frost, but till now, man has been largely ineffective in controlling these factors. They must be treated simply as 'non-controllable' in any policy analysis, but nonetheless must always be recognized and accounted for.

Finally, some effects of policy do not apply to the targets, or do not directly enter the community's welfare function, but should nevertheless be monitored because they are potentially significant. These are the X_s in the above framework, and are called the 'side effects' of policy. A policy to shift the production of energy from steam engines to internal combustion engines will have side effects that will not be significant for most situations. Internal combustion engines produce a variety of invisible pollutants in the air that are not a problem, until they reach certain dangerous threshold levels. These types of side effects must be watched, but may not affect the evaluation of policy until they reach problem proportions, in which case they may be shifted into the category of Y_i.

It is primarily a taxonomic device, and should be of value in elucidating what is being sought, the available means of reaching what is being sought, and at what cost. It helps the policy maker to keep things straight.

Action Systems: Instruments

In the context of development management, an action system may be conceived of as consisting of four elements: the manager/actor, the objectives, the conditions (physical, technological, economic, social and political), and the means or instruments. Their relationships can be indicated by a simple diagram, as given in Fig. 21.3. The manager or actor may be an employee of a public, private, cooperative, corporate or any other entity. The manager in any given system makes the decisions as to what means should be employed towards a given objective or set of objectives.

The objectives are what the manager wants to accomplish. They need to be clearly defined in operational terms. The conditions of an action system are all those technical and institutional circumstances beyond the control of the managers, at least with respect to the particular programme under consideration. The instruments must be adapted to, or compatible with, the conditions under which the programme must operate.

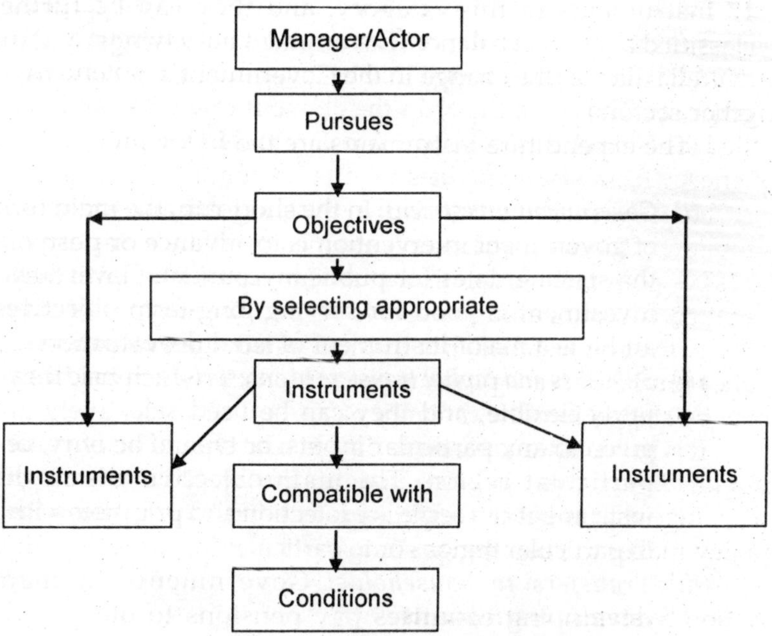

Fig. 21.3: An Action System

The instruments are the policy measures or programme provisions employed to achieve the objectives. There are often many different instruments that could possibly serve a certain objective. Knowledge of economics is especially useful in making a wise choice in the selection of instruments. The instruments can be grouped into public finance, money and credit, exchange rate, direct controls, and changes in the institutional framework; which are detailed below.

Instruments of Public Finance

The set of instruments covers most income and expenditure of the central, state and local governments. Government expenditure is largely devoted to the objective of the satisfaction of collective needs.

The main occasion for the use of the instruments of public finance is the annual budget; consequently many of these instruments can be employed at annual intervals. There are 17 instruments in this category, and they can be further classified as current balance (Government net savings) and the overall balance (the change in the Government's net claims on other sectors).

The expenditure instruments are the following:

(i) *Government investment*: In the short-run, the main form of government intervention is to advance or postpone the starting dates for public investment. Government investment is good for serving long-term objectives, and it is a major instrument of rural development.

(ii) *Subsidies and capital transfers to enterprises*: Subsidies are fairly flexible, and they can be used selectively and given to any particular inputs, or type of activity, or a particular region. The main objective which this instrument can serve is protection and priorities, either to particular regions or to particular inputs or activities.

(iii) *Transfers to households*: Governments in many developing countries pay pensions to old people, sickness allowances to invalids, unemployment benefits, and so on. Such expenditure is financed partly by contributions paid to the social security agencies, and partly by transfers from the central government.

(iv) *Government stock changes*: Governments sometimes build up stocks themselves by direct controls or subsidies for the satisfaction of collective needs and security of supply, *e.g.*, stockpiling of food grains, minerals, metals, coal, etc.

(v) *Current purchases of goods and services*: This instrument can be selective, for example, purchases in a particular region or from a particular sub-sector. Purchases can be delayed or advanced, with the objective of price stability or full employment.

(vi) *Wages and salaries*: Governments do not often attempt to manipulate their wage and salary bill for purposes of economic policy. Some expenditure on in-service education or training can serve to increase the mobility of labour, or to improve income distribution.

(vii) *Transfers to the rest of the world*: Transfers are usually made to very poor countries and international institutions, like the UNDP, ILO, etc.

The revenue instruments are the following:

(i) *Direct taxes on incomes of households*: There are fairly limits on the extent to which governments, in times of peace, can increase their revenue from personal income tax.

(ii) *Direct taxes on enterprises' incomes*: Company profits are taxed as a whole, that is, with no distinction between distributed and undistributed profits.

(iii) *Indirect taxes on internal transactions*: They are the largest of the income instruments.

(iv) *Customs duties*: Export duties are rarely used, but import duties are used universally; however, they can be both flexible and selective, but their use is limited by international agreements and the fear of reprisals by foreign governments.

(v) *Social security contributions*: They have been rarely used as instruments of economic policy.

(vi) *Taxes on property*: They include both taxes on wealth, and separate taxes on land and buildings, and serve as instruments for the distribution of incomes.

(vii) *Succession duties and inheritance tax*: They have some effect on income distribution.

(viii) *Transfers from the rest of the world*: Donations from the rich to the poor countries are important aids to development.

The main purpose of public expenditure is to satisfy collective needs, and this limits the extent to which it can be manipulated for other objectives. Political pressures and pressure groups can have a very strong influence on policies in the field of public finance.

Instruments of Money and Credit

This set of instruments includes those which serve to make it either more difficult or easier, for persons, companies or governments to borrow money. In contrast to budgetary measures, which can be described as open decisions openly arrived at, a great deal of mystery and mystique surrounds monetary and credit policy. It is not always possible to find out exactly what is being done. The important money and credit instruments are detailed in Tabel 21.1. The governments and Central Banks are responsible for promulgating these instruments.

Instruments of Exchange Rate

This instrument has the following three main characteristics:

(i) It is extremely powerful, can have considerable effects on the economy of the country concerned, and also on the countries from which it imports and exports.

(ii) It has a strong emotional content; the exchange rate of a country's currency gives its price in terms of gold and foreign currencies.

(iii) Any reduction brings with it the risk that it will lead to a loss of confidence in the national currency.

Table 21.1: Instruments of Money and Credit

Instruments	*Measures*
1. Government's new borrowing and lending	1. Lending abroad 2. Lending to households and enterprises 3. Borrowing from abroad 4. Borrowing from households and enterprises
2. Government operation in existing debt	1. Open market operations in short-term securities 2. Other open market operations
3. Interest rate instruments	1. Bank rate 2. Legal imposition of maximum rates 3. Government guarantees of loans
4. Instruments acting on credit creation by banks	1. Reserve ratios (statutory liquidity ratio and cash reserve ratio) 2. Quantitative stops on advances 3. Approval of individual loans 4. Other directives, recommendations and persuasion
5. Instruments acting on lending or borrowing by other agents	1. Control of borrowings of local authorities and nationalized enterprises 2. Control of borrowings or private companies by new issues 3. Control of hire purchase transactions 4. Control of other financial institutions

The exchange rate is a single instrument, not a family of instruments; however, there are different types of exchange rates, and consequently different types of changes in them. The exchange rate can be single or multiple, fixed or floating. Changes in exchange rate must either be revaluations or devaluations. The objectives of revaluation are price stability, and to a lesser extent, the international division of labour. Devaluations are always meant to improve the balance of payments, sometimes to expand production, and also for the international division of labour.

Instruments of Direct Controls

Direct controls are normally administered by the ordinary civil service departments. Because of their quick effect, these instruments are particularly used in crises, emergency and periods of war and to deal with short-term economic problems. Sometimes special institutions are set up for this purpose. In the field of international trade, decisions are taken in the framework of international institutions and agreements. Direct controls are very effective in the short term in holding back economic activity, but they are much less effective in stimulating it. Businessmen and consumers can be prevented by controls from doing certain things, but it is often virtually impossible to compel them to take positive action. The important instruments of direct controls are given in Table 21.2.

Direct controls have also been used much more to deal with short-term than with long-term or structural problems. Controls do not modify the underlying market forces which brought about the situation which needed control.

Table 21.2: Instruments of Direct Controls

Instruments	*Measures*
1. Control of foreign trade, foreign exchange and immigration	1. Control of private imports 2. State import trading 3. Control of private exports 4. Exchange control 5. Control of immigration
2. Control of prices	1. Price control of goods and services 2. Rent control 3. Dividend control 4. Control of wages
3. Other controls on the internal economy	1. Control of investment 2. Raw-material allocation 3. Control of operations 4. Regulation of conditions of work 5. Control of exploitation of natural resources 6. Rationing of consumer goods 7. Quality controls and standards

Changes in Institutional Framework

Changes in the institutional framework do not lend themselves easily to quantification, and usually require a change in the laws. Since it takes time to change the institutional framework, these changes are usually made with long-term rather than short-term objectives in mind. But there are occasions on which the institutional framework has been changed in order to facilitate the use of the instruments for short-term policy. Table 21.3 captures the major instruments in three categories.

Table 21.3: Instruments of Institutional Framework

Instruments	*Measures*
1. Institutional changes involving other instruments	1. Changes in the system of transfers to households (public finance) 2. Changes in the system of subsidies to enterprise (public finance) 3. Changes in the tax system (public finance) 4. Changes in the credit system (Money and credit) 5. Changes in the system of direct controls (direct control)
2. Institutional changes directly affecting production	1. Land reforms 2. Changing the conditions of competition (restriction on monopolies) 3. Changes in labour's influence in management 4. Changes in the extent of public ownership in industry 5. Creation of national institutions
3. Institutional changes in the international framework	1. Creation of international institutions

There are certain constraints on the use of changes in the institutional framework.

(i) The establishment of new institutions, or a major change in the institutional framework, is usually a fairly major policy step which often meets with more opposition than does the use of an existing instrument.

(ii) Since changes of this kind usually involve new laws, they have to go through a lengthy procedure of government approval.

In developing countries institutional changes constitute the most important instrument of promoting rural development. Institutional changes, particularly land reforms, contributed significantly to agricultural development in countries like China and Taiwan.

Conclusion

Developing countries have long history of government intervention in the rural sector, with a view to improve the socio-economic conditions of rural people, especially the poor. However, so far there are no comprehensive integrated national policies for agricultural and rural development reported from the developing countries. What is required is a long-term comprehensive integrated national policy, which clearly charts the future course of agricultural and rural development programmes targeting the new millennium. To achieve the objectives of rural development policy efficiently, it is necessary that a set of appropriate instruments be identified for each of the objectives of the policy, and that the chosen instruments are set at their optimal levels. Choice of appropriate instruments needs to be made carefully, keeping in view the prevailing socio-economic and political environment.

REFERENCES

Booth, D. (1994), *Rethinking Social Development: Theory, Research and Practice*, Longman Scientific and Technical, Harlow.

Eicher, Carl K. and John M. Stazz (1984), *Agricultural Development in the Third World*, The John Hopkins Press, London.

Griffin, Keith (1973), 'Policy Options for Rural Development', *Oxford Bulletin of Economics and Statistics*, Vol. 35, No. 4.

Lele, U. (1975), *The Design of Rural Development: Lessons from Africa*, The John Hopkins Press, London.

Johnston, B.F. and Clark, W.C. (1982), *Redesigning Rural Development: A Strategic Perspective*, The John Hopkins Press, London.

Singh, Katar (1999), *Rural Development: Principles, Policies and Management*, Sage Publications, New Delhi.

Bibliography

Acherman, Joseph, *et al.* (1962), *Land Economics Research*, John Hopkins Press, Baltimore.

Anderson, Lee G. (1977), *The Economics of Fisheries Management*, John Hopkins University Press, Baltimore.

Antle, John M. and Daniel A. Samner (1996), *The Economics of Agriculture: Selected Papers of D. Gale Johnson*, University of Chicago Press, Chicago.

Barnum, H.N. and Squine, L. (1979), 'An Econometric Application of the Theory of the Farm-Households,' *The Journal of Development Economics*, Vol. 6, March.

Bardhan, Pranab (1984), *Land, Labour and Rural Poverty: Essays in Development Economics*, Columbia University Press, New York.

Baumol, W.J. and Oates, W.E. (1979), *Economics, Environmental Policy and the Quality of Life*, Prentice Hall, Englewood Cliffs, New Jersey.

Baumol, W.J. and W.E. Oates (1988), *The Theory of Environmental Policy*, Cambridge University Press, Cambridge.

Beckerman, Wilfred (1974), *Two Cheers for the Affluent Society: A Spirited Defence of Economic Growth*, St. Martin's Press, New York.

Berndt, E. and Field, B. (eds.) (1981), *Measuring and Modelling Natural Resources Substitution*, MIT Press, Cambridge.

Berry, R. Albert (1979), *Agrarian Structure and Productivity in Developing Countries*, Johns Hopkins University Press, Baltimore.

Blaug (1985), *Economic Theory in Retrospect*, Cambridge University Press, Cambridge.

Bockstael, N.E. and McConnell, K.E. (1993), 'Public-hoods as Characteristics of Non-market Commodities,' *Economic Journal*, 103, 1244.

Booth, D. (1994), *Rethinking Social Development: Theory, Research and Practice*, Longman Scientific and Technical, Harlow.

Bose, P. (1997), 'Formal-Informal Sector Interaction in Rural Credit Markets, *Mimeograph*, Department of Economics, University of Memphis.

Boserup, E. (1965), *The Conditions of Agricultural Growth*, Aldine, Chicago.

Butlin, R. (ed.) (1981), *Economics of the Environment and Natural Resources Policy*, West View Press, Boulder, Colorado.

Caselli, F. (1997), 'Rural Labour and Credit Markets,' *Mimeograph*, Department of Economics, Harvard University.

Chambers, J.D. and Mingay, G.E. (1966), *The Agricultural Revolution, 1750-1880*, Schocken Books, New York.

Cohen, M.M. (1977), *The Food Crisis in Prehistory*, Yale University Press, New Haven.

Common, M.S. (1996), *Environmental Resources Economics: An Introduction*, Longman, Harlow.

Conrad, John M. and Colin W. Clark (1987), *Natural Resources Economics: Notes and Problems*, Cambridge University Press, Cambridge.

Dales, J.H. (1968), *Pollution, Property and Prices*, Toronto University Press, Toronto.

Daly, H.E. (1977), *The Steady State Economics*, W.H. Freeman, San Francisco.

Daniel Thorner, *et al.* (eds.) (1966), *The Theory of Peasant Economy*, Irwin Inc, Illinois.

Dasgupta, P.S. and G.M. Heal (1979), *Economic Theory and Exhaustible Resources*, Cambridge University Press, Cambridge.

Dorfman, Robert and Nancy S. Dorfman (1993), *Economics of the Environment: Selected Readings*, W.W. Norton, New York.

Dorner, P. (1972), *Land Reform and Economic Development*, Penguin, Harmonds Worth.

Drummon, Evan H. and John W. Goodwin (2001), *Agricultural Economics*, Prentice Hall, New Jersey.

Eicher, Carl K. and John M. Stazz (1984), *Agricultural Development in the Third World*, The John Hopkins Press, London.

Fassil G., Kiros (eds.) (1977), *Rural Development,* IDR, Addis Ababa University, Addis Ababa.

Freeman, A.M. (1979), *The Benefits of Environmental Improvement: Theory and Practice,* John Hopkins University Press, Baltimore, Maryland.

Freeman, A.M. (1993), *The Measurement of Environmental and Resource Values,* Resources for the Future, Washington DC.

Friedman, M. (1974), *Essays in Positive Economics,* University of Chicago Press, Chicago.

Furtado, Celso (1970), *Economic Development in Latin America,* Cambridge University Press, New York.

Griffin, Keith (1973), 'Policy Options for Rural Development', *Oxford Bulletin of Economics and Statistics,* Vol. 35, No. 4, November.

Griffin, K.B. (1974), *The Political Economy of Agrarian Change: An Essay on the Green Revolution,* Harvard University Press, Mass.

Halcrow, Harold G. (1984), *Agricultural Policy Analysis,* McGraw Hill Book Company, New York.

Hanley, N. (1989), 'Problems in Valuing Environmental Improvements from Agricultural Policy Changes: The Case of Nitrate Pollution', *Discussion Paper No.89/1,* Economics Department, University of Stirling.

Hanley, N. and Spash, C. (1993), *Cost-Benefit Analysis and the Environment,* Edward Elgar, Alder Shot.

Hansman, J.A. (ed.) (1993), *Contingent Valuation: A Critical Assessment,* North-Holland, Amsterdam.

Harriss, J. (1992), *Rural Development: Theories of Peasant Economy and Agrarian Change,* Huttchinson, London.

Hayami, Y. (1992), 'Agricultural Innovation, Economic Growth and Equity: A Critique of Michael Lipton,' *South East Asian Journal of Agricultural Economics,* 1 (June).

Helmberger, Peter G. and Jean Paul Chavas (1996), *The Economics of Agricultural Prices,* Prentice Hall, New Jersey.

Hollist, W. Ladd and Lamond Tullis (eds) (1987), *Pursuing Food Security: Strategies and Obstacles in Africa, Asia, Latin America and the Middle East,* Lynne Rienner Publishers, London.

Huppi, M. and G. Feder (1990), 'The Role of Groups and Credit Cooperatives in Rural Lending.' *World Bank Research Observor-5.*

Janson, Ann Mari, *et al.* (ed), *Investing in Natural Capital: The Ecological Economics Approach to Sustainability*, Island Press, Washington, DC.

Johanson, P.O. (1987), *The Economic Theory and Measurement of Environmental Benefits*, Cambridge University Press, Cambridge.

John, M. Antle and Daniel A. Sumner (1996), *The Economics of Agriculture: Selected Papers of D. Gale Johnson*, University of Chicago Press, Chicago.

Johnston, B.F. and Kilby, P. (1973), *Agriculture and Structural Transformation: Economic Strategies in Late Developing Countries*, Oxford University Press, New York.

Johnston, B.F. and Clark, W.C. (1982), *Redesigning Rural Development: A Strategic Perspective*, John Hopkins University Press, London.

Just, R.E., Hueth, D.L. and Schnitz, A (1982), *Applied Welfare Economics and Public Policy*, Prentice Hall, Englewood Cliffs, New Jersey.

Kneese, Allen V., *et al.* (1970), *Economics and the Environment: A Materials Approach*, Resources for the Future, Washington DC.

Kneese, Allen V. and Charles L. Shultze (1975), *Pollution, Prices and Public Policy*, The Brookings Institution, Washington, DC.

Krueger, A.O. and Schiff, M. and Valdes, A. (eds) (1991), *Political Economy of Agricultural Pricing Policies*, John Hopkins University Press, Baltimore.

Laurens van der Laan H., *et al.* (eds) (1999), *Agricultural Marketing in Tropical Africa*, African Studis Centre, Leiden.

Lele, U. (1975), *The Design of Rural Development: Lessons from Africa*, The John Hopkins Press, London.

Lipton, M. and Lonhurst, R. (1989), *New Seeds and Poor People*, Unwin Hyman, London.

Mandal, R.B. (1982), *Land Utilization: Theory and Practice*, Concept Publishing Company, New Delhi.

Meadows, Donella H., *et al.* (1972), *The Limits to Growth*, Universe Books, New York.

Mellor, J.W. (1966), *The Economics of Agricultural Development*, Cornell University Press, Ithaca, NY.

Nair, Reji D. (2003), *Land Economics: Issues in Land Use*, Centre for Studies in Development Strategy, Thiruvananthapuram.

OECD (1989), *Economic Instruments for Environmental Protection*, OECD, Paris.

Otuska, H., H. Chuma and Y. Hayami (1992), 'Land and Labour Contracts in Agrarian Economies', *Journal of Economics Literature*, Vol. 30.

Pearce, D.W. and Moran, D (1994), *The Economic Value of Biodiversity*, Earth Scan, London.

Penson, John B., *et al.* (2002), *Introduction to Agricultural Economics*, Prentice Hall, New Jersey.

Pim, A. (1946), *Colonial Agricultural Production*, Royal Institute of International Affairs, London.

Pinstrup-Anderson, P. and Rosegrant, M.W. (1999), *World Food Prospects: Critical issues for the Early Twenty-First Century*, International Food Policy Research Institute, Washington DC.

Powelson, J.P. and R. Stock (1987), *The Peasant Betrayed: Agriculture and Land Reform in the Third World*, Gunn and Hain, MA: Oelgeschlager, Boston.

Price, Colin (1989), *The Theory and Application of Forest Economics*, Basil Blackwell, Oxford.

Ray, Debraj (1998), *Development Economics*, Princeton University Press, New Jersey.

Robson, Peter and Dennis A. Lury (1969), *The Economies of Africa*, Allen and Unwin, London.

Salter, A. Leonard (1967), *A Critical Review of Research in Land Economics*, The University of Wisconsin Press, London.

Sandbrook (1982), *The Politics of Basic Needs*, Heinemann.

Schultz, T.W. (1953), *The Economic Organization of Agriculture*, McGraw Hill Book Company, New York.

Schultz, T.W. (1964), *Transforming Traditional Agriculture*, Yale University Press, New Haven.

Scott, Anthony (1985), *Progress in Natural Resources Economics*, Clarendon Press, Oxford.

Sen, A. (1981), *Poverty and Famines: An Essay on Entitlement and Development*, Oxford University Press.

Singh, Katar (1999), *Rural Development Principles: Policies and Management*, Sage Publication Inc.

Sterner, Thomas, (ed.) (1994), *Economic Policies for Sustainable Development*, Kluwer Academic Publishers, Norwell.

Tietenberg, T.H., *Emissions Trading: An Exercise in Reforming Pollution Policy*, Resources for the Future, Washington DC.

Tietenberg, Tom (1996), *Environmental and Natural Resources Economics*, Harper Collins College Publishers, New York.

Todaro, M. (1992), *Economics for a Developing World*, Third Edition, London and New York: Longman.

Turner, R.K. and Bateman, I. (1990), *A Critical Review of Monetary Assessment Methods and Techniques*, Environmental Appraisal Group, University of East Anglia.

UNDP, *Human Development Reports*, Various years.

Vaze, P. (ed.) (1998), *UK Environmental Accounts: 1998*, The Stationery Office, London.

Vink, A.P.A. (1967), *Land Use in Advancing Agriculture*, Springer-Verlag, New York.

Von, Brunn J., *et al.* (1993), *Aid to Agriculture: Reversing the Decline*, International Food Policy Research Institute, Washington, DC.

World Commission on Environment and Development (WCED) (1987), *Our Common Future*, Oxford University Press, Oxford.

Yotopoulos, P.A. (1968), 'On the Efficiency of Resource Utilization in Subsistence Agriculture,' *Food Research Institute in Agricultural Economics*, Trade and Development, Vol. 8, No. 2.

Yudelman, Montague, *et al.* (1971), *Technological Change in Agriculture and Employment in Developing Countries*, OECD, Paris.

Index